Palgrave Studies on Children and Development

The series focuses on the interface between childhood studies and international development. Children and young people often feature as targets of development or are mobilized as representing the future in debates on broader development problems such as climate change. Increased attention to children in international development policy and practice is also fuelled by the near universally ratified United Nations Convention on the Rights of the Child and the recently adopted Sustainable Development Goals.

Nonetheless, relatively little has been written on how the experience of childhood and youth is shaped by development as well as how young people as social actors negotiate, appropriate or even resist development discourses and practices. Equally, the increased emphasis in research on children and young people's voices, lived experiences and participation has yet to impact policy and practice in substantial ways. This series brings together cutting-edge research presented in a variety of forms, including monographs, edited volumes and the Palgrave Pivot format; and so furthers theoretical, conceptual and policy debates situated on the interface of childhood and international development. The series includes a mini-series from Young Lives, a unique 15-year longitudinal study of child childhood poverty in developing countries. A particular strength of the series is its inter-disciplinary approach and its emphasis on bringing together material that links issues from developed and developing countries, as they affect children and young people. The series will present original and valuable new knowledge for an important and growing field of scholarship.

More information about this series at
http://www.palgrave.com/gp/series/14569

Katarzyna Grabska · Marina de Regt
Nicoletta Del Franco

Adolescent Girls' Migration in The Global South

Transitions into Adulthood

palgrave
macmillan

Katarzyna Grabska
Institute of Social Studies
Erasmus University
The Hague, The Netherlands

Nicoletta Del Franco
University of Parma
Parma, Italy

Marina de Regt
VU University Amsterdam
VX Amsterdam
Noord-Holland, The Netherlands

Palgrave Studies on Children and Development
ISBN 978-3-030-00092-9 ISBN 978-3-030-00093-6 (eBook)
https://doi.org/10.1007/978-3-030-00093-6

Library of Congress Control Number: 2018953826

Cover credit: Katarzyna Elzbieta Grabska
Cover design by Fatima Jamadar

This Palgrave Macmillan imprint is published by the registered company Springer Nature Switzerland AG
The registered company address is: Gewerbestrasse 11, 6330 Cham, Switzerland

Foreword

Contemporary migration flows include migrants who are highly visible on the global stage, especially those who reach, or are trying to reach rich countries, and others, whose journeys and circumstances rarely touch the lives of the politically and economically dominant classes in the countries in the North. This book documents and analyses the lives and circumstances of one such less well-known migratory flow—that of girls and young women under 20 years old, who are moving within and between countries in the Global South. Many migrated as, or are, children; they are or were under 18. As such they come under the protection of the Convention on the Rights of the Child. There has been considerable international (and sometimes national) effort in the last 15 years to identify and protect such child migrants, rightly so. Some of these efforts recognize that the needs of those who are legally children may vary with age: migrating aged 10 or 11 is usually a more dangerous enterprise than moving aged 16, or 17.

The authors of this study chose to identify these young migrants as adolescents, rather than children, so highlighting the significant processes of maturation that occur as children move into legal and social adulthood, and beyond. As they point out, there is a whole policy and research framework that highlights this life stage as marked by a series of key transitions: transitions in education, in work, in sexual activity and in family building. These transitions contribute to identity formation, itself an important work that adolescents do.

This is a time when youngsters, whatever their circumstances, look for opportunities. Each, and every one of the girls in this study has found these opportunities lacking at home in their places of origin. The families of some of the Ethiopian, Eritrean and Bangladeshi migrants can scarcely ever make a secure rural living, becoming destitute when men die or abandon them, with profound effects on young female family members. Young Eritreans migrate to escape the demands of a repressive political regime. In other cases, it is violent, neglectful or abusive living situations, or gender coercive norms that curtail opportunity.

The researchers rightly stress that it is in many cases girls themselves who make the decision to migrate: with a deliberate effort to make things better for themselves and in some cases their families. But, migrating across borders, or into the city, girls are subject to coercive gender norms that not only control behaviour but stigmatize them, and make them very vulnerable. They find themselves inserted into gender orders that curtail their work choices, prescribe restrictive norms of behaviour, and allow a range of male predatory behaviour, as well as a generalised judgemental control.

By any standards their lives in the capital cities are difficult, dangerous and precarious. They are at best ignored, at worst stigmatized or criminalized. Some migrant girls are particularly vulnerable because of their undocumented status, their stigmatized ethnicity, or by earning a living in stigmatized ways. Work is hard to come by, yields little income and is very insecure. Places to live are hard to find, often temporary and conditions awful. Some must hide from the authorities, with religious institutions and self-help groups being the only sources of public support, and then only for a few.

However, this is not the only story. This book goes beyond these hardships, to look at how girls protect themselves, for example, by building social capital, and at the resilience many show in the face of setbacks. They survive, resist and many move forward, even though this may not be in the ways they hoped for when they set off on their journeys. One of the great merits of this research is the methods adopted. As well as using a portfolio of different qualitative methods, and collecting some statistics, they adopted a feminist standpoint. Each country study recruited migrant girls as researchers, with many playing a key role in contacting other migrants and some collecting and analysing data and writing reports. These methods, together with the authors' familiarity with the fieldwork contexts from previous research, provides a view that is not only richer, but crucially more long-term. This research uncovers the complex trajectories of some of the migrant girls and is able to explore how the young women who migrated as children assess these trajectories.

In the final chapter of this book the researchers turn to the central intellectual project that drove the design and execution of the research: namely how does migration—itself a transition—intersect with those other transitions which are occurring, or beginning to occur, at adolescence? Moving has facilitated a transition into work, which was rarely available in their home communities, but hopes that migrant girls might have had of continuing or improving their education are rarely met, although they acquire other kinds of new knowledge. How migration affects marriage, family making and becoming adult is more complex.

The detailed case studies find that migrant girls challenge the existing patterns of transition into adulthood, particularly by postponing marriage, or seeking to get married on their own terms. In these ways they have opened other pathways to becoming women, acquiring in the process a greater sense of selfhood. By their small, (and we might say heroic), acts to survive and make a life in the city, young female migrants are bringing about social transformation by their challenges to, and renegotiation of, existing definitions of gendered adult identities. These new identities are however uneasily worn, and not fully embraced by the young female migrants themselves. There are too many costs and too many severe difficulties of daily living for this to be the case.

Brighton, UK

Ann Whitehead
Emeritus Professor of Anthropology
School of Global Studies
University of Sussex

Acknowledgements

This book would have not been possible to complete without the efforts, support, collaborations, openness and friendships of so many people. The idea of the research emerged during a workshop on child migration organized by Prof. Ann Whitehead in September 2012 at the University of Sussex to which the three of us, Marina de Regt, Nicoletta Del Franco and Katarzyna Grabska, were invited. Ann's particular attention to migration of children, how it was framed in policy discourses and in development interventions, and her insistence on the need to better understand the agency of children and adolescents in migratory processes prompted us to ask important questions. Thanks to this intellectual space that Ann created, the three of us met and had the opportunity to interact with various academics, policy-makers and activists involved in research and advocacy with and on behalf of migrant children and youth. This was the beginning of our friendship but also of the academic collaboration that ensued. Based in three different countries (The Netherlands, Switzerland and Italy), speaking three different languages, and having worked in three different regions of the world, we were united by our feminist approaches to research. We shared similar interests to better understand migratory experiences of adolescent girls, as we felt they were invisible in research and policy frameworks. Ann generously supported us in our endeavours to write a research proposal and secure funding.

During the life of this project, new friendships were formed, a new life was born, and sadly, some lives of our close-ones were lost. Our friendship but most importantly a truly feminist approach to our collaboration meant that the others' of us stepped in when one of us was faced with personal challenges. It was this joint strength with the continuous support and mentoring from Ann Whitehead that carried us through the research (2014–2016) and collaborative writing of this book (2017–2018). Our approach to writing this book was unique, as we jointly prepared the research, carried out the fieldwork, analysed our data, and wrote each chapter of the book together. It was due to continuous meetings in person during our fieldwork and filming, workshops, write-shops, meetings and conferences in Addis Ababa, Amman, Amsterdam, Geneva, the Hague, London, Rome, Warsaw, but also over Skype, WhatsApp and email that each page of the book was negotiated and emerged as a result. A truly collaborative experience in which we have learned a lot from each other!

There are many institutions and people who should be thanked for the support they offered throughout this project. First of all, we acknowledge the generous support of the Swiss Network of International Studies (SNIS) that provided the main funding for the research (2014–2016). Co-funding for the research and documentary film was also received from Terre des Hommes, University of Sussex, Vrije Universiteit Amsterdam, Feminist Review Trust, and Girl Effect Ethiopia. We are very grateful to them for making this project financially possible. The project was carried out under the umbrella of the Global Migrations Centre at the Graduate Institute of International and Development Studies (IHEID) in Geneva. Thanks go to Prof. Vincent Chetail for hosting the project and to Prof. Alessandro Monsutti for his collaboration and support. Special thanks go to Dr. Géraldine Ruiz for her administrative assistance and patience! Jacqueline Barrin M.A. candidate at the Graduate Institute and Terre de Ridder, M.A. candidate at the Department of Social and Cultural Anthropology, Vrije Universiteit Amsterdam provided invaluable assistance in collecting of literature for the research. Rebecca Glade, M.A. candidate at the Ahfad University, provided analysis of some of the policy documents in Sudan. Thank you all!

We would like to acknowledge the co-researchers who made the research possible. In Ethiopia, special thanks go to the two main researchers, Felegebirhan Belesti and Arsema Solomon, who were responsible for the largest part of the data collection, and to Madereshaw Tafesse and Aynadis Yohannes who carried out the interviews with returned women from the Middle East. We also want to thank the staff of Girl Effect Ethiopia, and in particular Rebecca Smith and Fiker Abebe, for their support during the data collection. The support of

NIKAT Charitable Foundation, and in particular of Hanna Hagos, has been instrumental for the success of the project. Other organizations that facilitated the research were Timre Le Hiwot, CHAD-ET and OPRIFS, for which many thanks.

In Bangladesh, we thank Valentina Lucchese and Manuela D'Andrea together with the staff of Terre des Hommes Italy in Bangladesh, ARBAN (Association for the Realization of Basic Right), Aparajeyo Bangladesh, RMMRU (Refugee and Migratory Movement Unit) at the University of Dhaka and ZXY International for their valuable support during the fieldwork.

In Sudan, special thanks go to the Regional Institute of Gender, Rights, Diversity and Justice at the Ahfad University for Women in Omdurman, and especially to Professor Balghis Badri for offering institutional support. Also, the French Research Centre, CEDEJ in Khartoum, and particularly Dr. Alice Franck, have contributed in diverse and significant ways to the success of the project.

Special thanks to Ignacio Packer from Terre des Hommes Federation who immediately recognized the importance of the project already in December 2012 during our first meeting in Geneva. You have been an advocate of the project and its results and we thank you for all the support you have offered and for the advocacy on behalf of migrant girls. Also, Laura Cello from Terre des Hommes Federation participated actively in dissemination of the findings, including the preparation of the final conference of the project in June 2016 at the Graduate Institute in Geneva.

The biggest contribution, however, comes from adolescent migrant girls and young women in Addis Ababa, Dhaka and Khartoum who opened up their lives, their homes, and their hearts to us. Without you, this research and the book would not have had happened! We would like to thank all those who agreed to participate as researchers, as respondents, and as informants. We would in particular like to thank Kidist Tamasgen, Kidist Worku, Bana Goitom Gaim, Bisrat Solomon, Ruta Zekarias, Hibret Ghebregziabher Tesfay, Bushra Mahmuda, Kakoli Shaha, Ushree Barua, Rupa Mollick, Khadeja, Bably Akter, Mim Akter, Hazera Akter, Eity Yeasmin and Rokunuzzaman. Without you this project would not have had happened! We would like to express our deepest gratitude and special thanks to all the research participants who shared their stories with us and provided insights into their very complex and vulnerable lives. This book is a testimony to your struggles, your resilience, and your quest for a better life.

The documentary films entitled *Time to look at girls: adolescent girls' migrants in Bangladesh and Ethiopia* and *2 Girls* that were produced in collaboration with research participants and with a film crew offered a new way for us to share our research findings. They also opened up a space to discuss these issues outside of small academic circles and create debates for wider publics. Marco Speroni and Riccardo Russo were responsible for directing and shooting the footage for the documentaries that were made as part of this research, which was a great addition. Working with them was a lot of fun, for which we thank them.

Finally, we want to thank Roy Huijsmans for encouraging us to submit our book proposal to Palgrave Macmillan, and Alina Yurova and John Stegner at Palgrave Macmillan for the pleasant cooperation. Deborah Eade had a lot of patience with us and did a great job editing the manuscript.

Last, but not least, to our great source of support and inspiration: Ann Whitehead. You have been so patient, sharing, cooperative and supportive. This had made the whole project a lot of fun and made us truly believe in feminist collaborative work. Thank you.

April 2018

Katarzyna Grabska
Marina de Regt
Nicoletta Del Franco

Contents

List of Figures

CHAPTER 1

Girls, Transitions and Migration

Time to Listen to Girls

Adolescent girls are increasingly understood in development policies to be a crucial segment of the population, whose successful transition into adulthood is of major importance for their own lives and of those around them. Adolescence is important for key transitions such as to work, marriage and parenthood and in defining one's self and social identity (Bucholtz 2002; Del Franco 2012; Johnson and Hanks 2002; Punch 2002; Temin et al. 2013). In 1990, the United Nations Children's Fund, UNICEF, made "the girl child" one of its priorities, and numerous development projects and campaigns were launched to improve the lives of girls worldwide (Croll 2006). In 2012, the United Nations established 11 October as the International Day of the Girl Child. An increasing number of national and international development organizations have started investing in girls, mainly in education in order to reduce early marriage, teenage pregnancy, maternal mortality rates and gender-based violence (GBV). The overall aim is to break the cycles of poverty and, in so doing, work towards the social and economic development of the population as a whole (see, for example, Temin et al. 2013; UNICEF 2011)[1]. Policy-makers and development agencies see girls

[1] See also https://www.odi.org/projects/2590-transforming-lives-adolescent-girls, retrieved 7 September 2017.

K. Grabska et al., *Adolescent Girls' Migration in The Global South*, Palgrave Studies on Children and Development,
https://doi.org/10.1007/978-3-030-00093-6_1

Fig. 1.1 Girl Effect slogan in Ethiopia

as change-makers in whom it is worth investing as this will benefit society overall. Global campaigns such as *Girl Effect, Girls Empowerment* and *Girls Are Powerful* are therefore receiving large-scale public and private funding (see Koffman and Gill 2013) (Fig. 1.1).

Migrating girls have also emerged more recently as a focus on development and humanitarian interventions (see TDH children on the move; IOM campaigns; and UNHCR's attention to the displacement of girls). Despite the growing awareness of the participation of adolescent girls in internal and international migration, few academic studies deal with this important phenomenon and its wider consequences (see, for example, Derks 2008; Hertrich and Lesclingand 2012; Jacquemin 2009, 2011). In 2013, the Population Council published *Girls on the Move: Adolescent Girls & Migration in the Developing World* (Temin et al. 2013), and international and non-government organizations (NGOs) have published a growing number of reports in recent years. Very often, however, the focus of policy debates is on the negative aspects of adolescent girls' migration, emphasizing the risks and dangers such as trafficking and exploitation.

The migration projects of adolescent girls are part of a wider flow of children and young people worldwide who move in search of earning a better living and protection as well as to meet family obligations and individual aspirations. Since the turn of the century, the number of children who are leaving their place of origin has been increasing rapidly. The large majority of these children are adolescents, many of them girls (see Temin et al. 2013). In the literature on migration and development, independent migrants who are under 18 years of age are mainly described also as victims of trafficking and exploitation (O'Connell Davidson 2011) or as being forced to migrate by situations of dire vulnerability, poverty and war (see Hopkins and Hill 2008). The focus on exploited and abused child migrants has made it difficult to recognize and address the needs of other children and adolescents who migrate in diverse circumstances. The problem with such framing is not only that it denies adolescent girls' their own agency, but the type of interventions and policies that are designed to 'rescue' and 'rehabilitate' the victims. Moreover, younger children and adolescents are all framed as minors; policies aiming to protect people under 18 years of age do not always consider important differences among them due to age, socio-economic conditions, actual experiences and the different ways in which adulthood is constructed in different cultural settings. The 'social age' of girls and boys does not necessarily correspond to their chronological age. Social age can be described as "the socially constructed meanings applied to physical development and roles attributed to infants, children, young people, adults and elders, as well as their intra- and inter-generational relationships" (Clark-Kazak 2009, p. 1310). This consideration is also important in approaching the phenomenon of the so-called unaccompanied migrants and refugee children, who are the focus of controversial policies and interventions in the countries of destination. Once they reach the age of majority, girls and boys are no longer formally entitled to the kind of protection granted to children under the provision of the United Nations Convention on the Rights of the Child (CRC).

From different perspectives, a number of studies have criticized approaches based strictly on chronological age, which frames legal minors as always vulnerable and subject to other people's decisions and choices. Whitehead et al. (2007), Jacquemin (2009) and Hashim and Thorsen (2011), for example, have shown that children and adolescents often make their own decision to migrate, and that their reasons are in many cases very similar to those of young adults of between 20 and 25 years of age. A growing body of literature addresses children's agency in the process of migration (Coe et al. 2011; Ensor and Gozdziak 2010; Huijsmans 2011, 2017; Veale and Donà 2014) and attempts to conceptualize it by emphasizing children's resilience and capacities to negotiate their own position, and the importance of relational and collective agency, without losing sight of the potential risks and vulnerabilities (Razy and Rodet 2016; Veale and Donà 2014). The need to listen to children's and adolescents' words and experiences has also been highlighted (Dobson 2009), as well as the methodological and ethical dilemmas arising from giving them voice (see Razy and Rodet 2016, pp. 7–8).

The vast majority of studies on young people's migration have focused on boys and young men (Gardner 2012; Hashim and Thorsen 2011; Punch 2007; Thorsen 2006; White et al. 2011). Adolescent migrant girls are almost invisible in both quantitative and qualitative studies despite their generally increasing numbers, in most regions of the world both within their regions and countries and across the globe (Temin et al. 2013). Exceptions are academic studies, mainly of domestic workers in African countries (e.g. Erulkar et al. 2006; Erulkar and Mekbib 2007) and South East Asia (e.g. Camacho 2006; Muttarak 2004; Guo et al. 2011) or occasionally of sex workers (e.g. Van Blerk 2008). The studies on domestic or sex workers usually take a gender lens as they focus on young women without combining it with that of generational perspective. In this way, they fail to ask how age might be a relevant dimension in understanding gendered experiences of migration and work. A few studies in West Africa have taken a more in-depth view (Hertrich and Lesclingand 2012, 2017; Jacquemin 2009, 2011). In 2017, a comprehensive quantitative study of 28 countries (Montgomery et al. 2016) sought to quantify urban migration of adolescent girls in low- and middle-income countries by examining data collected through a large number of censuses and surveys and supported by some country-specific studies (Agarwal et al. 2016; Bunmak 2012; Hertrich and Lesclingand 2012; Lin and Tong 2008). According to this study, the census-based data in a number of countries shows that 40% of adolescent girls from 10 to 19 years of age are recent in-migrants in urban areas, whether coming from rural villages or other towns (Montgomery et al. 2016, p. 574). Over the last twenty years, women and girls migrate more often than men and boys of the same age, especially in South East Asia. An example from Cambodia shows that from the age 15 years onwards, a higher percentage of urban Cambodian girls than boys are recent migrants (Montgomery et al. 2016, p. 577).

Although the links between migration and wider social transformations have been addressed to some extent (see Bakewell 2010; Castle 2010; Grabska 2013, 2014), there has been less focus on the particular effects of migration on an individual's life course (Bretell 2002), and scholars have not much examined the link between transitions into adulthood and migration. Punch (2002, 2016) discussed key linkages between migration transitions and youth transitions in the case of young Bolivians moving to Argentina. Crivello (2009), in longitudinal research among Peruvian girls and boys, examined the links between education and migration with transitions into adulthood. Guo et al. (2011) described how the pattern of reverse and circular migration of young Chinese women to Beijing is linked to changes in their life course. The authors in the volume edited by Veale and Donà (2014) take a methodological approach, focusing on the intersection between the development of the individual life course and migration trajectories for boys and girls.

The migration of adolescent girls, whether as part of a household strategy or an individual endeavour, has major implications for their transition into adulthood as it intersects with other important decisions in their lives. While girls' migration is often described in negative terms, such as when they are trafficked and exploited, it may also offer them new and better opportunities with positive implications for their future. This book sets out to provide a nuanced, complex, comparative analysis of adolescent girls' migration and mobility in the Global South. The stories and the narratives of young migrant girls collected in Bangladesh, Ethiopia and Sudan over a period of more than two years will guide us in drawing the contours of their lives on the move, a complex, fluid scenario of choices, constraints, setbacks, risks, aspirations and experiences in which internal or international migration plays a pivotal role.

According to the Population Council's report (Temin et al. 2013), adolescent girls migrate for four main reasons: work, education and training, marriage, and in response to a shock or crisis. Migration is a response to the lack of opportunities in their home communities; for some it is a response to acute family needs, for others to their unmet aspirations. Many girls migrate for work or to earn an income, and adolescents' labour migration can be seen as a manifestation of processes of social change in rural areas that affect employment opportunities (Huijsmans and Baker 2012). Even so, finding employment is not always the main factor behind girls' decision to move (Jacquemin 2009, 2011; Thorsen 2007, 2014). Migration can also offer girls an escape from difficult circumstances, such as respite from the heavy social pressures of being young and female at home, or to flee an arranged marriage (see, for example, Erulkar et al. 2006). It can be a way to express agency, to escape dominant gender regimes, and to build independent resources (Castle and Diarra 2003; Hertrich and Lesclingand 2012; Van Blerk 2008; Whitehead and Hashim 2005). Girls' migration is also often inspired by a longing for a different type of life, away from the boredom of village life (Guo et al. 2011; Mills 2005) and the drudgery of agricultural and domestic work (Balakrishnan 2005). In studying these complex situations, we concur with scholars who argue that while migrant girls and boys are social actors exercising agency, this agency is often constrained in more or less severe ways (Huijsmans and Baker 2012; Klocker 2007; Yaqub 2009).

This book presents the findings of research carried out in Bangladesh, Ethiopia and Sudan, which we believe offers valuable comparisons among them. Why did we select these three countries, which at first sight may not have much in common? First, because international and local NGOs in these countries consider the migration of adolescent girls and young women as an important but under-researched issue. Second, the countries are in three different regions—South Asia, the Arab world and East Africa—which reveal migration flows within and between countries that have to date been largely understudied despite their growing numerical importance (UNDP 2013). The Sudan case study provides a strong methodological link with Ethiopia, as a large number of adolescent Ethiopian girls migrate to Sudan. Contrasting Ethiopian internal and international migration with Eritrean refugees in Sudan enables us to better understand complexities of migratory trajectories. Ethiopia and Bangladesh provide an interesting comparison of internal migration, where there are profound differences in the social and cultural context. Last, but not least, as individual researchers each of us has long-standing experience in one of these three countries. Nicoletta Del Franco has more than 20 years' experience in issues related to gender and development, young people, adolescence and the transition to adulthood in rural and urban Bangladesh (see Del Franco 2012). Katarzyna Grabska has carried out extensive research in Sudan, especially in what used to be Southern Sudan, and among South Sudanese refugees in Kenya and Egypt since 2002, with a particular focus on gender and generational relations in situations of forced displacement and the impact of (forced) migration on youth (see Grabska 2006, 2014). Marina de Regt has been studying the gendered aspects of migration between Ethiopia and Yemen since the early 2000s, focusing mainly on Ethiopian domestic workers in Yemen, and also including the historical aspects of migration of these two close but rather distinct countries (see De Regt 2010, 2012).

Setting the Scene

Adolescence: A Broader Approach

We focus on adolescent girls and adolescence because the phase between 11 and 20 years of age is in many respects crucial in the course of an individual's life. We deliberately decided to use the term *adolescent girls* instead of young female migrants, or girl child, to emphasize this specific gendered period in the life course. We are aware that the adolescent girl has now fully entered the UN talk and international development discourse in rather problematic ways (see, for example, Jauhola 2011). Yet, we find reference to adolescent girls rather than youth an important analytical and political position. First, the term 'youth' in development and migration policies and studies have mainly been associated with male migration (see, for example, Howard 2017). In addition, 'youth' is rather a broad age category, often including young people up to 30 or 35 years old. Our intention is to draw attention to how the period of adolescence intersects with gender and how migration might become a defining factor of transitions in that particular phase of life for girls. Second, we did not want to use the language of 'girl child' in order to critique but also to distance ourselves from the international discourses influenced by the Convention of the Rights of the Child and related campaigns that frame all people below 18 years of age as children. While legally being still children, girls between ages of 11 and 20 in the countries that are the case studies for this book as well as elsewhere, are no longer considered as small children, but rather as getting ready to enter the phase of adulthood, even if that phase is not necessarily ethnographically defined as adolescence in the three contexts presented here. Yet, this particular phase of preparation for full adulthood, how it intersects with age and gender, interests us as a critical point of transitions at which many different life-changing decisions are being made. Lastly, our decision to refer to use the term adolescence is also to engage with the problematic policy discourses that have been pervading development policies and projects.

Adolescence can be seen as a 'process' characterized by critical transitions when major life decisions are taken, albeit in context-specific ways (Bucholtz 2002; Del Franco 2012). The spatial shift implied in migration can be read as one such critical transition that intersects with other life choices being made (Crivello 2009; Gardner and Osella 2003; Gardner 2009; Grabska 2010). Whether we talk about adolescents or youth, however, we engage with an unstable terrain that cannot be easily defined only in terms of chronological age. Bourdieu rightly argued that "divisions, whether into age-groups or into generations, are entirely variable and subject to manipulation" (1993, p. 95). Both terms refer to social categories that can be understood only in relation to local and context-specific practices and norms as well as to "complex and changing historical network of institutions, economic structures, state policies, adult initiatives and youth self-activities" (Austin and Willard 1998, p. 3). We concur with Crivello that "the relationship between biological age and social age is complex and is produced and practiced in culturally-specific ways, yet embedded in both local and global systems of power and hierarchy" (Crivello 2009, p. 4).

Following Stuart Hall (1905), medical science and psychology have characterized adolescence as a problematic and fragile state, regarding adolescents as unfinished human beings at risk of deviant behaviour. In this view, a successful transition to adulthood would necessarily imply adults' intervention to ensure a smooth socialization process. These psycho-biological interpretations were founded on the idea that the phases of individual growth are shaped by genetically determined physiological changes. Puberty and sexual maturation were seen as the starting point of a universal phase of individual development, which ends with full adulthood and adult responsibilities. This universal view of adolescence and its psycho-biological processes was initially challenged from an anthropological perspective by Mead's account of adolescence in Samoa (Mead 1928). Mead specifically sought to question the biological determinism that views adolescence as a period of stress, storms and turmoil, and to show the importance of culture and culturally determined socialization processes in shaping children's and adolescents' behaviour in different contexts.

In the field of psychology, Erikson and his followers substantially broadened the interpretation of adolescence (Erikson 1968; Marcia 1980; Muuss 1996). Erikson problematized its supposedly universal character and the identity crisis it implies, by recognizing that the emergence of adolescence "as an even more marked and conscious period" is linked to the technological and economic changes that prolong the period between school life and access to specialized employment (Erikson 1968, p. 128). In this sense, Erikson recognized that as a developmental stage in a person's life, adolescence might vary in different societies in terms of "duration, intensity and ritualization" (ibid., p. 155). He also acknowledged that in the process of identity formation that characterizes this life phase there is a continuous interplay between the psychological and the social: "we deal with a process located in the core of the individual and also in the core of its communal culture" and a "process which establishes in fact the identity of those two identities" (ibid., p. 22). History and society can thus variously shape the constitution and duration of social adolescence.

We problematize approaches that confine adolescents (and children) to the passive status of incomplete human beings, who are in the process of being socialized into adult social roles, as found in a "socialization" framework (see Schlegel and Barry 1991). Rather, we emphasize that adolescents and young people are active agents in complex social contexts, engaged in creating their social identities through on-going processes of negotiation within social relations (Bucholtz 2002). Rather than treating young people in adult terms either as resisters, victims or in the process of acquiring predetermined adult identities, we see them as cultural agents in contexts where identities are shaped by elements of local culture as well as by globalization and transnationalism. We refer to the young women in our research as adolescents because this places them within a developmental phase which entails a complex and multifaceted process of transition, involving physical, psychological and social dimensions. The young women are at the centre, voicing their perceptions, experiences and aspirations. We look at their agency as it is expressed in contexts of strong social embeddedness, also drawing on theorizations (see Coleman 2010) of the process of individuation in developmental psychology, where emotional disengagement from one's parents can be no longer seen as a fundamental characteristic of the move towards independence. Many now argue that autonomy can co-exist with "social responsibility" (Greenberger 1984), "interdependence" (Youniss and Smollar 1985) or "connectedness" (Grootevant and Cooper 1986, quoted in Coleman and Hendry 1999, p. 76). Rather than being based on severing affective links with one's parents, these authors see the acquisition of selfhood and identity as being linked to the development of qualitatively different family relations, implying greater symmetry of reciprocal influence. Thus, adolescents' increased degree of self-assertion and decision-making autonomy is not incompatible with keeping the relationships going but is in fact favoured by it.

We thus consider that the acquisition of identity is defined not only in terms of occupational, marital or any other social position, but more profoundly as a sense of selfhood that is also but not solely created from one's social position. Identity is a contested and problematic concept. Erikson (1968) and the School of "Ego Psychology"[2] he represents, recognize that the process of forming an identity can be seen as having a relative and contingent character but that, in his view, social identity implies a strong sense of coherence and continuity. His conceptualization of social identity is founded on a very culture-specific concept of the self as linked to an inner identity which constitutes the individual's essence. Anthropologists have long shown, however, that "the Western transcendental subject and the Western concept of the person are far from universal" (Moore 1994, p. 33). Social identity is rather something that "has to be established socially through a set of discourses which are both discursive and practical" (Moore 1994, p. 37) or, as Stuart Hall (1991) argues, building on Foucault, as the relationship between subjects and broader discursive practices. In this perspective adolescence, as much as youth is "a socially constructed multiple identity whose relations to other social formations is constantly in flux" (Austin and Willard 1998, p. 3). Moreover, "social becoming" in the contexts that we are studying is much more a collective endeavour and experience than an individual process.

[2]The school of Ego Psychology to which Erikson belongs focuses on the study of the so-called realistic Ego or self.

Gendered Adolescence

Gender has important implications for how the social phase of adolescence and the process of transition to adulthood are constructed and lived in different socio-cultural contexts. The study of initiation ceremonies by which adulthood is acquired and age sets and age grades are defined, which characterized British social anthropology before the 1970s, mainly concerned boys. For girls, the transition to adult status was mainly linked to biological events such as menarche or the birth of the first child. In the three contexts discussed in this book, attaining womanhood is strongly linked to marriage and fertility. In Sudan, among migrants and refugees from Ethiopia and Eritrea, adolescence for girls is often interpreted as being linked not to a certain age, but to the social status of being unmarried and without children. In Bangladesh, puberty used to correspond to the immediate acquisition of adulthood for girls, since marriage before or soon after menarche was a predominant reality. In rural Ethiopia, marriage is still considered one of the main ways for girls to achieve adulthood, yet perceptions in urban areas are changing, as this research also points out.

Both Bangladeshi and Ethiopian societies are notably hierarchical (Blanchet 1996; Del Franco 2012; Heinonen 2011; Pankhurst 1992; Poluha 2004) with strong gender-based and generational inequalities. Gender norms are similar in Eritrea, although there was some progress towards achieving gender equality during the national liberation struggle, in which women were very active in combat and in the liberation movement. In all three contexts gender norms regulate and influence the life of children from birth, as girls are less valued than boys at home and in the wider community. Boys are more valued because they will continue the patrilineal family line and traditionally would continue to live with their parents after marriage while married girls move to live with their husband's family. Gender norms determine how girls are treated, their responsibilities and the type of domestic and farming work they have to do, their education, their freedom of movement, their relationships with friends, and their ambitions and aspirations for the future. The sexuality of adolescent girls is strictly controlled and premarital relationships are not accepted. This is a defining moment of how adolescence is experienced differently by boys and girls in the Bangladeshi, Ethiopian and Eritrean societies. As a girl's virginity is highly valued in order to secure a good marriage and achieve respectability, parents and guardians often "protect" girls from engaging in sexual relations. Adolescence is a key moment when girls are eager to experiment with their sexuality but are at risk of boys and men perceiving them as sexual objects. Parents and guardians thus often stop girls from going to school, where they fear the negative consequences of co-education.

It emerges from our research, however, that in rural and urban Bangladesh and in Eritrea a girl's engagement in premarital relationships might jeopardize good marriage opportunities, in the Amhara region in Ethiopia parents are also afraid of the potential abduction of girls into marriage. In all three contexts, parents and guardians see arranged marriages at a young age as a way to control girls' sexuality. Educated urban girls have greater potential to delay marriage in the three contexts considered, where profound processes of socio-economic change influence the way in which different phases in the lives of women and men are lived and understood. Migration is one of these processes and young girls' choice to migrate is a factor that can contribute to postponing marriage and starting a family, and open up new life trajectories for girls and new ways of becoming an adult woman and the meanings attached to it.

Migration and Transitions

Our study conceptualizes migration as a physical movement within and across geopolitical borders, initiated for a variety of factors. We acknowledge that there are significant differences between the two, and also in the reasons for movement in the first place. By focusing on the spatial dimension of migration, we see it as more than an act or an event in a person's life, but as a process, and how it links to other transitions.

The concept of transition through different life phases is controversial, however. In mainstream sociological and psychological approaches, it has implied the idea of a linear progression from one phase of an individual's life to another. In anthropology, too, the classical studies on the rites of passage inspired by Van Gennep (1908) have focused on institutionalized moments in which people moved from one status to another. These approaches and the use of the term transition to identify significant turning points have been criticized from various perspectives in different geographical contexts (see Punch 2015). As Johnson Hanks (2002, p. 865) underlines, criticizing the use of the life-cycle model, "most vital events—such as marriage, mother-hood, and migration—are negotiable and contested, fraught with uncertainty, innovation, and ambivalence", and thus the transition to adulthood is a fluid and non-coherent process. While agreeing with Johnson Hanks' and other scholars' critique of a linear view of the process of becoming an adult, we draw on Punch's holistic notion of transition as "a time of key changes for many young people", not necessarily implying a particular direction or content (Punch 2015, p. 263). We therefore refer to life phases rather than life stages when discussing the different transitions during a life course.

Both adolescence and migration connote a journey. The term adolescence contains the ideas of both transition and development, coming from the Latin verb *adolescere* to grow up, and its past participle *adultum*, which means grown up (Bucholtz 2002, p. 532). Migration implies both a temporal and spatial shift (see Grabska 2016). In this book, we look at how the process of migration intersects in different contexts with the processes of transition to adulthood, which shape and transform young women's sense of selfhood, affect the kind of social person they want to be/can become and their capacities to choose, control and shape their own lives. Besides being a significant moment in the individual psychosocial development in relation to one's sense of selfhood and self-identity, adolescence has been interpreted as a period in which individuals redefine their social world by distancing themselves from the kind of social relations that characterized childhood and by occupying wider social spaces. Through their adolescent journeys, girls face transitions related to education, work, sexual initiation, marriage and having children. As Gigi Durham Meenakshi argues, "the psychological transition of adolescence, already charged in terms of gender and sexuality, is then imbricated with the conundrums of the other transition—the diaspora identity that demands delicate negotiations of race/ethnicity, nation, class, language, culture and history" (2004, p. 141). Our approach to *adolescence transitions* allows us to explore how concepts of adolescence and adulthood for girls are being transformed in the context of migration and to elaborate on the type of choices that young female Bangladeshi, Ethiopian and Eritrean migrants are making and the possible pathways these choices open for them. We look mainly at how life-course transitions to work, education, marriage and having children, and the establishment of new sets of relationship beyond the girl's birth family, are interconnected and how they intersect with the process of migration.

The literature shows that girls' and boys' migration and education choices potentially intersect and affect each other in different ways.

Some studies show high levels of independent child migration in communities where very many children have never attended school (Custer et al. 2005; Hashim and Thorsen 2011) and where children drop out of school in order to migrate (Khair 2008). Some studies show that despite the growing importance given to education (Kabeer 2000), migration for work is increasingly a choice in a context where education is not perceived as or is not actually providing employment opportunities or when the costs of education are very high compared to its quality. This is true, for example, in India (Jeffrey et al. 2008) as well as in Gambia and Ghana (Jones and Chant 2009; Langevang 2008). In contrast to the view that migration has negative impacts on educational levels, other studies show that migration for education is becoming increasingly important (Crivello 2009) and that children sometimes migrate in order to cover the costs of their education over a long time frame (Hashim 2007; Hashim and Thorsen 2011). It is highly likely that there are relevant gender differences. Girls appear to drop out of school for other reasons too, such as poverty, early marriage and negative attitudes towards their education (Giani 2006; Kifle 2002; Lloyd 2005). Migrant girls often come from communities where fewer girls than boys attend school. On the other hand, migration is sometimes a way to continue education, for example, when relatives in towns and cities are willing to host young girls and send them to school in exchange for domestic help (see Camacho 2006) and when girls' labour migration contributes to the school costs of their siblings (see Afsar 2003; Camacho 2006).

In terms of internal migration to cities, whether from rural areas or other urban areas, the study by Montgomery et al. (2016) mentioned earlier shows that urban girl migrants have higher levels of education than rural non-migrant girls, but lower than urban non-migrant girls of the same age. Migrant girls in urban areas are also less likely than non-migrant girls to be enrolled in school, although the data also show that a significant percentage of migrant girls are, thus demonstrating, according to the authors of the study, a positive correlation between migration and the acquisition of human capital (Montgomery et al. 2016, pp. 590–591). In addition, as Hashim and Thorsen (2011) argue, migrant adults and children may decide on the basis of their own perception what education means. More than formal schooling, they may value informal training for life and skills they can build on for their future work.

When education is not seen as leading to desirable forms of employment, migration for work becomes an alternative. Here a key area of investigation relates to the impact of work on girls' economic and social empowerment. Again, there are both positive and negative outcomes reported as well as significant differences with boys. Migrant girls are often employed in the formal economy in low-paid, low-skilled jobs, in poor conditions and with high levels of risk. Siddiqui (2009), for example, emphasizes the exploitative nature of garment work in Bangladesh, risks of accidents, sexual harassment and abuse, as do Pearson and Kusakabe (2012) for young women workers in Thai garment factories. The same is true for India, Indonesia and the Philippines (Heissler 2013). Other research has suggested that this must be set against the positive effects of entry into the workforce. In Bangladesh, garment factory workers' greater contribution to the household budget has been interpreted as leading to an improved family status (Kabeer 2000; Kabeer et al. 2011; Kabeer and Mahmud 2004). In addition, girls have become more mobile and more visible in public spaces (Hossain 2012). Migration and work might also lead to a change in gender relations. For South Sudanese refugee girls, returning to their country helped to transmit new ideas about more equal gender relations through greater access for girls to education and work (see Grabska 2011, 2014). On the other hand, Bangladeshi women who migrate independently to the Gulf States to work in garment factories or as domestic workers are often stigmatized when they return home, and may lose status in their community, despite their financial contribution to the family (Blanchet 2002). There is a significant gender differential here. For boys, earning a living through work can be directly connected with the transition to manhood, as in the case of rural Beninois adolescents who migrate to work in Nigerian mines (Howard 2017), and with the acquisition of valued adult status even when they are employed in low-status work (Rao 2014). For girls, however, womanhood is strongly associated with marriage, and being employed in low-status jobs can jeopardize their future marriage prospects (Heissler 2013).

How decisions about sexual initiation, marriage and reproduction intersect with the decision to migrate is particularly important for girls and may have lasting significance in relation to fertility. As well as intersecting in different ways with the choice of when and whom to marry, migration decisions involve girls' aspirations about work and education and affect their future life trajectories (Temin et al. 2013). It was previously believed that the migration of adolescents leads to early sexual initiation and pregnancy, but this is not borne out by other studies. Longitudinal research in Mali, for example, showed that the increase in girls' migration was accompanied by a delay in the age of marriage for boys as well as girls, who also appear to have gained more control over their choice of partner (Hertrich and Lesclingand 2012). In Bangladesh, girls who migrate to take up jobs in the garment factories and for higher education tend to marry later (Del Franco 2010; Hossain 2012). South Sudanese refugee girls in Kenya and Egypt also postponed marriage and becoming mothers (see Grabska 2010, 2015). A similar situation has been observed in a few demographic studies on internal migration in Kyrgyzstan (Nedoluzhko and Andersson 2007; Nedoluzhko and Agadjanian 2009), and in research on Ethiopian domestic workers in Yemen (de Regt 2012). The postponement of marriage reduces the rate of early pregnancy and the associated health risks for mothers and babies (Finlay et al. 2011). Women who defer marriage are less at risk of spousal violence, and tend to have fewer children, who in turn are more likely to survive and to go to school (Lloyd 2006).

The quantitative study by Montgomery et al. (2016) mentioned earlier does not provide insights into the relation between marriage and migration among girls who migrate internally to urban areas. The authors acknowledge the difficulty of doing so without qualitative life histories data. Census data and surveys show, however, that most girls were unmarried at the time of migration and the authors suggest that "migration may be one phase in a longer-term strategy by which a girl prepares herself—in terms of acquisition of skills and capital so that when she does eventually marry that transition takes place on more favourable terms" (Montgomery et al. 2016, p. 584). Migration can have a fundamental impact on the timing of marriage and might also change the prospects, decision-making, circumstances and purpose of marriage. Small qualitative case studies in China and South East Asian countries (Bunmak 2012; Lin and Tong 2008; Ngan and Ma 2008; Yang 2008) show, for example, that living and working in a city may expose young migrants to new forms of relationships with the other sex, favoured by the use of mobile technology, and giving rise to a new language of "love" romance and dating. Our data also show how this might challenge dominant views of marriage.

Finally, migration choices and processes affect and are affected by a set of social relationships that migrants establish in their migratory journeys as well as by those they leave behind. Adolescence and migration both open extended networks of social relations with many significant others in different social domains, such as school, work and peers, to mention just a few. Here, individuals can play an active part in shaping social relations as much as being shaped by them. This is also recognized in recent developments in the field of psychology (see Coleman 2010), which have underlined how the process of defining one's selfhood is relational and based on "interdependence" rather than on severing links with parents. In anthropological terms this means that migrant girls, while opening up to new social relationships in the place of destination, are still in different ways bound by an "intergenerational contract" (Kabeer 2000) which defines the terms of their relationships with their family members. These relationships are characterized by "negotiated and constrained interdependence" (Punch 2015) and, as we will see in our three case studies, girls' transitions are always embedded in a complex net of social relationships.

Our Methodological Approach

In this book, we analyse the narratives of adolescent migrant girls in Addis Ababa, Dhaka and Khartoum through a relational approach (Huijsmans 2012, 2016, 2017). As Huijsmans states, it "includes highlighting age and space as important structuring relations, the role of networks in shaping young people's migrations, the field of the household as a key relational space in which migration dynamics unfold and that itself is reworked through migration, and the connections between early involvement in migration and wider processes of social change and continuity" (2017, p. 52). Our approach puts particular emphasis on the *social* in understanding how relational agency is grounded in social relations of power. Here, we conceptualize gender as social relations and gender relations as historically specific and socially constituted relations of power between women and men, and among women and men (see Whitehead 1979). Thus, we argue that in order to understand migrant girls' experiences, the agency they express, the ways in which they tackle the challenges they face and the kind of social persons they become, we have to take into account how their lives are embedded in multiple social relational dimensions, with gender being at the core. In all three contexts, there is an emphasis on commitments to family and complex networks of social relationships that cross-cut class and gender and have profound implications for how young people experience and confront the process of transition to adulthood. According to Ewing (1991), who discusses the case of two Pakistani women, the possibility of agency is linked to an individual's self-esteem and can be seen as the ability to negotiate social relations while also remaining part of their network. Ewing argues that even in the context of an extended family, as in the Pakistani case, where the place of a new bride is strictly defined by age and gender hierarchies, there must be some flexibility "behind the scenes". Following Moore, even if persons are bound into complex webs of relationships "this does not make the individuals concerned as incapable of agency and intention" (Moore 1994, p. 33). While acknowledging that many adolescent girls migrate under circumstances of structural gender, age and class inequality and experience situations of abuse and exploitation, we look for spaces of agency and self-assertion in their everyday lives and in the major decisions they take in their adolescent journey.

It is vitally important to explore the link between migratory choices and adolescence as a phase in life in which critical transitions take place. We take a broader view of this life phase and argue that, contrary to approaches that confine adolescents (and children) to the passive status of incomplete human beings in the process of being socialized into adult social roles, young people are active agents engaged in the construction of their social identities through on-going processes of negotiation within social relations.

In view of the preceding discussion, the main questions our research set out to answer concern first of all adolescent girls' migration choices and trajectories, the motives for their first migration and for their subsequent choices, and the circumstances in which the decision to migrate was taken. We looked at their life-course transitions and how migration as a spatial shift intersects with other transitions in the lives of adolescent girls and in what ways it affects their life trajectories in terms of education, marriage, work and having children. We also studied the factors that made girls vulnerable in the process of migration and the sources of support on which they could rely.

Outline of the Book

The book is organized into ten chapters. Chapter 2 discusses our methodological approach in more detail. Inspired by feminist methodologies, we used participatory methods and tried to break away from hierarchical power dynamics and minimize harm and control of the research process. We present our methodological choices and the methods used such as ethnographic research, focus group discussions (FGDs), the collection of life stories, and following girls over a longer period of time to get a better insight into their life trajectories and choices. We reflect on the involvement of migrant and refugee girls as research assistants and researchers in the three different contexts, and on the advantages and disadvantages of collaborative and comparative research. We also explain our choice to make a documentary film about migrant girls in Bangladesh and Ethiopia, and the ways in which the film was used not only for dissemination but was also one of our data-analysis methods.

Chapter 3 contextualizes adolescent girls' migration in the three countries. In Bangladesh and Ethiopia, girls' rural–urban migration is an age-old phenomenon. In Ethiopia, rural girls migrate mainly to become domestic workers for (often distant) relatives, sometimes in exchange for education, but an increasing number now become sex workers. In the past few decades in Bangladesh, with the rise of the garment export industry, the number of girls migrating to Dhaka has rapidly increased, although there are no official statistics available. Another form of migration is that of Garo girls and women, an ethnic minority, who work predominantly in beauty parlours or as domestic workers for foreigners. While there is limited independent internal migration of adolescent girls in Sudan, the country hosts large numbers of adolescent girls from Eritrea and Ethiopia, both as migrants and as refugees. The chapter also discusses the economic, social and political contexts in Bangladesh, Ethiopia and Sudan and policies on migrants, refugees and migration. We compare and contextualize migrant girls' experiences in the three capital cities: Dhaka, Addis Ababa and Khartoum. Gender, age and migration intersect in such ways that migrant girls are extremely vulnerable and are exposed to great risks. At the same time, the cities also offer chances to pursue different choices and to expand girls' options in terms of the lives that they desire.

Chapter 4 starts with the life story of Helen,[3] who escaped Eritrea to Sudan when she was 18 years old. Helen's life story goes against the dominant discourse, which presents migrant girls' motivations mainly in terms of helping the family, sacrificing themselves for their parents and

[3]All names of research participants have been changed to protect their anonymity.

siblings, and having no other choice. As a result, migrant girls are mainly presented as victims of constrained circumstances. Notwithstanding the importance of poverty and human rights violations, the girls' narratives reveal more complex and multifaceted decision-making processes. They show elements of agency, as well as pressures, in the choice to migrate and in the way the decision to do so is taken. Girls' choices can result from diverse factors: the struggle to survive versus following their own aspirations and desires. In this chapter, we present and analyse a number of (forced) migration stories and in so doing contribute to the theoretical debates on children and young people's mobility and agency.

In Chapter 5 the story of Sharmeen, a rural girl who moved to Dhaka and works in the garment industry, is a starting point to present and discuss the lives of migrant and refugee girls in the three cities. Based on the girls' narratives, we describe the ways in which they arrived and settled, their first encounters with the local population and other migrant girls, and their living conditions. We compare the situation in each capital city and discuss how migrant and refugee girls try to develop a space of their own. We elaborate on their working conditions, as garment workers, domestic workers, waitresses, sex workers and tea-sellers, and the relationship between their working and living conditions. In each of the three case studies, adolescent girls experience strong systems of social control, and often stigmatization, discrimination and harassment. At the same time, the cities also increase girls' options in terms of lives to which they aspire, and enlarge their view of themselves in the world.

Chapter 6 discusses the risks, threats and set-backs girls face through the story of Tigist, who escaped an abusive household and became a sex worker on the streets of Addis Ababa. Her narrative shows the different forms of abuse migrant girls may encounter, but also illustrates their resilience in trying to make something of their lives. The sources of vulnerability for migrant and refugee girls and young women are multiple: their position as girls and as women, from a specific ethnic and national background, their legal situation as foreigners and the absence of parents, guardians or relatives. In addition, the nature of their work, their level of education, and the almost non-existent support from international, national and community organizations, increase their vulnerability. Our longer-term perspective on the experiences of adolescent girl migrants and refugees reveals overwhelmingly volatile lives marked by protracted uncertainty and precariousness. Some of these difficulties might be mitigated by the available institutional support system, but also by the girls' own agency in expanding their social capital.

Chapter 7 starts with the story of Tsirite, who navigates an adverse environment in Khartoum working as a live-in domestic for Sudanese families. In this chapter, we examine the sources of protection and support on which migrant and refugee girls can rely on the three countries. We argue that while adolescent migrant girls are clearly visible in the landscape in each of the capital cities, they are largely invisible for those planning and implementing development interventions. Government institutions have no particular policies focusing on migrant and refugee girls, and national and international organizations' interventions rarely distinguish them as a distinct group. Girls rely mostly on informal sources of support, such as those offered by social and religious networks. They build social capital by supporting each other and sharing resources, housing, money and food. In this way, they are better able to protect themselves than those who have a very limited social network.

In Chapter 8 we present the story of Lamia, who moved to Dhaka at the age of 16 to work in the garment industry and support her mother and sister. Girls and young women are often aware of the hazards of the journey, as well as the dangers of different migratory destinations, but they decide to face them in order to improve their situation. Their narratives show that some are capable of creating a liveable environment by navigating the political and social constraints after migration. We argue that, faced with protracted and volatile uncertainty, the actions of adolescent girls and young women are evidence of their agency and a desire for a different (gender) identity as girls and as women. In the face of constant adversity, they often remain flexible in a world of deep uncertainty and unpredictability.

Arsema's narrative is central to Chapter 9. She migrated from Ethiopia to Sudan at the age of 16. Through the narratives of women who migrated as adolescent girls over the last 10–25 years as well as those who migrated more recently, we present findings related to sending remittances, supporting family members, investing in the future, and the impact on households and on the status of migrants in relation to their families. As the research shows, the increasing participation of young girls in the labour market in their place of destination, their increasing contributions to household finances, even if minimal, have effects on gender and generational relations both within families and in societies at large. In the short term, the effects of migration on girls and their families are rather negative. Yet, one needs to also pay close attention to how migrants, refugees and their families conceptualize change. While positive changes might not be immediately visible, small steps of transformation do take place.

In the concluding chapter, we reflect on how the choice to migrate and the experiences of migration have affected the young migrants' life trajectories and how they have intersected with their transition to adulthood. In all three case studies, the gender order has had profound effects on the decisions, experiences and consequences of migration for the girls and their families. We look specifically at social relations and at gender norms. Finally, we conclude by reflecting on whether migration is good for girls.

References

Afsar, R. (2003). *Internal Migration and the Development Nexus: The Case of Bangladesh*. Paper presented at Regional Conference on Migration, Development, and Pro-Poor Policy Choices in Asia, Dhaka, Refugee and Migratory Movements Research Unit and DFID.

Agarwal, S., Jones, E., & Verma, S. (2016). Migrant Adolescent Girls in Urban Slums India: Aspirations, Opportunities and Challenges. *Indian Journal Youth Adolescent Health, 3*(4), 8–21.

Austin, J., & Willard, M. N. (1998). Introduction: Angels of History, Demons of Culture. In J. Willard & M. N. Willard (Eds.), *Generations of Youth: Youth Cultures and History in Twentieth-Century America* (pp. 1–20). New York: New York University Press.

Bakewell, O. (2010). Some Reflections on Structure and Agency in Migration Theory. *Journal of Ethnic and Migration Studies, 36*(10), 1689–1708.

Balakrishnan, R. (2005). Rural Women in Household Production: Increasing Contributions and Persisting Drudgery. In *Rural Women and Food Security in Asia and the Pacific: Prospects and Paradoxes*. RAP Publication 2005/30. Bangkok: Food and Agriculture Organization of the United Nations (FAO).

Blanchet, T. (1996). *Lost Innocence, Stolen Childhoods*. Dhaka: The University Press.

Blanchet, T. (2002). *Beyond Boundaries: A Critical Look at Women Labour Migration and the Trafficking Within*. Drishti Research Centre. Submitted to USAID, Dhaka.

Bourdieu, P. (1993). Youth 'Is Just a Word'. *Sociology in Question* (pp. 94–102). London: Sage.

Brettell, C. (2002). Gendered Lives: Transitions and Turning Points in Person, Family, and Historical Time. *Current Anthropology, 43*(S4), S45–S61.

Bucholtz, M. (2002). Youth and Cultural Practice. *Annual Review of Anthropology, 3*(1), 525–552.

Bunmak, S. (2012). Cell Phone Networks and Migrant Networks: The Case of Nayu Migrant Workers in Malaysia. *Malaysian Journal of Society and Space, 8*(1), 38–49.

Camacho, A. Z. V. (2006). *Children and Migration: Understanding the Migration Experiences of Child Domestic Workers in the Philippines.* The Hague: Institute for Social Sciences.

Castle, S. (2010). Understanding Global Migration: A Social Transformation Perspective. *Journal of Ethnic and Migration Studies, 36*(10), 1565–1586.

Castle, S., & Diarra, A. (2003). *The International Migration of Young Malians: Tradition, Necessity or Rite of Passage.* London: London School of Hygiene and Tropic Medicine.

Clark-Kazak, C. R. (2009). Towards a Working Definition and Application of Social Age in International Development Studies. *Journal of International Development, 45*(8), 1307–1324.

Coe, C., Reynolds, R., Boehm, D., Hess, J. M., & Rae Espinoza, H. (Eds.). (2011). *Everyday Ruptures, Children, Youth and Migration in Global Perspectives.* Nashville, TN: Vanderbilt Press.

Coleman, J. C. (2010). *The Nature of Adolescence.* London: Routledge.

Coleman, J. C., & Hendry, L. (1999). *The Nature of Adolescence.* London: Routledge.

Crivello, G. (2009). *'Becoming Somebody': Youth Transitions Through Education and Migration in Peru. Young Lives* (Working Paper No. 43). Oxford. Young Lives, University of Oxford.

Croll, E. J. (2006). From the Girl Child to Girls' Rights. *Third World Quarterly, 27*(7), 1285–1297.

Custer, C., et al. (2005). *Adolescent Migration in Udaipur District: An Investigation into the Causes and Consequences.* Udaipur: Seva Mandir.

de Regt, M. (2010). Ways to Come, Ways to Leave: Gender, Mobility, and Il/Legality Among Ethiopian Domestic Workers in Yemen. *Gender & Society, 24*(2), 237–260.

de Regt, M. (2012). Ethiopian Women's Migration to Yemen: Past and Present. *ChroniquesYémenites, 17,* 1–17.

Del Franco, N. (2010, March). Aspirations and Self-hood: Exploring the Meaning of Higher Education for Girl College Students in Rural Bangladesh. *Compare: A Journal of Comparative and International Education, 40*(2), 147–165.

Del Franco, N. (2012). *Negotiating Adolescence in Rural Bangladesh: A Journey through School, Love and Marriage.* New Delhi: Zubaan Books.

Derks, A. (2008). *Khmer Women on the Move: Exploring Work and Life in Urban Cambodia.* Honolulu, HI: University of Hawaii Press.

Dobson, M. E. (2009). Unpacking Children in Migration Research. *Children's Geographies, 7*(3), 355–360.

Durham Meenakshi, G. (2004). Constructing the "New Ethnicities": Media, Sexuality, and Diaspora Identity in the Lives of South Asian Immigrant Girls. *Critical Studies in Media Communication, 21*(2), 140–161.

Ensor, M., & Gozdziak, E. (Eds.). (2010). *Children and Migration: At the Cross-Roads of Resiliency and Vulnerability*. Basingstoke: Palgrave Macmillan.

Erikson, E. H. (1968). *Identity: Youth and Crisis*. New York, NY: Norton & Company.

Erulkar, A., & Mekbib, T. (2007). Invisible and Vulnerable: Adolescent Domestic Workers in Addis Ababa, Ethiopia. *Vulnerable Children and Youth Studies, 2*(3), 246–256.

Erulkar, A., Mekbib, T., Simie, N., & Gulema, T. (2006). Migration and Vulnerability Among Adolescents in Slum Areas of Addis Ababa, Ethiopia. *Journal of Youth Studies, 9*(3), 361–374.

Ewing, K. (1991). Can Psychoanalytic Theory Explain the Pakistani Woman? Intra-psychic Autonomy and Interpersonal Engagement in the Extended Family. *Ethos, 19*(2), 131–161.

Finlay, J. E., Ozaltin, E., & Canning, D. (2011). The Association of Maternal Age with Infant Mortality, Child Anthropometric Failure, Diarrhea and Anaemia for First Births: Evidence from 55 Low- and Middle-Income Countries. *BMJ Open, 1*.

Gardner, K. (2009). Lives in Motion: The Life-Course, Movement and Migration in Bangladesh. *Journal of South Asian Development, 4*(2), 229–251.

Gardner, K. (2012). Transnational Migration and the Study of Children: An Introduction. *Journal of Ethnic and Migration Studies, 38*(6), 889–912.

Gardner, K., & Osella, F. (2003). Migration, Modernity and Social Transformation in South Asia: An Overview. *Contributions to Indian Sociology, 37*(1&2), 5–28.

Giani, L. (2006). *Migration and Education: Child Migrants in Bangladesh* (Sussex Migration Working Paper No. 33). Brighton: University of Sussex.

Grabska, K. (2006). Marginalization in the Urban Spaces of the Global South: Urban Refugees in Cairo [Special Issue: Urban Refugees]. *Journal of Refugee Studies, 19*(3), 273–286.

Grabska, K. (2010). Lost Boys, Invisible Girls: Stories of Marriage Across Borders. *Gender, Place and Culture, 17*(4), 479–497.

Grabska, K. (2011). Constructing 'Modern Gendered Civilised' Women and Men: Gender Mainstreaming in Refugee Camps. *Gender and Development, 19*(1), 81–93.

Grabska, K. (2013). The Return of Displaced Nuer in Southern Sudan: Women Becoming Men? *Development and Change, 44*(5), 1135–1157.

Grabska, K. (2014). *Gender, Identity, and Home: Nuer Repatriation to Southern Sudan*. Oxford: Boydell & Brewer, James Currey.

Grabska, K. (2015). Threatening Mini Skirts?: Returnee South Sudanese Adolescent Girls and Social Change. In L. Akensson & M. E. Baaz (Eds.), *Africa's Return Migrants: The New Developers?* London: Zed Books.

Grabska, K. (2016). *Time to Look at Girls: Eritrean and Ethiopian Adolescent Migrant in Sudan, Research Report.* Geneva: Swiss Network of International Studies.

Greenberger, E. (1984). Defining Psychosocial Maturity in Adolescence. In P. Karoly & J. Steffen (Eds.), *Adolescent Behaviour Disorders.* Lexington, MA: Heath.

Grootevant, H., & Cooper, C. (1986). Individuation in Family Relationships. *Human Development, 29,* 82–100.

Guo, M., Chow, N. W. S., & Palinka, L. A. (2011). Circular Migration and Life Course of Female Domestic Workers in Beijing. *Asian Population Studies, 7*(1), 51–67.

Hall, S. (1905). *Adolescence (1&2).* New York, NY: Appleton.

Hall, S. (1991). Old and New Identities, Old and New Ethnicities. In A. D. King (Ed.), *Culture Globalization and the World System* (pp. 41–68). Minneapolis, MN: University of Minnesota Press.

Hashim, I. (2007). Independent Child Migration and Education in Ghana. *Development and Change, 38*(5), 911–931.

Hashim, I., & Thorsen, D. (2011). *Child Migration in Africa.* London: Zed Books.

Heinonen, P. (2011). *Youth Gangs and Street Children: Culture, Nurture and Masculinity in Ethiopia.* New York, NY and Oxford: Berghahn.

Heissler, K. A. (2013). Rethinking 'Trafficking' in Children's Migratory Processes: The Role of Social Networks in Child Labour Migration in Bangladesh. *Children's Geographies, 11*(1), 89–101.

Hertrich, V., & Lesclingand, M. (2012). Adolescent Migration and the 1990s Nuptiality Transition in Mali. *Population Studies, 66*(2), 47–166.

Hertrich, V., & Lesclingand, M. (2017). When Girls Take the Lead: Adolescent Girls' Migration in Mali. *Population, 72*(1), 63–91.

Hopkins, P. E., & Hill, M. (2008). Pre-flight Experiences and Migration Stories: The Accounts of Unaccompanied Asylum-seeking Children. *Children's Geographies, 6,* 257–268.

Hossain, N. (2012). *Women's Empowerment Revisited: From Individual to Collective Power Among the Export Sector Workers of Bangladesh* (IDS Working Paper No. 38). Brighton: Institute of Development Studies.

Howard, N. (2017). *Child Trafficking, Youth Labour Mobility and the Politics of Protection.* London: Palgrave Macmillan.

Huijsmans, R. (2011). Child Migration and Questions of Agency. *Development and Change, 42*(5), 1307–1321.

Huijsmans, R. (2012). Beyond Compartmentalization: A Relational Approach towards Agency and Vulnerability of Young Migrants. *New Directions for Child and Adolescent Development, 136,* 29–45.

Huijsmans, R. (Ed.). (2016). *Generationing Development: A Relational Approach to Children, Youth and Development.* London: Palgrave Macmillan.

Huijsmans, R. (2017). Children and Young People in Migration: A Relational Approach. In C. Ní Laoire, A. White, & T. Skelton (Eds.), *Movement, Mobilities and Journeys* (Vol. 6, pp. 45–66). Singapore: Springer.

Huijsmans, R., & Baker, S. (2012). Child Trafficking: Worst Form of Child Labour, or Worst Approach to Young Migrants? *Development and Change, 43*(4), 919–946.

Jacquemin, M. (2009). "Petites nièces" et "petites bonnes" à Abidjan. Les mutations de la domesticité juvenile. *Travail, Genre et Sociétés, 22*, 53–74.

Jacquemin, M. (2011). Migrations juvéniles féminines de travail en Côte-d'Ivoire. *Journal des Africanistes, 81*(1), 61–86.

Jauhola, M. (2011). 'The Girl Child of Today is the Woman of Tomorrow': Fantasizing the Adolescent Girl as the Future Hope in Post-tsunami Reconstruction Efforts in Aceh, Indonesia. *Rhizomes, 22.*

Jeffrey, C., Jeffery, P., & Jeffery, R. (2008). *Degrees Without Freedom? Education Masculinities and Unemployment in North India.* Palo Alto, CA: Stanford University Press.

Johnson-Hanks, J. (2002). On the Limits of Life Stages in Ethnography: Toward a Theory of Vital Conjunctures. *American Anthropologist, 104*(3), 865–880.

Jones, G. A., & Chant, S. (2009). Globalising Initiatives for Gender Equality and Poverty Reduction: Exploring "Failure" with Reference to Education and Work Among Urban Youth in The Gambia and Ghana. *Geoforum, 40*(2), 184–196.

Kabeer, N. (2000). Inter-generational Contracts Demographic Transitions and the Quantity–Quality Trade Off: Parents, Children and Investing in the Future. *Journal of International Development, 12*(4), 463–482.

Kabeer, N., & Mahmud, S. (2004). Globalization, Gender and Poverty: Bangladeshi Women Workers in Export and Local Markets. *Journal of International Development, 16*(1), 93–109.

Kabeer, N., Mahmud, S., & Tasneem, S. (2011). *Does Paid Work Provide a Pathway to Women's Empowerment?* (IDS Working Paper No. 375).

Khair, S. (2008). *Child Migration for Work.* Dhaka: RMMRU.

Kifle, A. (2002). *Ethiopia: Child Domestic Workers in Addis Ababa—A Rapid Assessment.* Geneva: International Programme on the Elimination of Child Labour (IPEC)/ILO.

Klocker, N. (2007). An Example of "Thin" Agency: Child Domestic Workers in Tanzania. In R. Panelli, S. Punch, & E. Robson (Eds.), *Global Perspectives on Rural Childhood and Youth: Young Rural Lives* (pp. 83–94). New York and London: Routledge.

Koffman, O., & Gill, R. (2013). "The Revolution Will be Led by a 12-Year-Old Girl": Girl Power and Global Biopolitics. *Feminist Review, 105*, 83–102.

Langevang, T. (2008). "We Are Managing!" Uncertain Paths to Respectable Adulthoods in Accra, Ghana. *Geoforum, 39*(6), 2039–2047.

Lin, A., & Tong, A. (2008). Mobile Cultures of Migrant Workers in Southern China: Informal Literacies in the Negotiation of (New) Social Relations of the New Working Women. *Knowledge, Technology, and Policy, 21,* 73–81.
Lloyd, C. B. (2005). *Growing Up Global: The Changing Transitions to Adulthood in Developing Countries.* Panel on Transitions to Adulthood in Developing Countries, National Research Council and Institute of Medicine. Washington, DC: National Academics Press.
Lloyd, C. B. (2006). Schooling and Adolescent Reproductive Behavior in Developing Countries. Background Paper to *Public Choices, Private Decisions: Sexual and Reproductive Health and the Millennium Development Goals.* New York, NY: UN Millennium Project.
Marcia, J. E. (1980). Identity in Adolescence. In J. Adelson (Ed.), *Handbook of Adolescent Psychology.* New York, NY: Wiley.
Mead, M. (1928). *Coming of Age in Samoa.* Ann Arbor, MI: Morrow.
Mills, M. B. (2005). Engendering Discourses of Displacement. *Ethnography, 6*(3), 385–419.
Montgomery, M. R., Balk, D., Liu, Z., Agarwal, S., Jones, E., & Adamo, S. (2016). Urban Migration of Adolescent Girls: Quantitative Results from Developing Countries. In J. Michael (Ed.), *International Handbook of Migration and Population Distribution* (pp. 573–604). Dordrecht: Springer.
Moore, H. (1994). *A Passion for Difference.* Cambridge: Polity Press.
Muttarak, R. (2004). Domestic Service in Thailand: Reflection of Conflicts in Gender, Class and Ethnicity. *Journal of Southeast Asian Studies, 35*(3), 503–529.
Muuss, R. E. (1996). *Theories of Adolescence.* New York, NY: McGraw Hill.
Nedoluzhko, L., & Agadjain, G. (2009). Marriage, Childbearing, and Migration in Kyrgyzstan: Exploring Interdependences. *Demographic Research, 22,* 159–188.
Nedoluzhko, L., & Andersson, G. (2007). Migration and First-Time Parenthood: Evidence from Kyrgyzstan. *Demographic Research, 17*(25), 741–774.
Ngan, R., & Ma, S. (2008). The Relationship of Mobile Telephony to Job Mobility in China's Pearl River Delta. *Knowledge, Technology, and Policy, 21,* 55–63.
O'Connell Davidson, J. (2011). Moving Children? Child Trafficking, Child Migration, and Child Rights. *Critical Social Policy, 31*(3), 454–477.
Pankhurst, H. (1992). *Gender, Development and Identity: An Ethiopian Study.* London and Atlantic Highlands, NJ: Zed Books.
Pearson, R., & Kusakabe, K. (2012). *Thailand's Hidden Workforce: Burmese Migrant Women Factory Workers.* London: Zed Books.
Poluha, E. (2004). *The Power of Continuity: Ethiopia Through the Eyes of Its Children.* Uppsala: Nordic Africa Institute.
Punch, S. (2002). Youth Transitions and Interdependent Adult–Child Relations in Rural Bolivia. *Journal of Rural Studies, 18*(2), 123–133.
Punch, S. (2007). Negotiating Migrant Identities: Young People in Bolivia and Argentina. *Children's Geographies, 5*(1&2), 95–112.

Punch, S. (2015). Possibilities for Learning Between Childhoods and Youth in the Minority and Majority Worlds: Youth Transitions as an Example of Cross-World Dialogue. In J. Wyn & H. Cahill (Eds.), *Handbook of Children and Youth Studies* (pp. 689–701). Singapore: Springer.

Punch, S. (2016). Exploring Children's Agency Across Majority and Minority World Contexts. In F. Esser, M. S. Baader, T. Betz, & B. Hunderland (Eds.), *Reconceptualising Agency and Childhood: New Perspectives in Childhood Studies* (pp. 183–196). Abingdon: Routledge.

Rao, N. (2014). Migration, Mobility and Changing Power Relations: Aspirations and Praxis of Bangladeshi Migrants. *Gender, Place and Culture, 21*(7), 872–887.

Razy, E., & Rodet, M. (Eds.). (2016). *Children on the Move in Africa: Past and Present Experiences of Migration.* Woodbridge: Boydell & Brewer.

Schlegel, A., & Barry, H. (1991). *Adolescence: An Anthropological Enquiry.* New York, NY: Free Press.

Siddiqui, D. M. (2009). Do Bangladeshi Factory Workers Need Saving? Sisterhood in the Post-sweatshop Era. *Feminist Review, 91*, 154–174.

Temin, M., Montgomery, M. R., Engebretsen, S., & Barker, K. M. (2013). *Girls on the Move: Adolescent Girls and Migration in the Developing World. A Girls Count Report on Adolescent Girls.* New York, NY: Population Council.

Thorsen, D. (2006). Child Migrants in Transit: Strategies to Assert New Identities in Rural Burkina Faso. In C. Christiansen, M. Utas, & H. E. Vigh (Eds.), *Navigating Youth, Generating Adulthood: Social Becoming in an African Context* (pp. 88–114). Uppsala: Nordic Africa Institute.

Thorsen, D. (2007). *"If Only I Get Enough Money for a Bicycle!" A Study of Childhoods, Migration and Adolescent Aspirations Against a Backdrop of Exploitation and Trafficking in Burkina Faso* (Working Paper). Development Research Centre on Migration, Globalisation and Poverty. Brighton: University of Sussex.

Thorsen, D. (2011). Non-formal Apprenticeships for Rural Youth—Questions That Need to Be Asked. *NORRAG NEWS, Towards a New Global World of Skills Development? TVET's turn to Make its Mark, 46*, 71–73.

Thorsen, D. (2014). Jeans, Bicycles and Mobile Phones: Adolescent Migrants' Material Consumption. In A. Veale & G. Donà (Eds.), *Child and Youth Migration: Mobility-in-Migration in an Era of Globalization* (pp. 67–90). Basingstoke: Palgrave Macmillan.

UNDP. (2013). *Internal Migration in Bangladesh: Characters, Drivers and Policy Issues.* Dhaka: United Nations Development Programme.

UNICEF. (2011). Adolescence an Age of Opportunity. *The State of the World's Children Report.* New York: UNICEF.

Van Blerk, L. (2008). Poverty, Migration and Sex Work: Youth Transitions in Ethiopia. *Area, 40*(2), 245–253.

Van Gennep, A. (1908). *The Rites of Passage*. London: Routledge & Kegan Paul.
Veale, A., & Donà, G. (2014). Complex Migrations, Migrant Child and Family Life Trajectories and Globalization. In A. Veale & G. Donà (Eds.), *Child and Youth Migration: Mobility-in-Migration in an Era of Globalization*. Basingstoke: Palgrave Macmillan.
White, A., NíLaoire, C., Tyrrell, N., & Carpena-Méndez, F. (2011). Children's Roles in Transnational Migration [Special Issue on Transnational Migration and Childhood]. *Journal of Ethnic and Migration Studies, 27*(8), 1159–1170.
Whitehead, A. (1979). Some Preliminary Notes on the Subordination of Women. *IDS Bulletin, 10*(3), 10–13.
Whitehead, A., & Hashim, I. (2005). *Children and Migration*. Background paper for DFID Migration Team. Unpublished.
Whitehead, A., Hashim, I., & Iversen, V. (2007). *Child Migration, Child Agency and Intergenerational Relations in Africa and South Asia* (Globalisation and Poverty Working Paper No. T24: Development Research Centre on Migration). Brighton: University of Sussex.
Yang, K. (2008). A Preliminary Study on the Use of Mobile Phones Amongst Migrant Workers in Beijing. *Knowledge, Technology, and Policy, 21*, 65–72.
Yaqub, S. (2009). *Child Migrants with and without Parents: Census-based Estimates of Scale and Characteristics in Argentina, Chile and South Africa*. Discussion Paper No. IDP 2009-02. Florence: Unicef Innocenti Research Centre.
Youniss, J., & Smollar, J. (1985). *Adolescent Relations with Mothers, Fathers and Friends*. Chicago, IL: University of Chicago Press.

CHAPTER 2

Doing Research Among Migrant and Refugee Girls

Doing research among marginalized and often invisible populations poses challenges, which are marked by huge power hierarchies between researchers and those whose lives are being studied. Migrant and refugee adolescent girls often try to stay invisible in their place of migration in order not to expose themselves to risks and to protect themselves (see Chapter 7). Inspired by feminist methodologies, we used participatory methods in the research and tried to break away from hierarchical power dynamics and to minimize harm and control of the research process. This does not mean that we were not aware of the intersectional power dynamics between us as researchers and the research participants, but we took the difference, following Henrietta Moore's dictum (1988), as a point of departure that guided our reflections on the research process. Moreover, the choice of a three-country study, as explained in Chapter 1, allowed us to contribute to the rather scant literature and research that addresses migration dynamics in the Global South in a comparative manner (see the exceptions of Salway et al. 2011; Bosswick and Husband 2005). In this way, we were able both to make some advances and innovations in migration research more generally, and also to elaborate on the methodological and theoretical challenges related to comparative research. We will return to these issues at the end of this chapter but now turn to our methodological approach and the realization of the research.

K. Grabska et al., *Adolescent Girls' Migration in The Global South*, Palgrave Studies on Children and Development,
https://doi.org/10.1007/978-3-030-00093-6_2

Research Approach: Feminist Methodologies

We locate our methodological approach in feminist methodologies. Following Harding's (1987) argument that there is no one feminist method, and recognizing that there are multiple feminist epistemologies and feminist projects, our research approach was based on a general concern to examine adolescent interests in and experiences of migration while striving towards a science that minimizes harm and control of the research process. While our research focused on girls' and young women's perceptions in particular, in order to contextualize their views and experiences, we also interviewed their parents and family members and also peers who had not decided to move. We chose feminist methodologies also because they question positivist value-free methodologies and seek alternative epistemological and methodological paradigms to better explain the often invisible power relations embedded in gender and its intersection with age, ethnic background, religion and class. Feminist methodologies appealed to us because of their central commitment to reflexivity and making biases and stand on issues visible and explicit. In this way, in close collaboration with local researchers in each country and among ourselves, we were able to bring our own preconceptions and interpretations to the subject under study, resulting in the production of "partial truths" rather than one overarching interpretation.

We follow standpoint theory, which underscores the situated nature of knowledge and the particularities of knowledge production by those in marginal positions (Intemann 2010). The situated knowledge approach argues that a "social location systematically influences experience, shaping and limiting what we know, such that knowledge is achieved from a particular standpoint" (Intemann 2010, p. 783). Following the understanding that all knowledge is situated (see Harding 1991, 2004), we were committed to listening and including different voices. In order to better understand the voices and experiences of adolescent girls who had migrated, we needed to listen and acknowledge the voices of those who had not. The second element of the standpoint theory is the privileging of the viewpoints of the oppressed and marginalized groups[1]

[1] Here the references to the standpoints of the oppressed and marginalized imply a "multi-axis standpoint approach that captures the simultaneous, multiple oppressions such as race, class, and gender that affect people's vantage points on reality" (Archer Mann and Patterson 2015, p. 223).

in relation to other perspectives (within certain limits and specific contexts) (Intemann 2010).

In our feminist approach to the research, gender was an important dimension that not only structured and regulated our access to the field, but also influenced our data analysis and subsequent theorization. We employed this methodology in order to shed light on those whose life-worlds are repeatedly rendered invisible and silenced. Adolescent girls, owing to the often oppressive gender norms in their places of origin or migration, but also because of their need to protect themselves, remain marginal and often invisible to researchers. At the same time, their concrete experiences in specific geographical locations cannot be understood without linking them to the analysis of the regional, international and global contexts, regulated by cultural, socio-economic and geopolitical hierarchies of power. Thus, the migratory trajectories and experiences of adolescent girls and young women in our study are framed within wider globalization processes.

Our choice to work closely with migrant and refugee girls and to include them in data gathering, analysis and writing was one way to confront hierarchies that are deeply rooted in the research process. This was an attempt, often imperfect, towards a knowledge that was co-constructed in the process of listening, discussing and negotiating. By including them in the research on equal grounds and regarding them as researchers, our aim was to create spaces of transformation and possibly emancipation, leading towards the transformation of social relations of power.

For the research, we adopted a common methodology for each of the country studies. Data were collected using a mixed multi-method while privileging a qualitative approach to ensure the participation and involvement of migrant and refugee girls and young women. In each country, we worked with a research team. Prior to the fieldwork, the teams were trained in the methodology and research methods. We also adopted a collaborative approach to research design, data analysis and writing up. Together with Ann Whitehead, our academic advisor, we three main researchers met several times throughout the research to discuss and share our perceptions, to analyse and to write together. We then shared our discussions with our respective research teams and asked for their inputs.

This book is also a result of joint analysis and writing. In this way, we were able to comment on each other's findings and approaches, and draw more thematic comparisons and contrasts across the three case studies.

Research Methods and Research Participants

In all three countries, data were collected in different phases. In Bangladesh, the fieldwork took place between January and December 2014 and was conducted by Nicoletta Del Franco, supported by a research team comprising a research assistant, a counsellor from ARBAN (Association for Realization of Basic Needs), a project coordinator from Terre des Hommes Italy, and five adolescent girls who helped with administering the qualitative questionnaires. The fieldwork in Ethiopia took place between March and September 2014. The research was carried out by a team of Ethiopian researchers under supervision of Marina de Regt. The main researchers were Felegebirhan Belesti and Arsema Solomon, who focused on internal migrants in Addis Ababa. AynadisYohannes and MedareshawTafesse interviewed with young women who had returned from the Middle East. Two migrant girls assisted in identifying other girls who had migrated internally for interviews and carried out interviews themselves. The fieldwork in Sudan took place between March 2014 and September 2015 and was conducted by Katarzyna Grabska, supported by a research team comprising four research assistants, who were recruited among the Eritrean and Ethiopian migrant and refugee adolescent girls and young women. They were involved in designing and administering the qualitative questionnaires, translating and transcribing interviews, conducting life story interviews and focus group discussions, analysing data and jointly co-writing a research report and an academic article (Fig. 2.1).

In each country study, we used semi-structured and in-depth interviews, small-scale qualitative surveys, life stories, and focus group discussions (FGDs) with migrant girls and women, as well as with their families and peers. In order to gain a longer perspective on the lives of adolescent girl migrants, we also interviewed women who had migrated as adolescents ten or more years earlier. Initially, we planned to interview about 30 'older' women migrants in each country. However, it proved very difficult to find women who have stayed for so long in their migration destinations. Many moved back to their places or origin or migrated further across national borders in search of a better life. This observation revealed the dynamic nature of migratory processes, and migrants' mobility. Ethnographic methods were used to contextualize the lives of the research participants, as well as to gain a more grounded view of general circumstances of migration in these places.

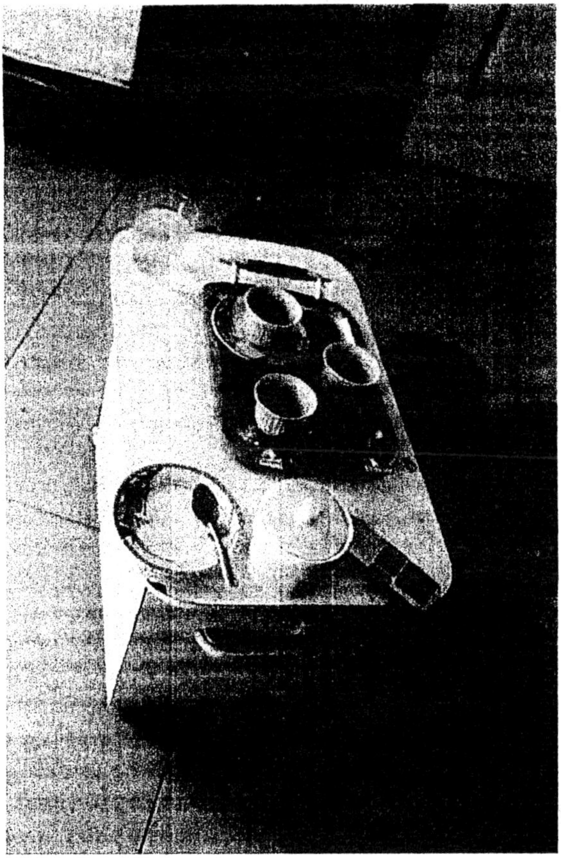

Fig. 2.1 Fieldwork in Sudan, Khartoum, 2014

In **Bangladesh**, the research focused on adolescent girls and women who had migrated to Dhaka from rural areas and looked at two main groups: young women and girls working in the garment manufacturing sector, and those employed in 'beauty parlours'. The first group consisted of 47 Bengali migrants, who ranged in age from 12 to 34 years at the time of the study, mainly women who have worked or are working in the garment sector and a minority who have worked or are working in other sectors. Eleven Bengali girls moved to Dhaka when they were not yet 13 years of age, 30 of them between 13 and 17 and six between 18 and 20. The second group of migrants, who were working in beauty parlours, comprised 13 girls and young women belonging to the Garo ethnic minority. Most of these migrants (11) moved to Dhaka when they were between 13 and 17 years of age, and two between the ages of 18 and 20. Despite the initial plan to interview equal numbers of recent migrants and older women who had lived for 10 or more years at their destination (30 of each), the team led by Nicoletta Del Franco interviewed only 17 (11 Bengali, six Garo) migrants who had been living in Dhaka for more than a decade. The majority of the respondents 37 (33 Bengali, four Garo) had migrated up to five years before. Family members of eight migrants were also interviewed in their village of origin, as were some non-migrant adolescent girls.

In **Ethiopia**, the research focused on two groups of young migrants (total 60 participants), domestic workers and sex workers, as they form the large majority of adolescent internal migrants in Addis Ababa. Fifteen migrants in this group were between 12 and 17 years of age when they were interviewed and 15 between 18 and 24. They were all aged between 12 and 18 years when they migrated. The second group comprised 30 young women who migrated to the Middle East before they were18 years of age and who returned to Addis Ababa where they were interviewed. Twenty-four of them were 18–24 years of age at the time of the interviews and six of them over the age of 24.

Migrant and refugee girls from Ethiopia and Eritrea were the focus of the research in **Sudan**. All 60 of them had moved across borders when they were under 22 years of age (and mainly under 20 years). At the time of the interviews, the majority of both Ethiopian and Eritrean respondents were between 18 and 24 years of age, with only three below the age of 18. Most migrated when they were between 13 and 20 years of age. Only one had migrated when she was less than 13 years old and eight Eritreans had migrated when they were over the age of 20 (up to 22). Some family members of migrant girls who came to visit or live in Khartoum were also interviewed, as were some Eritrean refugee girls and young women who were born in Sudan in order to get a different perspective from that of more recent refugees.

In our efforts to obtain more comparative data, we collaboratively designed qualitative questionnaires that were then tested, translated and adapted for each case study. In **Bangladesh**, 60 questionnaires were completed by interviewing migrants, of whom 13were from the Garo community working in beauty parlours, and 47 from the Bengali community who at the time were mainly working in garment factories. In **Ethiopia,** 30 questionnaires in Amharic were carried out with internal migrants, of which 15 were with sex workers and 15 with domestic workers. Thirty questionnaires, also in Amharic, were completed by interviewing returnees from the Middle East, of whom 15 had been deported during the large-scale deportation campaign in 2013–2014, and 15 had returned for other reasons. In **Sudan**, 32 questionnaires in Tigrinya were carried out with Eritrean adolescent migrant girls who had come to Khartoum in the past six years and 16 were conducted in Amharic with Ethiopian adolescent girls and women who had migrated to Khartoum between two and 30 years ago. These qualitative questionnaires allowed us to provide more numerical comparative analysis across cases. However, the method proved only partially successful, as most answers given in the questionnaires were too simplistic, hiding the diversity and richness of individual circumstances (see Chapter 4). It was only when we spent more time with the respondents, and used other research methods, such as life histories, that we could more precisely decode the general categories that appeared in the survey. General answers such as 'poverty was a reason for movement' became more nuanced and often belied by the contextualization provided in life histories or by ethnographic methods.

Life stories provided rich data that offered many insights. In **Bangladesh**, 16 life stories were collected by visiting and talking more than once during 2014 with some of the girl migrants. Meetings with these girls took place both in their homes and in other locations and on different occasions such as the botanical garden and the cinema. The life stories were transcribed in Bengali and some were translated into English. In **Ethiopia**, 20 life stories were collected and recorded—ten with migrant girls who had migrated to Addis Ababa in the past five years and ten with women who migrated to Addis Ababa as adolescent girls, but had been living in the city for more than five years. Of the 20 life stories, ten each were from sex workers and domestic workers. The life stories were transcribed and translated into English. In **Sudan**, life stories of 15 Eritrean and 10 Ethiopian girls and young women were collected, recorded in Tigrinya or Amharic, transcribed and translated into English. This group included Eritrean adolescent girls and young women (up to 25 years of age) who had migrated to Khartoum in the previous six years. Life stories were recorded in girls' and women's homes, in workplaces, as well as at the researcher's home.

Focus group discussions (FGDs) with migrant girls, their families, or peers who did not migrate, provided valuable contextual information that helped us to make sense of the individual life stories of migrants and refugees. In **Bangladesh**, seven FGDs were conducted: one with young girls working in beauty parlours; two with migrants who were living in either Bauniabandh or Bhola slums; one with (mainly) young domestic workers who are receiving some assistance from two local NGOs through a project funded by the European Union (EU); two with women who were about to migrate to Middle Eastern countries; one with a mixed group of migrant women who are members and beneficiaries of AWAJ Foundation, an organization that campaigns for garment workers' rights. The FGDs were recorded and transcribed in Bengali and some were translated into English. In **Ethiopia**, six FGDs were conducted. Two were with migrant girls in Addis Ababa (one with domestic workers and one with sex workers); two with peers of migrant girls outside Addis Ababa (one in Amhara region and one in Shashemene); one with migrant girls who had returned to their place of origin (in Amhara region) and one with migrant girls staying in a shelter in Shashemene (waiting to return to their place of origin). The FGDs were recorded and transcribed into English. In **Sudan**, five FGDs were conducted with Eritrean refugee girls, two with girls in an Eritrean refugee school, which included girls who had arrived in the last five years and those who were either born in or came as small children to Sudan. Two FDGs included groups of girls who had arrived in the past five years, and one included girls who had arrived more than five years earlier. The FGDs were recorded and transcribed into English.

Another important method to comprehend the programmatic and political framework of girls' migration were interviews with experts. We designed common guidelines for the interviews in each country. In **Bangladesh**, six expert interviews were conducted with representatives of local and international NGOs working on issues related to internal migration and adolescence. In **Ethiopia**, a total of 20 interviews were carried out with representatives of (non-governmental) organizations involved in migration policies and programmes—ten in Addis Ababa, five in Estie/Amhara region and five in Shashemene. The expert interviews in Addis Ababa were not recorded digitally, but those in the places of origin of some of the migrants (Estie and Shashamene) were recorded and transcribed into English. In **Sudan**, 15 interviews were carried out with representatives of international and local NGOs involved in migration policies and programmes. One donor government representative working on migration issues in Sudan and the region was also interviewed, as were five researchers working on similar issues in Khartoum. All interviews took place in Khartoum, and handwritten notes were taken. Unfortunately, it was not possible to interview government representatives due to the sensitivity of the subject.

In addition, in all three countries secondary data, such as research and policy reports, were collected and reviewed. In some cases, however, it was difficult to obtain any statistical data or policy reports from government institutions. While the importance of adolescent girls' migration is acknowledged by many stakeholders in the three countries, there are limited specific policies or interventions and no reliable statistics.

The most invaluable research methods were informal conversations with research assistants, interviewees, family members and friends of the interviewees, other migrants, people working in NGOs, slum residents and others. In Sudan, for example, Katarzyna's presence in Khartoum for over two years (January 2014–June 2016) gave her insights into the everyday life of migrant communities. Observation in churches, community gatherings, schools, markets, workplaces, at home, and attending ceremonies were invaluable in understanding the general context of migration to Khartoum. Katarzyna's lengthy stay also allowed her to see the changing circumstances of migrant and refugee women and girls, with arrivals and departures of visiting or migrating family members, changing economic conditions in the country, and migration dynamics in the region. Nicoletta's long-term engagement with Bangladesh, her fluency in Bangla and work at Terre des Hommes made it easy to quickly build up close relations and friendships with the migrant girls involved in this study. For Marina, it was more difficult because the data was mainly collected by the local researchers, but her close contacts with them and her regular visits to Ethiopia enabled her to build strong connections, including with some of the migrant girls. All three of us still remain in touch with some of the research participants or migrant researchers. This longitudinal view provides us with an opportunity to comment on the volatile and dynamic experiences and migratory trajectories of adolescent girls and young women.

Challenges, Constraints and Limitations

Addis Ababa, Dhaka and Khartoum are hosts to large numbers of internal and international migrants. Adolescent girls and young women blend into the city, which makes it challenging to find them and follow their lives. In our research, we experienced various constraints in obtaining access to the different groups and had to design differentiated strategies that would allow us to gather the data we sought. Our navigation through the urban landscapes of the three cities was also a good indicator of the challenges that migrants and refugees confront.

In Dhaka, it was relatively easy to locate migrants, since most of those who move from rural areas to work in garment factories tend to find cheap accommodation in slum areas. We decided to focus on two slums where Nicoletta Del Franco had previously worked and where Terre des Hommes Italy, with its partners ARBAN and Aparajeyo Bangladesh, have been running development projects for over 12 years, mainly in the field of education. The collaboration of these NGOs was essential in facilitating access to the slums and locating the migrants. Collaboration with adolescent girls who were known to these NGOs was crucial in identifying their migrant peers in the Bauniabandh area. Together with the girls, Nicoletta visited every slum household and asked about the presence of migrants. Other respondents were identified through the Aparajeyo Bangladesh office, where a first FGD with 12 migrant girls living in the Bhola slum was organized. With respect to the Garo/Mandi migrants, most of those interviewed were already known to Nicoletta from her previous visits to Bangladesh. The research team established a strong rapport with some of the migrants, and allowed us to follow up the main events in their lives and the changes in their circumstances.

The main obstacle was the very limited free time the garment workers have. Working hours are on average from 9 a.m. to 7–8 p.m., including overtime, six days a week. Almost all the garment factories in Mirpur, where the Bengali respondents were employed, are closed only on Fridays, and in busy periods not at all. This meant that we had to concentrate most of the interviews in one day a week or during holidays. Overall, the migrants were very interested in the research and eager to participate. They were happy to connect Nicoletta and her team with their parents to follow up the migratory links from the rural areas.

In Khartoum and Addis Ababa, we faced different challenges and limitations. First, it is generally difficult to connect with domestic workers and sex workers. In both cities, most families have a domestic worker, but it is almost impossible to approach and interview these girls. Most of them live and work in their employer's home and have almost no time off. In Sudan, contacts had to be negotiated mainly through Sudanese employers, who were not always willing to cooperate. They also insisted on being present during the interviews, which made it difficult to judge the trust and openness of the respondents. This was one of the reasons why there were fewer Ethiopians interviewed (16 instead of the planned 30). In Ethiopia, most of the domestic workers were met through a school that gives evening classes to boys and girls unable to attend school during the day. The school director was willing to facilitate the research, but the time for interviews and for establishing a general trust and rapport with respondents was limited. In addition, this restricted the selection of research participants to those who were able to attend evening school. Fortunately, we were also able to interview some domestic workers whom we got to know via the migrant girl assistants.

Sex workers have much more freedom of movement. Often they live on their own or with friends, but their work schedule (evening and nights) makes it difficult to find them since they sleep for part of the day. With these constraints, it is not easy to build up a relationship of trust and confidence and gain more insight in the lives of these migrants, by sharing their lives, as anthropologists commonly try to do. Access to sex workers was facilitated by two local NGOs in Addis Ababa. NIKAT is a sex workers' organization established in 2006 with the aim of improving the living conditions of sex workers in Ethiopia, and to fight against poverty and HIV and AIDS. NIKAT has a drop-in centre where sex workers can come to relax, rest, meet others and have access to information. The second NGO was Timret Le Hiwot (TLH), which was established in 2004 with the aim of preventing the spread of HIV and AIDS. TLH also has programmes aimed at sex workers and their clients. With the help of TLH, we found a number of adolescent sex workers for interviews. Financially, our research was facilitated by Girl Effect Ethiopia, which supports girls in Ethiopia in a variety of ways. Girl Effect offered us office space but had no active role in the research as such.

In Khartoum, the research was carried out with the support and under the aegis of the Ahfad University for Women in Omdurman. Katarzyna carried out interviews mainly in respondents' homes, at workplaces and social gatherings. Some were also conducted in public (safe) spaces, including churches and restaurants. Good collaboration with three key research assistants, who became researchers during the project, was key in securing access to diverse Eritrean and Ethiopian groups and individuals and building trust in the community.

One of the main challenges both in Dhaka and Khartoum was the high mobility of migrants. Eritrean migrants move because of security reasons but also because they want to migrate beyond Sudan to seek better life opportunities. This made it challenging to find Eritrean and Ethiopian respondents who had both migrated as adolescent girls and had spent more than seven to eight years in the country. In Dhaka, one of the reasons we could not find many older migrants might be that after some years of work and/or after marriage, with a better economic situation, the migrants move to a different area of the city. We found this was the case for five of our respondents. As we focused our search for adolescent migrants in two *bustee* (slum) areas, we tended to find only those who had migrated recently, who were single and whose income was not enough to afford better housing.

One of our objectives was to carry out research in cooperation with adolescent girls and young women since we believed that this would greatly improve the quality of the research findings. This was also our core feminist commitment. This was not always possible to the extent we had hoped. In Ethiopia, the two migrants who assisted in administering the questionnaires were very helpful and the accounts of their lives and their responses to the stories of other sex workers gave the local researchers more insight into the issues regarding adolescent girls' migration. We were not able to involve them more than this, which is a pity, as is the absence of a domestic worker as a migrant girl assistant. In Sudan, the principal researcher asked migrant and refugee girls to administer some of the questionnaires. Eritrean refugee girls were also involved in data gathering, identifying respondents, transcribing data and doing initial analysis and some writing. Katarzyna also worked closely with the refugee researchers on data analysis by discussing the findings and the reports and including their inputs. In Bangladesh, the possibility of involving the migrants in collecting data was ruled out because of their time constraints. As garment workers they did not have time to do research. Instead, five adolescent girls who had been living in the slum for a long time, selected in cooperation with the local NGOs, helped in administering the questionnaire and in locating the migrants.

Another challenge in all three cases was linked to interviewing family members of the migrant girls and women. In Ethiopia, none of the interviewed girls was willing to give the contact details of their relatives back home. Their reasons varied: in some cases, their relatives did not know their whereabouts and the girls did not want them to find out, in other cases, they had lost contact with their relatives, or their relatives did not know what type of work they were doing in Addis Ababa. Instead of visiting the families of the interviewed girls, we decided to do fieldwork in two areas outside Addis Ababa; one that is known as a rural migrant-sending area (in Amhara region), and one a town (Shashemene) which is a hub for migrants from the southern part of the country. In this way, we were able to gain a wider perspective on the places of origin and the dynamics of their home communities.

In Bangladesh, it was mainly due to time constraints that we were not able to visit more households in the migrants' places of origin. The migrants interviewed in Dhaka were mainly from a wide spread of districts—Bogra, Netrakona, Jamalpur, Mymensingh, Barisal and Bhola—and from different villages in the same district. We chose five girls from two districts and visited their households and communities. Netrakona district was selected because it includes the hilly northern areas where the Garo girls come from, while Bogra district was chosen because of the very good rapport that had been established with two girls from that area. Three other households of migrant girls were also visited in Bogra.

Doing research in Eritrea is currently very problematic if not impossible, so we were unable to interview the families of those who had migrated to Sudan. Ethiopian participants, like the girls in Addis Ababa, did not want to facilitate contact with their families. In order to gain insights into the perspective of migrant girls' family members, we interviewed relatives of migrants and refugees who had come to visit them or to reside in Khartoum.

In every case, confidentiality and anonymity were important priorities. All interviews were coded, files were safeguarded, and pseudonyms were used in order to protect all the respondents. The names of the research participants were also changed in this and other reports, and the stories slightly altered in order not to endanger the girls and young women. The information from migrants and refugees in Sudan was often very sensitive, due to their irregular status as illegal residents or as refugees in vulnerable situations.

In Sudan, the young women who worked in the project initially as research assistants, and subsequently as co-researchers, had often been through traumatic experiences themselves and Katarzyna was concerned that listening to other traumatic stories would place a tremendous emotional strain on them. After each visit, the interview was discussed to ensure that the refugee researchers were able to process the information. The team took breaks in the fieldwork, as the stories were sometimes too dramatic and there was a need for space to reflect and disconnect. The co-production of knowledge here included more participatory action-oriented research and was geared towards personal transformation. During the fieldwork, several young women and girls were identified as being in critical situations that needed immediate intervention. By using her knowledge networks in Khartoum, Katarzyna, together with the Eritrean researchers, assisted several girls and young women in obtaining access to potential protection and assistance services, as necessary. Some of the researchers expressed interest in attending training related to gender-based violence, refugees' rights, and services available for those who suffered abuse in Khartoum. As a result of the research, two of the researchers became very active in helping their own communities and identifying those who needed urgent assistance. At the end of the project, they commented that their participation in the research had been a transformative experience for them. They commented that thanks to the research they realized how much knowledge about refugees and migrants is produced by researchers, often with no collaboration from refugees themselves. This particular commitment to involving research participants in the research and writing process in Khartoum gave them a space to provide direct input into the type of knowledge that was created as a result of the project. In addition, it helped in mediating the interpretative process of research and writing up. Such an approach, however, requires time and training, as well as being open to collaborative work across different viewpoints and intersectional power dynamics.

In Bangladesh, the findings of the research were shared with the staff of Terre des Hommes, ARBAN and Aparajeyo as the fieldwork progressed. The preliminary results were thoroughly discussed and fed into the design of two three-year projects that are now halfway through the implementation phase, funded by the European Union (EU) and Italian Cooperation respectively. Two of the five girls who helped in administering the questionnaires now have a leading role in them, coordinating their peers in the two slums. Thus, the experience in the research led to some transformative effects.

In Ethiopia, the local researchers learned a lot from the migrant girls who assisted them during the research process, and at the same time, the migrant girls obtained knowledge about how to carry out interviews. In addition, Marina learned from the local researchers and vice versa. We exchanged knowledge and discussed the findings on a regular basis, which was beneficial for everyone individually and for the group. Marina regularly discussed the preliminary research findings with Girl Effect Ethiopia, which was interested in using them in future activities.

Collaborative Film-Making

While feminist researchers have attempted to minimize power differentials between the researcher and the researched (Minh-ha 1989; Patai 1991; Scheper-Hughes 2009; Wolf 1996), the result has been rather unsatisfactory (Wolf 1996). To a varying extent, we also experienced this frustration throughout fieldwork and writing up in our project. This is partly to do with the nature of fieldwork and the process of knowledge production in general. For by maintaining control and distance even feminist researchers end up "benefiting the researcher more than those studied and furthering the gap between the researcher and the researched" (Wolf 1996, p. 3). Thus, another aspect of our attempt to break the hierarchies in research and also in research dissemination was to make a documentary film based on our findings (see also Rollwagen 1996) (Fig. 2.2).

Our initial idea of making a documentary was to break away from the rather fixed parameters of dissemination of academic knowledge, which is dominated by written documents read by a narrow group of people. Our aim was to disseminate the research findings beyond academia, among policy-makers and practitioners, and the general public (see Parkin and Coomber 2009). In addition, in the spirit of our co-production of knowledge, we were interested in finding a way to disseminate the research that could be easily shared with research participants. Film is a much more accessible medium than an academic article or a book. We also aimed at involving the girls as much possible in the process of film-making, another dimension of our approach towards breaking the hierarchies in research. Our rationale was thus threefold: the power of the visual; visual as part of an activist and transformative strategy beyond research; and providing a space for the girls to speak in their own voice.

Although the research focused on three countries, we decided not to film in Sudan for political and security reasons. For research participants, researchers and film-makers it would have created numerous logistical

Fig. 2.2 Filming in Bangladesh, February 2015

and security problems. The film therefore focused on the lives of two sex workers in Ethiopia and two garment workers in Bangladesh.

We decided to work with a team of professional film-makers, a director and a camera operator. The latter has a research background and has mainly produced films that focus on social issues. Although we had some filming experience, we felt that working with professionals would ensure better-quality film material. The collaboration between professional film-makers with feminist researchers and protagonists created various points of tension, which led us to reflect on the ethical considerations regarding the use of film, filming technics, and visual methods as such. Such reflections are not new in visual anthropology. Back in 1975, Margaret Mead considered the role of visual anthropology in a verbal discipline, Timothy Ash (1988) reflected on collaboration in ethnographic film-making, and Maurice Godelier (1988) wrote his reflexions on the use of audiovisual methods in anthropology. Peter Loizos (1993) also discussed the role of film in studying refugees. Guidelines and reflection on collaborative work with research participants, and visual methods being part of a transformative action–research project, have also been discussed (Englehart 2003; Elder 1995; Pink 2011; Ruby 2000; Stadler 2003; White 2003). Film—as any other medium—is one of many perspectives (see Rouch 1973), but in many ways it is an even more contested terrain of 'knowledge production'.

Our main commitment was that girls participate in the film-making on their own terms. We asked several of the research participants whether they would be interested in participating in the film. Some girls expressed interest and we worked with them. In each country, we filmed four or five young women who migrated as adolescent girls. Each filming session took between three and five weeks, but was preceded by at least a year's research. In each country, we developed slightly different filming strategies. In Bangladesh, Nicoletta developed deep personal relations with the girls and was also able to film their families in their home villages. In Ethiopia, Marina worked with local researchers and so was much more detached from the girls' stories. We were lucky that one of the research participants and assistants in the project was an extremely powerful character. She took on the role of film coordinator and saw the film as her own project and strategy to expand life possibilities.

At different moments of film-making, various power dynamics and hierarchies between professional film-makers, protagonists and researchers emerged. Different stages of film-making require different skills—and this is how various power dynamics and hierarchies came about. We all needed to find creative ways to overcome them in order to create a collaborative experience. During the filming the young women were asked about what they wanted to talk about and show in the film. They also could also decide whether they wanted their faces to be visible. In the editing stage, we researchers provided inputs to the film director in terms of the storylines, and then consulted with main film protagonists to check that their experiences were correctly reflected. Although the film-making process brought to the surface another set of power hierarchies, and questions of whose voice counts and when, the dissemination of the research through film was successful. We were able to make two versions of the film: a shorter one designed for education and awareness-raising purposes and also used by us and by NGOs with which we had collaborated in the project. It was also used by the protagonists themselves, especially one of the young women in Ethiopia, who was able to screen the film and talk about the issues of adolescent girl migrants in the country on a couple of occasions. The longer version was screened across the globe at over 30 festivals and received several prizes and recognition. The main value of the longer version was its ability to convey the message and the research findings to a much wider audience that might not be interested in the academic side of the research.

Visual and film methods in particular can be problematic for feminist researchers, however. The combination of a visual medium and research can be a very powerful way to show and share research findings. Yet, there are some key issues to address. Visual methods have a greater interpretative power and impact, but at the same time can be interpreted in different ways. Thus, the form of visual dissemination needs more of a commentary than a report would. Furthermore, collaborating in the production of a visual materials means having to reconcile different stands and points of view. It forces the researchers to address the issues of research ethics much more seriously, as the guarantee of respondents' anonymity and protection is more problematic. Can we truly guarantee anonymity and confidentiality in using this type of research method or form of dissemination? To what extent is a process of collaborative film-making truly collaborative when participants have a variety of knowledges and skills?

Towards Comparative Co-production of Research on Migration and Displacement

By engaging in a comparative study of migration dynamics in three countries in three regions, our aim was also to go beyond simple descriptions of migration patterns within and across borders in each of the countries, in order to point to various ways in which cross-national comparative research can potentially enhance methodological innovations and rigour in issues regarding girls' migration and transitions into adulthood. This approach challenged us to engage in both ideological and methodological critical reflexivity. Similarly, by discussing social constructions of gendered adolescence, transitions and adulthood across the different contexts we hoped to raise awareness of the need to understand the socially and historically embedded nature of concepts, methods and generated 'knowledge'. By moving beyond fixed 'groups' and 'categories' of 'youth', 'refugees' and 'migrants', this collaborative research encouraged us to look at processes of identification, inclusion and exclusion. We believe that such research also facilitates going beyond specific country case studies, towards multilevel analysis of local, national and global influences on young people's migration and life trajectories.

By developing a feminist approach to such comparative research on migration, we employed various methods. Our methodologies are to some extent an experimental approach to gathering data, but the fundamental difference is how the research questions are developed and then worked through. While research questions were initially designed by the three of us in collaboration with our academic advisor, we then discussed them extensively at the beginning of the fieldwork in each of the countries with the local co-researchers and research assistants. In particular, we sought the insights from adolescent migrant and refugee girls as to whether the type of questions we were asking were of importance to them. In addition, we designed our particular research tools in collaboration with those adolescent migrant girls and young women who participated in the research. Their insights were important in shaping our approach both in terms of research tools but also the ways to carry out research. Our feminist commitment meant that in situations where we realized that the questions we as researchers initially thought of addressing were inappropriate or other questions were more important for the research participants, we adjusted and tuned into the views of those whose migratory trajectories we set out to understand. By privileging their situated knowledge(s), and remaining flexible in our research approach, we attempted to stay as close as possible to the premises of the feminist methodologies.

Acknowledging that knowledge is socially constructed and situated, in this process we sought to pay attention to the knowledge and experiences of those who have been marginalized, whose voices have not been recognized. Current approaches to participatory research are not only about *giving a voice* to the marginalized groups, a highly problematic and patriarchal assumption to start with, but are also, as we tried to do, about how to create inclusive, fully participatory research processes that create an environment of co-construction of knowledge, and minimize some of the power hierarchies in the research process. It is about an emphasis on and commitment to dignity and recognition in the research process. Each of the chapters in this book and all its findings emerge through such a collaborative constitutive process of co-creation of knowledge, where different viewpoints were shared, acknowledged, and discussed, before arriving at more general interpretations presented in what follows.

Moreover, our collaborative approach to the whole research project, including fieldwork, data analysis and writing, enabled conceptual and methodological development through the exchange of ideas and experience among diverse researchers, including research participants. Here, screening of the short version of the film among migrants and refugees in the three countries, and also among policy-makers and development workers who deal with youth migration, was very beneficial. It allowed us collectively to comment on and analyse some of the findings.

Yet, at the same time, cross-country comparative research has to address significant challenges in developing conceptual frameworks that are meaningful in diverse contexts. In a way, there is a tendency to reify concepts and essentialize migrant/minority 'groups' in an effort to harmonize across countries (see Salway et al. 2011). We tried to overcome this by bringing in individual stories of migrant and refugee girls without making them emblematic and generalized experiences. At times, however, we found it difficult to generate integrated insights across the three case studies. In what follows, by staying close to our feminist premises, we tried to bring a more holistic view of the experiences of migrant and refugee girls beyond their portrayal of victims or heroines, at the same time acknowledging both the gendered context-specific and the structural constraints that they face as young women on the move.

References

Archer Mann, S., & Patterson, A. S. (2015). Intersectionality Theories. *Feminist Theory: From Modernity to Postmodernity* (pp. 218–298). Oxford: Oxford University Press.

Ash, T. (1988). Collaboration in Ethnographic Filmmaking: Personal View. In J. R. Rollwagen (Ed.), *Anthropological Perspectives on the Production of Film and Video for General Public Audiences* (pp. 1–30). New York, NY: Hardwood Academic Publishers.

Bosswick, W., & Husband, C. (2005). *Comparative European Research in Migration, Diversity and Identities*. Bilbao: University of Deusto.

Elder, S. (1995). Collaborative Filmmaking: An Open Space for Making Meaning, Amoral Ground for Ethnographic Film. *Visual Anthropology Review, 11*(2), 94–101.

Engelhart, L. (2003). Media Activism in the Screening Room. *Visual Anthropology Review, 19*(1–2), 73–85.

Godelier, M. (1988). An Internview. In J. R. Rollwagen (Ed.), *Anthropological Filmmaking*. Chur: Harwood.

Harding, S. (1987). Introduction: Is There a Feminist Method? In S. Harding (Ed.), *Feminism and Methodology*. Bloomington, IN: Indiana University Press.

Harding, S. (1991). *Whose Science/Whose Knowledge?* Milton Keynes: Open University Press.

Harding, S. (2004). Introduction: Standpoint Theory as a Site of Political, Philosophical, and Scientific Debate. In S. Harding (Ed.), *The Feminist Standpoint Reader: Intellectual and Political Controversies*. New York, NY and London: Routledge.

Intemann, K. (2010). 25 Years of Feminist Empiricism and Standpoint Theory: Where Are We Now? *Hypatia, 25*(4), 778–796.

Loizos, P. (1993). *Innovation in Ethnographic Film. From Innocence to Self-Consciousness, 1955–85*. Manchester: Manchester University Press.

Minh-ha, T. (1989). *Woman, Native, Other: Writing Postcoloniality and Feminism*. Indianapolis, IN: Indiana University Press.

Moore, H. (1988). *Feminism and Anthropology*. Cambridge: Polity Press.

Parkin, S., & Coomber, R. (2009). Value in the Visual: On Public Injecting, Visual Methods and Their Potential for Informing Policy (and Change). *Methodological Innovations Online, 4*(2), 21–36.

Patai, D. (1991). U.S. Academics and Third World Women: Is Ethical Research Possible? In S. B. Gluck & D. Patai (Eds.), *Women's Words: The Feminist Practice of Oral History* (pp. 137–153). New York, NY: Routledge.

Pink, S. (2011). Images, Senses and Applications: Engaging Visual Anthropology. *Visual Anthropology, 24*(5), 437–454.

Rouch, J. ([1973] 2003). The Camera and Man. In S. Feld (Ed.), *Cine-Ethnography Jean Rouch* (pp. 29–460). Minneapolis, MN and London: University of Minnesota Press.

Rollwagen, J. R. (Ed.). (1996). *Anthropological Perspectives on the Production of Film and Video for General Public Audiences* (4th ed.). New York: Hardwood Academic Publishers.

Ruby, J. (2000). *Picturing Culture: Explorations of Film and Anthropology*. Chicago, IL: University of Chicago Press.

Salway, S. M., Higginbottom, G., Reime, B., Bharj, K. K., Chowbey, P., Foster, C., et al. (2011). Contributions and Challenges of Cross-National Comparative Research in Migration, Ethnicity and Health: Insights from a Preliminary Study of Maternal Health in Germany, Canada and the UK. *BMC Public Health, 11*(1), 514.

Scheper-Hughes, N. (2009). Making Anthropology Public. *Anthropology Today, 25*(4), 1–3.

Stadler, J. (2003). Narrative, Understanding and Identification in Steps for the Future: HIV/AIDS Documentaries. *Visual Anthropology Review, 19*(1–2), 86–101.

White, S. A. (2003). *Participatory Video: Images That Transform and Empower*. Thousand Oaks, CA: Sage.

Wolf, D. L. (1996). Situating Feminist Dilemmas in Fieldwork. In D. L. Wolf (Ed.), *Feminist Dilemmas in Fieldwork*. Boulder, CO and Oxford: Westview Press.

CHAPTER 3

Situating Girls' Migration in Three Contexts

The Context

Disasters driven by climate change in Bangladesh, famine and drought in Ethiopia and warfare and conflict in Sudan are what the general public tend to associate with these three nations. The countries are characterized by high levels of poverty, political instability, regional conflicts and political oppression and they rank very low on the United Nations Human Development Index: Bangladesh scores 139, Sudan 165 and Ethiopia 173 out of 189 countries (UNDP 2016). In this chapter, we contextualize adolescent girls' migration in Bangladesh and Ethiopia and into Sudan. Without knowledge of the historical, political and economic background of contemporary population movements in these countries, the migration of adolescent girls cannot be fully understood. We start with a section on migration trends, in which we briefly describe the historical background of each country, with an emphasis on the political and economic structures. We continue with a section on politics and policies with regard to migration, and end with a description of the capital cities Dhaka, Addis Ababa, and Khartoum, which were the main sites of our research.

K. Grabska et al., *Adolescent Girls' Migration in The Global South*, Palgrave Studies on Children and Development,
https://doi.org/10.1007/978-3-030-00093-6_3

Migration Trends

Bangladesh

The People's Republic of Bangladesh is one of the world's most populated countries with 162 million inhabitants and a population density of 1252 people per square kilometre.[1] The country was recognized in 1971 after the independence war with Pakistan, which left Bangladesh in a dire economic situation. Hundreds of thousands of Bangladeshis were killed, including many intellectuals and potential leaders, and it took years to build up the country. The flooding of the many rivers and large-scale crop failures led to famines, adding to the growing pains of the young nation. In the late 1970s, two-thirds of the population lived below the poverty line. Since then, although successive governments have made enormous efforts to improve the situation the country still faces many development challenges.

The macroeconomic indicators suggest that there have been significant changes in the structure of the economy. While agriculture used to be the main source of revenue, from 1980 to 2010 agricultural production as a share of Gross Domestic Product (GDP) dropped from 32 to 19%, while the share of industrial production rose from 21 to 28% (UNDP 2013, p. 6), among other factors because of the exponential growth of the ready-made garment (RMG) industry since 1976, which today accounts for 81% of total exports (Islam et al. 2016, p. 55). In 1982, in the context of the International Monetary Fund (IMF) structural adjustment policies, Bangladesh launched the so-called New Economic Policy, which relied mainly on export-led growth. This stimulated the growth of the textile export sector. In 1983–1984 there were 134 RMG factories, which had risen to 4222 by 2013–2014 (Islam et al. 2016, p. 53). In 2014, about 5000 garment factories already employed more than 3.5 million people (Islam et al. 2016, p. 55). From 2010 to 2015, the economy grew steadily and underwent structural changes; new employment was generated in the service sector, led by wholesale and retail trade and transport, storage and communication (65%) and manufacturing (35%) (World Bank 2017, p. 3). Despite a decade of economic and social gains for most of the population, however, Bangladesh

[1] https://data-worldbank-org.vu-nl.idm.oclc.org/indicator/EN.POP.DNST, accessed 19 February 2018.

remains one of the world's poorest with 21 million people living in extreme poverty (World Bank 2017, p. 3).

Migration is a major feature of the country's history, and today many Bangladeshis migrate internally and internationally. Internal migration has been on the rise since the 1970s, linked to the expansion of the manufacturing sector in urban areas and to the gradual worsening of livelihood options in rural areas. The urbanization rate as a correlate of internal rural–urban migration was 3.03% from 1975 to 2009, one of the highest in the world (UNDP 2013, p. 6). The number of landless households chasing low-paid agricultural work, together with increasing land scarcity and poor returns to farming, push rural people to look for work elsewhere. Such vulnerability is exacerbated by riverbank erosion and seasonal flooding in the south-western part of the country, and by drought in the north-east.

Historically, male rural workers have undertaken seasonal migration depending on the annual cycle of rains and dry periods, in particular from the north-eastern districts that are characterized by subsistence agriculture. Since the late 1990s, these rural–urban movements have become more permanent (UNDP 2013, p. 6). Climate refugees are a substantial reality in Bangladesh, since the coastal belt of the country is prone to cyclones and other natural phenomena intensified by climate change. The International Organization for Migration (IOM) stated back in 2009 that "climate exodus" had resulted in some 70% of Dhaka's slum dwellers who had moved there in order to escape some kind of environmental shock (IOM 2009, p. 193). Most of the garment workers are migrants from rural areas, 90% of whom were women and young girls in 2014 (Islam et al. 2016, p. 55).

International migration is mainly to the Middle East and South East Asia, although countries such as the United States (USA), the United Kingdom (UK) and, more recently, countries in southern Europe are also significant destinations. Bangladeshi workers started migrating to the Middle East and South East Asia for short-term labour contracts from the 1970s, after Northern countries adopted more restrictive immigration policies. Short-term migrants from Bangladesh are predominantly young men between the ages of 18 and 25, but the percentage of women has been increasing (see, for example, Rudnick 2009). In 2002, women workers constituted 0.54% of the total number of Bangladeshi workers who migrated overseas in that year, and by mid-2013 the percentage stood at 13% (ILO 2014, p. 11). Lebanon was the top destination for migrant women workers between 1991 and June 2013, followed by the United Arab Emirates (UAE), Jordan, Saudi Arabia, Mauritius, Oman, Kuwait and Malaysia. Women migrate to be employed as domestic workers, nurses and garment workers. They migrate mainly on short-term contracts via agencies and, in some cases, on the basis of international agreements with the destination countries. Women's international migration is subject to strict laws and regulations so that formally only women over 25 years of age can obtain the necessary authorizations from the government. In some cases, host governments also apply a quota.

Bangladeshi men and women also migrate to India. Despite the lack of official data, India's government estimated in 2016 that there were some 20 million Bangladeshis living in the country, which would make this migration corridor the largest in the world. Some are Hindu refugees while others are labour migrants. With regard to migration to Europe, most Bangladeshis migrate to the UK but also to other European countries, including Greece and Italy. In January 2016, the number of documented Bangladeshis in Italy was more than 142,000 (MLPS 2016, p. 16). Since 2015, a new influx of Bangladeshi migrants started arriving across Europe. In 2017, Bangladeshis were one of the top migrant groups leaving from Libya along a route more traditionally used by sub-Saharan Africans. More than 8700 Bangladeshis reached Italy by sea between January and August 2017. In the first six months of 2017, some 7413 Bangladeshis have applied for asylum, second only to Nigerians (ANCI et al. 2017, p. 82).

Ethiopia

Ethiopia is one of the most populated countries in Africa with more than 100 million inhabitants and, like Bangladesh, is also one of the world's poorest countries. Although the poverty rate decreased from 39% in 2004 to 30% in 2011, still more than 60% of the population lives on less than US$2 per day (The World Bank Group 2015, p. xv). The country was never colonized and became a nation at the end of the nineteenth century, under Emperor Menelik II. Emperor Haile Selassie introduced the first constitution, yet it gave almost absolute power to the emperor and, after decades of oppression, a popular revolution brought an end to his reign. Oppression continued, however, under the military regime of Mengistu, who stayed in power from 1974 to 1991. Since 1991 Ethiopia

Fig. 3.1 Making injera in Ethiopia

has constitutionally been a democracy, yet the ruling Ethiopian People's Revolutionary Democratic Party (EPRDF) has obtained almost absolute power (Fig. 3.1).

In the past decade, Ethiopia experienced rapid economic growth (10.3% in 2013–2014); the IMF even considers the country one of the five fastest-growing economies in the world. Since the early 1990s the Ethiopian government has followed a 'developmental state' model, envisaging that long-term public investments will lead to poverty reduction and rapid economic growth, including Agricultural Development-Led Industrialization (ADLI). The large majority of the population, around 85%, is rural and depends on small-holder farming and livestock. The agricultural sector is, therefore, Ethiopia's most important economic sector, employing 73% of the population (Schewel and Fransen 2018, p. 10). In particular, the newly developed horticultural sector is offering employment, followed by the service sector and finally the industrial sector, which accounts for only 10% of GDP (Broussard and Tekleselassie 2012, p. 3). Rural poverty has declined, and access to basic services such as education and health has increased. Despite this, around 25 million people live below the poverty line (UNDP 2016, p. 3). In addition, urban poverty seems to have increased (The World Bank Group 2015, p. xxi). Even though urbanization rates are relatively low in Ethiopia, rural–urban migration is on the rise, as is urban poverty. In 2000, 11% of Ethiopians living in poverty were city dwellers and this rose to 14% in 2011 (ibid., p. xxi).

The economic situation in Ethiopia, combined with its rapid population growth, has made it harder to tackle huge unemployment, especially among the increasingly younger population. In 2014, 45% of the population was under the age of 15 and 71% under the age of 30 (Central Statistical Agency 2014, p. 13). The most important factor affecting the Ethiopian labour market is rapid population growth, which reached 2.5% in 2016. As a result, the labour force is growing much faster than the population as a whole. Creating enough jobs to absorb the labour force is one of government's main challenges. Young people face not only the difficulties of obtaining productive employment, but also of securing decent work. Women comprise approximately 52% of the youth labour force. In both rural and urban areas, girls and women are more likely to be unemployed, or employed in the informal economy, often in very low-paid work. Interestingly, while male unemployment increases with higher education, women with higher education are more likely to find employment than their less educated peers (Broussard and Tekleselassie 2012, p. 24). Young women are primarily employed in the horticultural and manufacturing sectors, in wholesale and retail trade and in hotels and restaurants. In addition, women are more likely to be employed in the informal economy, principally in domestic work, but also many young women become sex workers, in particular rural migrants to urban areas.

Population movements have been part and parcel of Ethiopia's modern history, mainly comprising rural–rural and rural–urban migration but also of large-scale refugee flows to neighbouring countries and the North, in particular during the military regime. International migration has recently become very common. Rural poverty caused by, among other things, overpopulation, land scarcity, government agricultural policies, and a lack of agricultural resources, coupled with the desire to explore new opportunities, partly explain the increased migration (see Atnafu et al. 2014; Dom 2017). People between 18 and 25 years of age comprise the main group of internal and international migrants. While the educational opportunities in rural areas have improved, job opportunities are limited even in the agricultural sector, and many young people hope to find paid work in the city or abroad (see, for example, Atnafu et al. 2014; Crivello and van der Gaag 2016; Mains 2012; Schewel and Fransen 2018). Labour migration has become one of the main ways in which people seek to improve their livelihoods. In addition, urban–urban migration has also increased, including among the middle classes, who migrate to pursue higher education and in doing so hope to increase their social, cultural and economic status (Breines 2017).

Under the Mengistu regime, international labour migration was restricted. Many Ethiopians fled the country, and for some time Ethiopians were the largest group of African refugees in the world (Bariagaber 1995, p. 213). In 1991, freedom of movement became a constitutional right with the result that migration has increased. In the past 20 years, international migration to the Middle East and to South Africa has increased rapidly. The large majority of migrants to the Middle East are young women who enter domestic work, whereas migration to South Africa is largely male-dominated, particularly by men under 35 years of age who are from the southern regions. They travel by land, and often enter the country undocumented (see Kanko et al. 2013; Zack and Estifanos 2016). Most of them work in the informal economy and have little contact with the local population (see Gebre et al. 2011; Zack 2015). Similar to other African immigrants in South Africa, Ethiopians often encounter xenophobia and racism.

While Ethiopia has become a so-called migrant-sending country, it also attracts refugees and migrants, mainly from neighbouring countries. One of the largest groups of refugees is from Eritrea. Eritrea gained independence in 1993, after decades of guerrilla war, yet the friendly relationship between the governments of Meles Zenawi and Isaias Afeworki came to an end in 1998, with a bloody war which led to the death of hundreds of soldiers. Since then the border has been closed and mixed Eritrean–Ethiopian families have been divided. The Eritrean regime has become increasingly oppressive and consequently many Eritreans, in particular young people, have fled the country. Ethiopia and Sudan are the main host countries for Eritrean refugees, of whom there were 155,207 in 2015 (UNHCR 2015b, p. 1). The second largest group of refugees are Somalis, followed by South Sudanese. In addition, there are refugees from other African countries, such as Burundi, Congo and Rwanda (see Charpentier 2015).

Sudan

The Republic of Sudan is the third biggest country in Africa. Over the centuries it has experienced numerous wars and civil conflicts, and more recently the separation of South Sudan, that have marked its economic and political developments. In 1956, Sudan gained its independence from the Anglo-Egyptian condominium. Yet, as Douglas Johnson noted, at the onset of the twenty-first century Sudan was "mired not in one, but many civil wars" (2006, p. xi). The second civil war between the government of Khartoum and the South Sudan People's Liberation Army (1983–2005) led to the establishment of two countries in July 2011: the Republic of Sudan and the Republic of South Sudan. Politically, the country has been under authoritarian rule since 1989. After a military coup against Sadiq al-Mahdi, the National Congress Party has been in power. In 1993 the country became a totalitarian Islamic state under the guidance of Omar al-Bashir. In the same year, Sharia law was introduced. Opposition is not allowed, and many civil rights have been curtailed. As a result, an increasing number of Sudanese have fled the country. In addition, there are ongoing conflicts in the western part of Sudan (Darfur) as well as in the eastern part of the country.

According to the last population census, Sudan's population in May 2008 was over 39 million, twice that recorded 25 years before (NPC 2010). Its population, like that of Bangladesh and Ethiopia, is rather young, with 62.2% aged below 25 years, a child-dependency ratio of 81.6%, and women outnumbering men (NPC 2010). As the IOM noted in 2013, however, migratory flows from, to and through Sudan are an important source of demographic dynamics (IOM 2013). Since the colonial period, the migration of workers from Sudanese regions (such as Kordofan or Darfur) or from neighbouring countries, especially Ethiopia, have been also driven by economic opportunities and demands. These migrants, some of them seasonal, would primarily be involved in agricultural activities in certain regions, which had developed from large-scale state-directed agricultural projects that were a part of colonial economic development initiatives, such as in the Gezira—the plain between the two Niles—the largest irrigated agricultural scheme, the Zande and Kenana schemes established in 1925 to support the cultivation of cotton to be sent to British industries. The rapid expansion and diversification of capitalist agriculture during the 1950s influenced labour migration trends throughout Sudan and eventually led to the need for labour in newer agricultural zones such as the Gedaref region. After the separation of South Sudan and losing much access to oil fields in the South, Sudan suffered an economic downturn. This affected work opportunities for Ethiopian and Eritrean migrants and refugees in particular.

Sudan is marked by diverse population flows. Both a host and producer of refugees, internally displaced persons (IDPs) and migrants, the country faces some of the world's largest population movements—but there are no comprehensive statistics concerning international migration. Like Ethiopia and Bangladesh, there is strong internal migration due to the urbanization and development projects concentrated in the capital. Khartoum is the major destination for internal migrants, with the last census showing 1,847,103 arrivals from other states (NPC 2010, p. 44).

Sudan is also a migrant-sending country and a producer of refugees. Official sources indicate that between 1.7 and 2 million Sudanese migrated or are living abroad: 51% in neighbouring African countries and 48.7% in the Gulf States, Europe and North America (Babiker 2011, p. 3; NPC 2010). Refugees include those who had sought asylum in other countries due to long-standing conflicts and political and religious tensions in Sudan. Economic migrants include those who have migrated since 1973 to the oil-rich Gulf States, seeking employment opportunities and better wages.

According to figures from the United Nations High Commissioner for Refugees (UNHCR), in 2016 it was estimated that there were some 2.3 million IDPs in Sudan (UNHCR 2017), down from 2.9 million in 2014. In 2016, there were some 440,000 refugees and asylum-seekers in the country, mainly from Eritrea and South Sudan. In addition, some 350,000 South Sudanese remained in Sudan since separation in 2011 and remain at risk of statelessness. This makes Sudan a major refugee hub in East Africa and a major staging post for those hoping to reach other destinations. A large number of IDPs were created by conflicts in Darfur, the Nuba Mountains, and in the east of the country. The humanitarian environment in Sudan deteriorated over 2014–2015, with new conflict-induced internal displacement in Darfur and refugees from South Sudan.

After South Sudanese, Eritreans constitute the largest refugee group in Sudan. At the end of 2015, UNHCR estimated that more than 411,000 Eritreans were refugees, up from the end of 2011, when 159,000 Eritreans were registered (UNHCR 2015a). By 2015, almost 10% of the Eritrean population (estimated at 5.2 million) had sought refuge outside the country (Ratha et al. 2011). While 2015 statistics show 130,000 officially registered refugees from Eritrea in Sudan, the actual number is probably three to four times higher. It should be noted that almost all Eritreans receive refugee status in the country. Sudan has been a host to Eritrean refugee population since the independence struggle in the 1970s and the war with Ethiopia (Kibreab 1995, 2000, 2009). Until the 1990s, Eritreans had few official channels for resettlement to third countries. Most of the refugees reside in the camps in the eastern part of the country, and an increasing number live in towns and cities, especially Khartoum. In Khartoum, an assessment of urban refugees and asylum-seekers was completed in 2014, when it was estimated that there were some 32,000. Since the outbreak of civil conflict in South Sudan, an increasing number of people have arrived at refugee camps at the borders as well as in Khartoum. UNHCR estimates point to some 200,000 who arrived in Sudan between December 2013 and November 2015, mostly residing in the camps in the border areas (UNHCR 2015a).

There is a large Ethiopian population, and although there are no precise statistics some unofficial estimates put the figure at between 2 and 3 million. In 2015, the Ethiopian embassy launched a registration process of Ethiopians residing in Khartoum. By 2016, some 120,000 people had been registered according to the Ethiopian Association in Khartoum. However, most of the Ethiopian population resides in the eastern areas of the country and is extremely mobile. Many are seasonal workers; others spend a few years in Sudan and then move on, either to another country in the region or to Europe or return to Ethiopia. While a significant percentage of Ethiopians who arrived in Sudan during the

Ethiopian–Eritrean war and the Ethiopian civil conflict in the 1990s were perceived as refugees, those arriving more recently mainly come for other reasons.

Locating Adolescent Girls' Migration

Bangladesh

In Bangladesh, employment for rural women fell sharply from 1976 onwards as a result of mechanization of the post-harvest tasks, which provided jobs for men, taking over activities that women used to perform near their home. The scope for wage employment for women and girls in rural areas is now extremely limited. Women from the poorest landless families may take work as agricultural day labourers, where they work for very low rates, or more often as domestics in neighbouring houses, where they are usually paid in kind. These jobs, apart from being low-paid, are perceived as contrary to *purdah*[2] norms and women who have to take them are held in very low esteem. A few educated women may find employment in NGOs, or as teachers, but the demand for such jobs is much higher than the number of jobs available. Although the rate of girls' enrolment in secondary school has significantly increased in the 2000s, reflecting a widespread awareness of the importance of education, rural households, especially landless or functionally landless agricultural families, can hardly afford it up to higher levels despite the economic incentives provided by the state, such as the stipend programme.[3] Completing the first cycle of secondary school and obtaining a secondary school certificate (SSC) after 10 years of schooling, is expensive and not perceived to lead to any desirable form of employment for girls.

Thus, when a girl reaches a marriageable age, commonly between the sixth and tenth year of schooling, and decisions about her future have to be taken, the respective advantages and disadvantages of different

[2] Purdah, which literally means curtain, should not be understood only in the limited meaning of the physical seclusion of women inside the house. The Hindu and Muslim concept of purdah entails an ideal of modesty enforced through '*prohibition on movement, gesture, speech and association and the development of feminine characteristics like virtue and* shame' (Ahmed 1993, p. 60).

[3] Since January 1994, rural girls with good school results receive a six-monthly stipend from the government to cover education costs up to grade 12.

options are considered, as well as their costs. Since investment in education does not ensure a return, poor parents regard her marriage is the best way to secure a daughter's future. There is a consensus, however, that this scenario has been significantly altered with the expansion of the RMG industry, which has become the first form of mass wage employment for women and girls outside the home (Kabeer 2000). Migration for employment in the RMG sector has become a feasible alternative to early marriage and childbearing for rural teenagers. Women constitute 61% of employees in the sector (World Bank 2017, p. 4), 60% of them under 25 years of age (Hossain 2012, p. 19).

Moving to Dhaka to work in the RMG sector is not the only migratory path open to Bangladeshi girls. Another major trajectory is to take up paid work as domestics in Dhaka or in smaller towns. The choice between domestic work or garment work is often related to age, with younger girls (below the age of 12–14) and women over the age of 30 taking up paid domestic work because they are either too young to be employed in factories or too old to withstand the long working hours. The most recent available statistics on domestic work in Bangladesh are from 2006, when a joint ILO–UNICEF report estimated that there were about 2 million domestic workers of whom 421,000 of them were aged 14 and under (Ashraf 2016, p. 12). According to Phulki, an NGO that works with domestics and garment workers, some young girls who migrated to Dhaka to work return to their villages to get married while others continue to work in the garment industry. According to Hossain, in the 1990s the average length of time women remain in Dhaka used to be about four years, which has since slightly increased (Hossain 2012, p. 19).

The personal care industry has also developed and provides employment to about 100,000 women in about 2000 registered beauty parlours, mainly in towns and cities across the country.[4] Although beauty parlours are usually owned by Bangladeshis, the employees are often young women from the Garo ethnic minority. There are between 80,000 and 100,000 Garo living in Bangladesh (Bal 2007, p. 11), originally from the north but now scattered all over the country, with more than 2000 of them working and living in Dhaka (Bal 2007, p. 55). The Garo are mostly Christian, either Catholic or Baptists. Since the 1947

[4]See http://www.thedailystar.net/news-detail-76232 and http://www.thedailystar.net/news-detail-159817 (consulted 30 January 2018).

partition, the Garo, like the other 20–56 ethnic minorities, have a marginalized social, political and economic status in relation to the Muslim majority (Bal 2007). Garo women are mainly employed as cooks, housekeepers and babysitters as well as in beauty parlours, NGOs and church organizations. Men are employed as garment workers, drivers, night guards and NGO staff. Many Garo women and men also migrate to Dhaka to continue their education.

Another group of migrants are girls who move from rural villages to district towns and then to Dhaka to study at university, after completing the tenth year of school or after the twelfth year to enrol at university. These migrants are mainly from middle-class and upper-middle-class families who can afford to pay for their daughters' education and postpone their marriage, besides having relatives or good acquaintances in town who can function as guardians (Del Franco 2010).

Ethiopia

The increased migration aspirations of Ethiopians, and in particular of rural youth, are strongly related to the economic, political and social changes that have taken place in Ethiopia in the past two decades. As mentioned earlier, the Ethiopian government has made major efforts to improve the educational level of the population, but the labour market has not expanded to the same extent. The migration of children, including adolescent girls, is not a new phenomenon in Ethiopia: historically, children have migrated for seasonal agricultural labour and to work in other sectors, such as in the weaving sector and as domestic workers (Abebe 2007; Bonsa 2001; Bjeren 1985; Chuta and Morrow 2015). In the past decade, however, an increasing number of adolescent girls and young women have migrated, both internally and internationally. Rural poverty is one, but not the only, reason. Adolescent girls also migrate in order to escape oppressive gender regimes, for example, by fleeing forced (and early) marriage or from abuse and exploitation (see Chapter 4). In addition, the lack of educational and employment opportunities inspires migration to urban areas (see Atnafu et al. 2014). Often, secondary education is only available in rural towns, so if girls are to continue their schooling they have to move out of the village. In the past ten years, the Ethiopian government has invested in establishing universities all over the country (see Akalu 2014), which has led to an increase in the number of university students, including many young women. They live on campuses in town.

The most remarkable development with regard to gender and migration is the large number of young women who have migrated to the Middle East to fill the demand for domestic labour (de Regt 2010; Fernandez 2010; Jones et al. 2014; Kebede 2001; Minaye 2012). Lebanon, Saudi Arabia and the Gulf States have become major destinations for Ethiopian women migrants, but also economically less developed countries such as Sudan and Yemen. Initially, it was mainly young women who had finished at least some years of secondary education who migrated, but now adolescent girls with no or only basic education are also moving abroad. Some of these girls are recruited in their home villages but others have first migrated to small and middle-sized towns, and from there migrate abroad. Legally, only women over 18 years of age are allowed to migrate abroad, yet sometimes younger women also go, in particular those who go by land to Sudan or by sea to Yemen.

The dominant discourse on migration in Ethiopia focuses in particular on the negative effects of women's migration to the Middle East. In the past two decades numerous Ethiopian women have died while they were working abroad, sometimes killed by their employers, sometimes because they committed suicide, while others returned home with mental illnesses or with stories about their mistreatment by employers, such as heavy workloads, not being paid, lack of food and sleep, and mental, physical and sexual abuse. In response to the increasing reports of abuse and investigations by human rights organizations, in November 2013, the Ethiopian government announced a temporary ban on migration to the Middle East. Initially, the ban was for six months but it continued until August 2016. This left many women who were intending to migrate stuck in Ethiopia, unless they decided to migrate by land to Sudan or Yemen instead. In addition, migration via Kenya increased as Ethiopians do not need a visa to enter the country. Brokers facilitated the use of these irregular migration routes, with all their consequences. Thus, while the ban was intended to curtail human rights violations, irregular migration increased.

Sudan

Historically, there have been close relations between Eritrea, Ethiopia and Sudan. Before their formation as independent nations and the establishment of frontiers, nomadic groups such as the Rashaida[5] moved around freely. Ethiopians, for example, moved back and forth across borders as seasonal labourers, working mainly in agriculture. In the 1980s and 1990s, particularly under the Derg regime that came to power after the fall of Haile Selassie, most Ethiopians arriving in Sudan were refugees, fleeing the repressive regime and civil conflict. Since the EPRDF came to power, the number of refugees declined, although labour migration from Ethiopia to Sudan continued. While at first it was mainly men doing day labour or agricultural work, increasingly younger women and adolescent girls are arriving independently in Sudan (Dom 2017). This confirms the general trend of large numbers of young women migrating abroad to fill the demand for domestic labour.

Although international migration for Ethiopians is not officially permitted under the age of 18, many adolescent girls manage to obtain false identity papers or migrate without any documents, including even girls as young as 13 years of age (Jones et al. 2014). As mentioned above, as a result of the ban on migrating to the Middle East, many Ethiopian women and adolescent girls decided instead to migrate by land to Sudan, often facilitated by brokers. In response to the ban, Sudanese consulates stopped granting visas to young Ethiopians, especially women. As a result, undocumented migration and work in Sudan have increased, further endangering girls and younger women. Most of the young Ethiopian women work in the informal economy in Sudan, either as domestic workers, tea-sellers, or in restaurants (Abbas 2012). These sectors have become increasingly reliant on Ethiopian migrants following the departure of South Sudanese who had occupied these jobs until 2011 when South Sudan obtained independence (Jamie 2013).

Sudan has been a host to Eritrean refugees and migrants for at least 30 years. After the 1952 Federation with Ethiopia, and then the de facto annexation by Ethiopia, many moved first to Addis Ababa. In the 1950s, less privileged Muslims left for nearby Arab countries, first as migrant labourers, but later, as Eritrea's national liberation struggle against Ethiopia intensified in the 1960s, increasingly as political refugees (Connell 2013; Kifleyesus 2012). Most of the Eritrean refugees residing in Sudan arrived during the independence war against Ethiopia and

[5]The Rashaida, Rashaayda or Bani Rashid is a tribe of ethnic Bedouin Arabs descending from Banu Abs, who were native to the Hejaz region of Saudi Arabia. They live in the border areas between Sudan and Eritrea and move freely between the two countries.

there is a large Eritrean diaspora, possibly as many as a million Eritreans living across Africa, the Gulf, the Middle East, Europe, North America, Australia and Israel (ICG 2014). The Eritrean People's Liberation Front (EPLF) won de facto independence from Ethiopia in 1991, and legal independence in 1993. Many did return to build a new state and contribute to its growth. While relations between Ethiopia and Eritrea at first seemed to normalize, they deteriorated into war once again, a couple of years after Eritrea introduced its own currency in 1997. Another war broke out in May 1998 over a border dispute, but more concretely over differences relating to ethnic tensions and different economic policies. It resulted in 100,000 deaths and millions of dollars diverted from much-needed development into military activities and weapons procurement. It also led to the closure of the border between the two countries, dividing families as a result.

The new political situation did not result in an opening of political space, as authoritarian rule under Isaias Afwerki persisted despite initial promises, and multi-party system and governance reforms failed (ICG 2014). The highly militarized state was "shaped by war and run by warriors" (ICG 2014, p. 5). While this was initially supported by pastoralists and peasants who were not much affected by the rules, educated urban elites increasingly resisted the idea of permanent military service, instituted in 1995. Since 2001, a growing number of young people have deserted national service and crossed over to Ethiopia, Sudan or Djibouti in transit to countries with well-established Eritrean communities. They also sought to obtain meaningful asylum and better economic opportunities. The government instituted a 'shoot-to-kill policy' to deter potential deserters, but quickly this evolved into "a chaotic 'pay-to-leave' trade in which the threat from the Rashaida ex-paramilitaries[6] was crucial to generate revenues" (ICG 2014, p. 8).[7] Linking up with other Sahelian

[6] See 'Report of the Monitoring Group' (2011) and 'Report of the Monitoring Group on Somalia and Eritrea Pursuant to Security Council Resolution 2060 (2012)', UNSC S/2013/440, 19 June 2013 for further explanation on the connections between Eritrean officials and Raishada gangs.

[7] For reported Rashaida abuses of Eritrean migrants and ransom demands to family members, see Human Rights Watch (2014). '"I Wanted to Lie Down and Die": Trafficking and Torture of Eritreans in Sudan and Egypt'. New York: Human Rights Watch; also, for a more nuanced analysis of reported Rashaida involvement, Rachel Humphris (2013). 'Refugees and the Rashaida'. The Rashaida's leading politician and Sudanese minister, MabroukMabarakSalim, denies any involvement of his community, 'Sudan blames foreigners for proliferation in human trafficking', *Al-Monitor*, 31 January 2013.

and Saharan criminal elements (already active along traditional smuggling routes towards Europe), a complex smuggling network through which Eritrean migrants were channelled was established. This resulted in vicious human trafficking that exposed migrants and asylum-seekers to gross human rights abuses (HRW 2014).

Since 2002, with the introduction of obligatory national service in Eritrea, there has been a significant increase of emigration of young people. Some have referred to it as an 'exodus', claiming that some 40% of the young people have left (Andom 2015).[8] The precise figures are hard to confirm, but most Eritrean asylum-seekers reaching Sudan and Ethiopia are young men, and increasingly young women. There are also growing numbers of young children crossing the borders on their own (UNHCR 2014).

Politics and Policies

The political situation in the three countries affects adolescent girl migrants and refugees in various ways. This is most obvious in Sudan, where Ethiopian and Eritrean girls are subjected to the restrictive environment of a conservative Muslim society under Sharia law. They are not supposed to move around freely, and for single women to live alone without male protection has a negative impact on their social status. They are stigmatized and discriminated against and can be subjected to violence and abuse because they are women, non-Sudanese and non-Muslims. In Sudan, Eritreans and Ethiopians tended to and continue to be considered *Habesh*.[9] Limited political space in the authoritarian country, combined with international pressures to contain migration from the region towards Europe, results in an unfavourable context for

[8]In a 38-page letter addressed to the Eritrean people, four Eritrean Catholic Archbishops (of Asmara, Keren, Barentu and Segeneiti) described the situation in the country and appealed to the faithful to solve the economic crisis, exile and other predicaments from which they suffer, 'Eritrean Catholic Bishops ask: "Where Is Your Brother?"', *Awate* (awate.com), 7 June 2014.

[9]In Sudan, the term *Habesh* is used to have a derogatory meaning. It also elides Ethiopians and Eritreans into one society. *Habesha* is commonly used by Tigrinya speakers, Eritreans and the inhabitants of the Ethiopian side of the Plateau, such as Tigrinya, Amhara and Oromo, to point to their cultural, social and political connection. They do not perceive it as a derogatory term.

hosting refugees. Migrants and asylum-seekers have been increasingly subjected to identity checks, arrests and expulsions.

In Ethiopia, the political situation has deteriorated over the past decade, with heightened government oppression, especially since the rigged 2005 elections. There is almost no space for opposition parties, freedom of speech is severely restricted, and human rights advocates and journalists have been arrested and imprisoned. This political instability has affected the country's economic and security situation. Prices of consumer goods have gone up and rents have risen while salaries have stayed the same. This has affected the livelihoods of migrant girls, who are increasingly struggling to make ends meet.

In Bangladesh, the political situation has also deteriorated since 2014 when the Awami League, the party led by Sheik Hasina—daughter of Mujibur Rahman, the 'Father of the Nation'—was the only participant in the national elections, which were boycotted by all the opposition parties including the main one, the Bangladesh Nationalist Party of Khaleda Zia, widow of the late General Ziaur Rahman. The rivalry between the two leaders has marked Bangladesh politics since 1991. Moreover, since 2014 there have been several episodes of violence inflicted by radical Islamists against minorities, bloggers, secular intellectuals and foreign development workers. While this did not affect migrant girls directly, the fact so many girls migrate, leaving their families behind, shows that government have failed to guarantee human security for a major part of the population. Rural families are destitute, educated girls and boys see no future in their place of origin, and the limited number of jobs available for girls and young women are just a few examples of the impact of the political situation on migrant girls.

Migrant girls are also affected by the policy frameworks in the three countries. Internal migration in Bangladesh and Ethiopia is not regulated and anyone who wishes to migrate may do so. It is also permitted for minors to migrate and adolescent girls can move around freely in the respective countries. In Bangladesh, girls over 14 years of age can easily find work in the garment industry. In Ethiopia, adolescent girls under 18 years of age can be formally employed only if they have a legal guardian, which is why so many migrant girls become sex workers. Domestic employment agencies are not allowed to employ minors under 18 years of age, with the result that adolescent girls turn to illegal brokers, who often arrange work for them in hotels where they have to do sex work. Their only other option is to become domestic workers, but the pay and treatment are often so bad that girls prefer to become sex workers. In Bangladesh and Ethiopia, international migration is legally regulated, such as by stipulating agreements with destination countries and by enforcing strict regulations to discipline and control the employment agencies through which workers are employed. As mentioned earlier, girls under 18 years of age are not allowed to migrate internationally in Ethiopia; in Bangladesh the age limit is 25 years. This leads many adolescent girls to change their birth certificates or declare a different age when they request a passport, in order to be able to obtain a visa and work permits. In Eritrea, children from the age of six and up to the completion of military service are not allowed to leave the country. This puts young people in particularly dangerous situations of being potentially caught by military forces in Eritrea, Rashaida gangs on the border, and Sudanese police who often cooperate in cross-border controls with the Eritrean state. There have been numerous reports of torture, rape and monetary extortion suffered by young people fleeing Eritrea, including adolescents (see Van Reisen 2016).

International pressures to curtail migration towards Northern countries are often framed within a discourse on human trafficking. One such example is the so-called Khartoum Process. Sudan is leader of the 'EU–Horn of Africa Migration Route Initiative', an outcome of a conference that took place in Rome in November 2014, attended by ministers of the 28 EU member states and of several African countries—Djibouti, Egypt, Eritrea, Ethiopia, Kenya, Somalia, South Sudan, Sudan and Tunisia—as well as representatives of the African Union. The goal of this initiative is to give new impetus to regional cooperation between countries of origin, transit and destination, particularly regarding the route between the Horn of Africa and countries in the EU.[10] In reality, the Khartoum Process is intended to limit the number of people travelling to Europe via the Horn of Africa migration route. The initiative has been criticized

[10]The initiative includes developing cooperation between countries of origin, transit and destination in order to fight against irregular migration and criminal networks, especially through initiatives concerning technical assistance, training and exchange of information and of best practices, as well as identifying and prosecuting criminal networks. It also involves setting up or strengthening criminal law frameworks and fostering the ratification and the implementation of two additional protocols to the United Nations Convention against Transnational Organized Crime: the Protocol against the Smuggling of Migrants by Land, Air and Sea and the Protocol to Prevent, Suppress and Punish Trafficking in Persons, Especially Women and Children.

by the European Association for the Defence of Human Rights (known by its French acronym, AEDH) as attempting "to arrange the material conditions to avoid that they [migrants and refugees] come to Europe, especially by establishing asylum processing centres within African countries" (AEDH 2015, p. 3). The process foresees, among other things, the enhancement of law-enforcement powers and border controls in East African states.

The policy discourses in Ethiopia and Bangladesh emphasize trafficking, in particular of girls and women, with the result that other forms of migration, such as voluntary migration (also via irregular channels), are neglected and concealed. This is similar to the situation in Sudan, where much of the discourse and policies at national, regional and international level focus on combatting traffickers and smuggling. Legislation in Sudan focuses on punishing the traffickers, with little or no recourse for victims to seek protection. As the victims of trafficking enter the country without proper documentation, they can then be tried under the 1994 Immigration Law for illegal entry. This is the case for Ethiopian and Eritrean girls as most of them are smuggled into Sudan. They arrive without the necessary documents, although recently there has been some relaxation of the rules at the border. Some might be trafficked. There has been much international pressure on Sudan to combat trafficking and smuggling by curtailing irregular migration (such as the Khartoum Process and EU funding to Sudan to strengthen its border control), but the weak rule of law in Sudan in general and with respect to trafficking and smuggling in particular renders this pressure ineffective.

The fact that Ethiopian and Eritrean girls in Sudan are international migrants and refugees significantly affects their living and working conditions. Those who do not have refugee cards, obtained by registering with the Sudan Refugee Commission or UNHCR, are regarded as undocumented migrants. This makes them vulnerable to abuse and exploitation since they have no legal protection. In addition, their status as foreigners and as non-Muslims has a major effect on their lives. As mentioned earlier, they are stigmatized and discriminated against by the local population. In addition, much of the harassment of Ethiopian and Eritrean girls is based on the Public Order Act of 1991, which prohibits social gatherings attended by women and men, and has been the basis for the almost complete exclusion of women from public life. Women have been subjected to official harassment in the enforcement of dress codes and limitations on public association. Ethiopian and Eritrean girls are widely seen as 'loose', and easy to have sex with. This is very similar to the experiences of Ethiopian girls in the Middle East, who are also stigmatized and discriminated against because of their age, ethnic background and status as foreigners. The strict migration policies in countries across the Arabian Peninsula, where migrants are legally tied to their employers who sponsor them (the so-called *kafala* system), has a major impact on migrant girls; running away from situations of abuse and exploitation automatically makes them undocumented migrants at risk of arrest and deportation. During our fieldwork, between November 2013 and April 2014, after the end of a seven-month amnesty period, more than 160,000 Ethiopians, including many young women, were deported from Saudi Arabia because they were undocumented (see de Regt and Tafesse 2016).

City as a Space

The capital cities of Dhaka, Addis Ababa and Khartoum have undergone fundamental changes in the past three decades owing to rapid urbanization and modernization processes. While the cities differ in size—Dhaka being a megacity of more than 14 million people, while Addis Ababa and Khartoum have, respectively, 4 and 6 million inhabitants—all three cities are booming, with all types of consequences for those living there.

Dhaka: Exploding with Migrants

Dhaka, located in the eponymous district and division, lies along the east bank of the Buriganga River in the heart of Bangladesh and the Bengal Delta. It is like a microcosm of the entire country with all its diverse religious and ethnic communities. Proud of its mediaeval heritage, when it was the most important economic centre in the Mughal Bengal, still it is the country's economic cultural and political centre. After partition, as the capital of East Pakistan, Dhaka was the birthplace of the independence movement with the foundation of the Awami League in 1949. The political activism of students and intellectuals at Dhaka University, the country's most prestigious educational institution, culminated on 21 February 1952 with the mass demonstration organized by the Bengali Language movement against the decision of the Pakistani government to make Urdu the official language. Every year, from that day for a whole week the country commemorates the Pakistani army killing a huge

Fig. 3.2 The Bhola slum, Mirpur, Dhaka, Bangladesh

number of student and intellectuals; during the week, Dhaka University campus is filled with young people streaming through the book fair and the many cultural initiatives (Fig. 3.2).

Dhaka is a city of contrasts. The northern neighbourhoods of Gulshan, Baridhara, Banani and Uttara, where renting a flat can cost up to US$3000, where the upper-middle and upper class live, and where most embassies and international development agencies are located, sharply contrast with the old and decrepit buildings of historical Dhaka in the south, where only a few mansions and mosques testify to its former splendour. In almost every ward in the city, there are further contrasts between the new skyscrapers and condominiums with central air conditioning and the trash-strewn slums where the poorest live in shacks of corrugated iron. While in the early 1980s the city's wide avenues thronged with hundreds of rickshaws and bicycles, traffic jams of old buses, three-wheeled vehicles and private cars now make moving around a very difficult, expensive and time-consuming business. Dhaka's population has grown constantly over the years and is now estimated at 9 million while Greater Dhaka, including the conurbation surrounding the city, is home to more than 17 million.

For decades the city has attracted rural migrants in search of better livelihoods, but more recently internal migration has been on the rise due to phenomena related to climate change. Most of the internal migrants settle in the growing city slums, with migrants constituting 53% of their population (UNDP 2013, p. 7). Slums, known as *bustee*, are built on government or private land and are characterized by poverty, very poor housing, high population density, and limited access to services. Slum conditions do, however, vary. According to a survey conducted in 2006 (CES et al. 2006) in some areas of Dhaka, most *bustee* were affected by poor drainage, flooding and very poor housing, but only a minority were affected by even worse conditions such as lack of electricity, cooking gas, tap water, and insecure tenure, threat of eviction, and a large number of households having to share water sources and latrines.

Slums are usually controlled by local 'leaders' who are well connected to the local police and/or political party. These 'leaders', who are sometimes associated with mafia-like criminal gangs known as '*mastaan*', control the delivery of services and constitute a well-established informal power structure that may act in the name of the '*samaj*' (society or community). They are recognized as having the power to enforce the rules related to social life through a system of informal arbitration, where they act in the name of the community's honour and prestige. In our research, we came across instances where they punished young people involved in a premarital relationship and forced them to marry or fined the transgressors. When they are connected to criminal gangs, such interventions in the personal sphere are all part of a system of legitimized extortion. NGOs or organizations working in a particular *bustee* find they have to negotiate with these informal power structures when employing people, establishing services and so on (Camellia et al. 2012).

The Bengali girls who participated in the research were all living in Pallabi *Thana* (literally Police Station), a suburb of Greater Dhaka on the outskirts of the city. Most of the girls lived in two of the slum settlements: the Bhola *bustee* and the Baunibandh *bustee*, where Aparajeyo Bangladesh and ARBAN, respectively, have been working in partnership with Terre des Hommes Italy for more than 12 years. The Garo respondents were working in Mohammadpur, in Dhaka's city centre, and in Kalachandpur in the north of the city.

Addis Ababa: The New Flower Is Growing

Addis Ababa is a relatively young capital, established at the end of the nineteenth century as part of Emperor Menelik II's project to modernize and unify Ethiopia. South of the green hills and mountains of Entoto, Addis Ababa (which means New Flower in Amharic) is located in central Ethiopia, between the Christian and Muslim north of the country and the religiously and ethnically diverse south. The Ethiopian capital was meant to become the centre of a strong nation, a place which would represent the country's rich history and civilization and where at the same time development and modernization would be created and disseminated (Gulema 2013, p. 172). Equally important, the capital is the country's main political centre, where the state exercises its power and control. Haile Selassie invited urban planners from all over the world to help build a modern capital; roads were built, neighbourhoods were planned, land use was controlled and open spaces were preserved (Gulema 2013, p. 174). The city is divided into *sefers*, neighbourhoods, which are again divided into *kebeles*, the smallest administrative unit in Ethiopia. In 1958 the United Nations Economic Commission for Africa (UNECA) established its headquarters in the city and in 1963 the Organization for African Unity followed. As a result, many other African and international organizations came to Addis Ababa, and with them many people from all over the world. The intention to build a capital which would unify the nation failed dramatically as social inequalities, in particular between rich and poor, but also those based on gender, age and class, affected the city in various ways (Gulema 2013). These processes started decades ago but have intensified under the current regime.

In the past, Addis Ababa was characterized by green pine trees and mud and stone houses with corrugated iron roofs, which gave it a pleasant and calm rural image. While there are still few skyscrapers, modern buildings have replaced traditional housing and the character of many neighbourhoods has drastically changed. The heart of the city was Piazza, where small shops, coffee houses and restaurants are located, the name of the area a reference to Ethiopia's Italian past. Old Airport and Bole are traditional upper-class neighbourhoods, but large gated communities have been constructed on the city outskirts, where many upper-middle-class families reside. Kasanchis and Haya Wulat used to be residential areas for the lower-middle classes, and popular places for entertainment and prostitution.

The city attracts tens of thousands of people from all over the country each year, although reliable statistics are lacking. According to the Central Statistical Agency, in 2014 there were 1,245,627 rural–urban migrants living in Addis Ababa, the majority female (727,208) and most of them between 20 and 29 years of age (CSA 2014, p. 22). The current government has invested greatly in improving the city's infrastructure and building large-scale housing projects (see Bonsa 2013; Demissie 2008). As a result, age-old residential areas have been demolished, new roads and a railway have been built, and many of the green areas in the city have disappeared. The construction sector is booming, creating opportunities mainly for migrants from the provinces. Yet, finding affordable housing is still a big challenge for many people. Large slum settlements have formed, both inside the city as well as on the outskirts. The new condominiums across Addis Ababa are supposed to offer affordable housing for lower-middle-class families but are also clear signs of the government's neoliberal policies. Moreover, hundreds of thousands of the city's inhabitants are unemployed.

Urban transport consists of minibuses, buses and private cars, and since the summer of 2015 a tram. Traffic jams are commonplace at the most important hubs. In the past decade, the city has undergone major transformation with the building or expansion of new roads, in an attempt to cut down the number of traffic jams. The newly built tram is supposed to provide affordable transport for the city's residents but reaches a limited number of areas and is often very crowded. Most people continue to use buses and minibuses.

Ethnically the city is very diverse. While Amharic is the lingua franca, Oromos, Gurages, Tigreans, and many other Ethiopians live there. The high rate of urbanization has contributed to this diversity. In addition, there are established communities of Armenians, Greeks and Italians, who are often socially integrated. Religiously the city's population is also very diverse. Although the Ethiopian Orthodox Church is the most visible, because of the many beautiful churches which daily attract numerous worshippers, Islam and Pentecostalism are also very present; an increasing number of mosques and Pentecostal churches have been built in the past decades. The city has become a crucible of different ethnicities, religions, socio-economic classes. While this could be considered a very positive development, it has also led to increasing social inequalities on many different levels. The girls who participated in the research were often forced to move house, being unable to pay the rent in the city centre, and moved to areas further away, on the outskirts of town.

Khartoum: A City with Many Faces

Set in the middle of the desert, Khartoum is located where the two Niles meet, at a point called *al-Mogran*, meaning the confluence. Divided by the Niles, Khartoum is a tripartite metropolis with an estimated population of over 6 million people, consisting of Khartoum proper, and linked by bridges to Khartoum North (*al-KharṭūmBaḥrī*) and Omdurman (*Umm Durmān*) to the west. It is a place of enormous power and privilege, discrepancies and contradictions, of aspirations, corruptions, dreams, and failed attempts to construct a 'new' life. The 'modernity dream' of making Khartoum a Dubai of North Africa clashes with the everyday reality and struggle for survival of those who are impoverished. This is most apparent in the 'unfinished' or 'in progress' architectural landscape, with skyscrapers in the Mugran area, new neighbourhoods on the Nile with large villas for the elites, unfinished apartment and office buildings from the era of the economic boom, and dirt roads full of pot holes, uncollected garbage, and unmaintained low-rise houses (Franck 2015). Khartoum exemplifies that contradiction: a dream of crossing into a different world yet often getting stuck in the daily experience of desperation, discrimination, and destitution.

During the 2004–2011 oil boom and before the separation with South Sudan, Khartoum offered a wide range of work opportunities for migrants and refugees. Since the creation of South Sudan and the cutting off of main oil supplies to the North, however, Khartoum's economic growth and expansion have declined. This is most visible from the unfinished construction projects that were going to transform the landscape of this historically sleepy and slow-pace city into a global bustling metropolis.

Khartoum is a largely low-rise, sprawling city, under an almost perpetual haze of dust. Arriving in Khartoum one is struck both by its chaotic arrangement and by its relatively slow pace. Its frequent power cuts and the oppressive heat infuse everything with a sticky torpor. Unlike Cairo to the north or Nairobi to the south, Khartoum lacks frenetic energy or drama. The country's international reputation for hard-line Islamism and ethnic warfare jars with the city's subdued mood.

Following the secession of South Sudan via a referendum in 2011, Khartoum is less diverse, as a large percentage of the southern minority moved to South Sudan. They have been, however, coming back since the eruption of the current conflict in South Sudan in December 2013. The city is quieter and poorer, suffering the economic loss of the South's resources and the loss of the southern territory smarting at a visceral, existential level. War still rages in the Nuba Mountains and tensions simmer in the east and west of the country. Rebel movements have twice approached and once entered Khartoum in the past five years.

Over the period of our fieldwork (2014–2016), it was noticeable that wealth in Khartoum is increasingly concentrated in the hands of the few, and the rest of the population has become poorer. With sanctions still in place against Sudan, the inflation rate has rocketed (in 2013 US$1 was exchanged for 8 SDG on the parallel market, whereas in April 2016 it reached 13.5 SDG, and by 2018 it had already reached 55 SDG). When South Sudan declared independence in July 2011, it took with it about 75% of the country's oil output. The Sudanese pound has lost 100% of its value since South Sudan's secession, pushing inflation rates to record levels given that Sudan imports most of its food. The population of Khartoum suffers from a lack of basic commodities, including shortages of bread, milk, gas and petrol. The prices of basic goods have almost doubled, while salaries remain low.

Although the city has immense class and ethnic diversity, spatially these are mingled, with unclear physical divisions between the very rich and the very poor. Large numbers of internal migrants and displaced people reside throughout the city, although mainly in the shanty towns in the city's outskirts. There are, however, some city neighbourhoods that are more popular among international migrants. The urban population assessment carried out by UNHCR in 2013–2014 (UNHCR 2015a) identified the following distribution of refugee and asylum-seekers throughout the city (in order of density): Jereif West, Daim, Al Sahafa, Jabra, Imtidad, Omdurman, Bahri, Arkaweet East and Taif, Jabal Awliya (including Kalakla, Mayo, Al Azhari). These areas were also the main residential areas for the Eritrean and Ethiopian girls and women who participated in this study.

Before the separation with South Sudan, Khartoum used to offer quite a number of job opportunities for migrants. Qualified Eritreans and Ethiopians worked as technical staff, often being better educated than the local population. Since the economic decline beginning in 2011, and the growing pressure from the young educated Sudanese entering the labour market, there are fewer lucrative opportunities in the city. Consequently, government regulations have become much stricter on issuing work permits for foreigners. Even well-educated Ethiopians and Eritreans are finding it increasingly difficult to obtain formal employment. Most migrants work in the food industry, whether running restaurants, or working as waiters or cleaners. Some are teachers, others are self-employed as rickshaw drivers, and some work in the construction sector. For girls and women, work opportunities are rather restricted. As the labour market is highly gendered and regulated by conservative Islamic norms, female international migrants take up jobs that Sudanese women are not allowed to do. This includes working as domestic workers, waitresses, working in fast-food places or as cleaners.

Contrasting yet Similar Settings

There are differences but also strong similarities among the girls living in the three cities. Adolescent migrant and refugee girls are in all three case studies subjected to strong systems of social control, and often experience stigmatization, discrimination and harassment, as will become clear in the rest of the book. Gender, age and migration intersect in such ways that migrant girls are extremely vulnerable and run great risks; the mere fact that they are living in cities without the protection of their parents, and in particular without male relatives, and so do not conform to dominant gender norms, has a great impact on their social status and consequently on their vulnerability. At the same time, the cities also offer chances to pursue different choices, and increase girls' options in terms of the lives to which they aspire. As we will see in the next chapters, however, although many girls had high hopes of their migration to the capital they faced many challenges, especially at the beginning.

References

Abbas, R. (2012, August 22). Ethiopian Servants in Sudan at the Mercy of Middle Men. *The Niles*.

Abebe, T. (2007). Changing Livelihoods, Changing Childhoods: Patterns of Children's Work in Rural Southern Ethiopia. *Children's Geographies, 5*(1&2), 77–93.

AEDH. (2015). *The Khartoum Process, a New Step in*. Declaration, see http://www.aedh.eu/The-Khartoum-Process-a-new-step-in.html.

Ahmed, S. (1993). Purdah: An Analysis of Ideal Versus Contextual Reality. *Journal of Social Studies, 60*, 45–58.

Akalu, G. A. (2014). Higher Education in Ethiopia: Expansion, Quality Assurance, and Institutional Autonomy. *Higher Education Quarterly, 68*(4), 394–415.

ANCI, Caritas, Cittalia, Fondazione Migrantes, Servizio Centrale SPRAR. (2017). *Rapporto sulla Protezione internazionale in Italia*. Rome.

Andom, N. (2015). *Demystifying Irregular Youth Hemorrhage from Post-2000s Eritrea: Driven by Politics or Economics*. Conference Paper for Migration and exile in the Horn of Africa: State of knowledge and currentdebates, CEDEJ, Khartoum, 16–18 November.

Ashraf, A. (2016). *Public Policy Formulation: A Case-Study of Domestic Workers in Bangladesh* (Migrating Out of Poverty, Working Paper No. 37). Brighton: University of Sussex.

Atnafu, A., Oucho, L., & Zeitlyn, B. (2014). *Poverty, Youth and Rural-Urban Migration in Ethiopia* (Migrating Out of Poverty, Working Paper No. 17). Brighton: University of Sussex.

Babiker, M. A. (2011). *Irregular Migration in Sudan: A Legal Perspective. CARIM-AS* 2011/64, Robert Schuman Centre for Advanced Studies, San Domenicodi Fiesole: European University Institute.

Bal, E. (2007). *They Ask if We Eat Frogs: Garo Ethnicity in Bangladesh*. Singapore: Institute of Southeast Asian Studies.

Bariagaber, A. (1995). Linking Political Violence and Refugee Situations in the Horn of Africa: An Empirical Approach. *International Migration, 33*(2), 209–234.

Bjeren, G. (1985). *Migration to Shashemene: Ethnicity, Gender and Occupation in Urban Ethiopia*. Uppsala: Scandinavian Institute of African Studies.

Bonsa, S. (2001). A History of Kistanemigration to 1974. *Azania: Archaeological Research in Africa, 36–37*(1), 172–186.

Breines, M. R. (2017). *Pursuing Progress: Urban-Urban Migration and Meanings of Being Middle Class in Ethiopia*. PhD dissertation, University of Sussex.

Broussard, N. H., & Tekleselassie, T. G. (2012). *Youth Unemployment: Ethiopia Country Study*. London: International Growth Centre, London School of Economics and Political Science.

Camellia, S., Khan, N. N., & Naved, R. T. (2012). Violence Against Unmarried Adolescent Girls. In R. T. Naved & S. Amin (Eds.), *Growing Up Safe and Healthy (SAFE): Baseline Report on Sexual and Reproductive Health and Rights and Violence Against Women and Girls in Dhaka Slums*. Dhaka: Iccdr,b.

Central Statistical Agency. (2014). *Ethiopia Mini Demographic and Health Survey 2014*. Addis Ababa: The Federal Democratic Republic of Ethiopia.

CES, et al. (2006). *Bangladesh: Urban Survey*. Measure Evaluation. http://www.cpc.unc.edu/measure.

Charpentier, É. (2015). L'Éthiopie des Congolais, Burundais et Rwandais réfugiés. *African Diaspora, 8*, 51–75.

Chuta, N., & Morrow, V. (2015). *Youth Trajectories Through Work and Marriage in Rural Ethiopia* (Young Lives Working Paper No. 135). Oxford: Young Lives, University of Oxford.

Connell, D. (2013). Refugees, Ransoms and Revolt: An Update on Eritrea. *Middle East Report, 266*(35), 28–32.

Crivello, G., & van der Gaag, N. (2016). *Between Hope and a Hard Place: Boys and Young Men Negotiating Gender, Poverty and Social Worth in Ethiopia* (Young Lives Working Paper No. 160). Oxford: Young Lives, University of Oxford.

de Regt, M. (2010). Ways to Come, Ways to Leave: Gender, Mobility, and Il/Legality Among Ethiopian Domestic Workers in Yemen. *Gender & Society, 24*(2), 237–260.

de Regt, M., & Tafesse, M. (2016). "Deported Before Experiencing the Good Sides of Migration": Ethiopians Returning from Saudi Arabia. *African and Black Diaspora, 9*(2), 228–242.

Del Franco, N. (2010). Aspirations and Self-Hood: Exploring the Meaning of Higher Education for Girl College Students in Rural Bangladesh. *Compare: A Journal of Comparative and International Education, 40*(2), 147–165.

Demissie, F. (2008). Situated Neoliberalism and Urban Crisis in Addis Ababa, Ethiopia. *African Identities, 6*(4), 505–527.

Dom, C. (2017). Migrating for Work from Rural Communities (2010–13). In A. Pankhurst (Ed.), *Change and Transformation in 20 Rural Communities in Ethiopia: Selected Aspects and Implications for Policy* (pp. 375–402). Addis Ababa: WIDE.

Franck, A. (2015). Urban Agriculture Facing Land Pressure in Greater Khartoum: The Case of New Real Estate Projects in Tuti and Abū Se'īd. In B. Casciarri, M. A. M. Assal, & F. Ireton (Eds.), *Multidimensional Change in Sudan (1989–2011) Reshaping Livelihoods, Conflicts and Identities*. Berghahn Books.

Fernandez, B. (2010). Cheap and Disposable? The Impact of the Global Economic Crisis on the Migration of Ethiopian Women Domestic Workers to the Gulf. *Gender & Development, 18*(2), 249–262.

Gebre, L. T., Maharaj, P., & Pillay, N. K. (2011). The Experiences of Immigrants in South Africa: A Case Study of Ethiopians in Durban, South Africa. *Urban Forum, 22*, 23–35.

Giani, L. (2006). *Migration and Education: Child Migrants in Bangladesh* (Sussex Migration Working Paper No. 33). Brighton: University of Sussex.

Girma, W., & Erulkar, A. (2009). *Commercial Sex Workers in Five Ethiopian Cities: A Baseline Survey for USAID Targeted HIV Prevention Program for Most-at-Risk Populations*. Addis Ababa: USAID.

Gulema, S. B. (2013). City as Nation: Imagining and Practicing Addis Ababa as a Modern and National Space. *Northeast African Studies, 13*(1), 167–213.

Hossain, N. (2012). *Women's Empowerment Revisited: From Individual to Collective Power among the Export Sector Workers of Bangladesh* (IDS Working Paper No. 38). Brighton: Institute of Development Studies.

Human Rights Watch. (2014). *I Wanted to Lie Down and Die: Trafficking and Torture of Eritreans in Sudan and Egypt*. HRW Report. http://www.hrw.org/news/2014/02/11/egyptsudan-traffickers-who-torture.

Humphris, R. (2013, March). Refugees and Rashaida: Human Smuggling and Trafficking from Eritrea to Sudan and Egypt. *New Issues in Refugee Research No. 254.*

International Crisis Group. (2014, August 8). *Eritrea: Ending the Exodus? Africa Briefing No. 100.*

ILO. (2014). *Gender and Migration from Bangladesh. Mainstreaming Migration into the National Development Plans form a Gender Perspective*. Dhaka: International Labour Organization.

IOM. (2009). *Compendium of IOM Activities in Migration, Climate Change and the Environment*. Geneva: ILO.

IOM. (2013). *Country Profile 2011: Migration in Sudan*. Geneva: IOM.

Islam, M. C., Rakib, M. A., & Adnan, A. T. M. (2016). Ready-Made Garments Sector of Bangladesh: Its Contribution and Challenges Towards Development. *Journal of Asian Development Studies, 5*(2), 50–61.

Jamie, F. O. M. (2013). Gender and Migration in Africa: Female Ethiopian Migration in Post-2008 Sudan. *Journal of Politics and Law, 6*(1), 186–192.

Johnson, D. (2006). *The Root Causes of Sudan's Civil Wars*. Oxford, Kampala, Nairobi, Bloomington & Indiana: The International Africa Institute.

Jones, N., et al. (2014). *Rethinking Girls on the Move: The Intersection of Poverty, Exploitation, and Violence Experienced by Ethiopian Adolescents Involved in the Middle East "Maid Trade"*. London: Overseas Development Institute.

Kabeer, N. (2000). *The Power to Choose: Bangladeshi Women and Labour Market Decisions in London and Dhaka*. London and New York: Verso.

Kanko, T. D., Bailey, A., & Teller, C. H. (2013). *Irregular Migration: Causes and Consequences of Young Adult Migration from Southern Ethiopia to South Africa*. Paper presented at the 27th IUSSP International Population Conference, 26–31 August, Busan, South Korea.

Kebede, E. (2001). *Ethiopia: An Assessment of the International Labour Migration Situation: The Case of Female Migrants* (GENPROM Working

Paper No. 3, Series on Women and Migration). Geneva: International Labour Organization.

Kibreab, G. (1995). Eritrean Women Refugees in Khartoum, Sudan 1970–1990. *Journal of Refugee Studies, 8*(1), 1–25.

Kibreab, G. (2000). Resistance, Displacement, and Identity: The Case of Eritrean Refugees in Sudan. *Canadian Journal of African Studies, 34*, 249–296.

Kibreab, G. (2009). Forced Labour in Eritrea. *Journal of Modern African Studies, 47*(1), 41–72.

Kifleyesus, A. (2012). Women Who Migrate, Men Who Wait: Eritrean Labor Migration to the Arab Near East. *Northeast African Studies, 12*(1), 95–127.

Mains, D. (2012). *Hope Is Cut: Youth, Unemployment and the Future in Urban Ethiopia*. Philadelphia, PA: Temple University Press.

Ministero del Lavoro e delle Politiche sociali (MLPS). (2016). *La comunità bengalese in Italia*. Roma: MLPS.

Minaye, A. (2012). Trafficked to the Gulf States: The Experiences of Ethiopian Returnee Women. *Journal of Community Practice, 20*(1–2), 112–133.

National Population Census (NPC). (2010). *Migration and Population Movement in Sudan*. Khartoum: General Secretariat, National Population Council.

Ratha, D., Mohapatra, S., & Silwal, A. 2011. Eritrea. In *The Migration and Remittances Factbook*. Washington, DC: World Bank.

Rudnick, A. (2009). *Working Gendered Boundaries: Temporary Migration Experiences of Bangladeshi Women in the Malaysian Export Industry from a Multi-sited Perspective*. Amsterdam: Amsterdam University Press.

Schewel, K., & Fransen, S. 2018. *Formal Education and Migration Aspirations in Ethiopia* (IMIn Working Paper No. 144). Amsterdam: University of Amsterdam.

UNDP. (2013). *Internal Migration in Bangladesh: Characters, Drivers and Policy Issues*. Dhaka: United Nations Development Programme.

UNDP. (2016). *Human Development Report: Human Development for Everyone*. New York, NY: United Nations Development Programme.

UNHCR. (2014). *Factsheet. Khartoum: Sudan*. Geneva: United Nations High Commissioner for Refugees.

UNHCR. (2015a). *Khartoum Urban Population Assessment Report*. Khartoum: United Nations High Commissioner for Refugees.

UNHCR. (2015b). *Factsheet Addis Ababa: Ethiopia*. Geneva: United Nations High Commissioner for Refugees.

UNHCR. (2017). *Global Trends: Forced Displacement in 2017*. Geneva, Switzerland: UNHCR.

The World Bank Group. (2015). *Ethiopia Poverty Assessment 2014*. Addis Ababa: The World Bank Group.

World Bank. (2017). Combined Project Information Documents/Integrated Safeguards Data Sheet (PID/ISDS).
Van Reisen, M. (2016). *The Involvement of Unaccompanied Minors from Eritrea in Human Trafficking*. Report, Rapid Social and Cultural Transformation, Tilburg University: Holland.
Zack, T. (2015). Jeppe: Where Low-End Globalization, Ethnic Entrepreneurialism and the Arrival City Meet. *Urban Forum, 26*, 131–150.
Zack, T., & Estifanos, Y. S. (2016). Somewhere Else: Social Connection and Dislocation of Ethiopian Migrants in Johannesburg. *African and Black Diaspora, 9*(2), 149–165.

CHAPTER 4

Becoming a Migrant, Becoming a Refugee

"*There Is No Room to Dream*": Helen's Decision to Leave

Helen left Eritrea for Sudan when she was 18 years old. She worked as a waitress in a Lebanese restaurant in Khartoum. She spoke good English and her dream was to study anthropology and archaeology. In August 2015, we decided to meet at a local café, *Solitaire*, in central Khartoum, a place frequented by well-to-do Sudanese. It is also one of the city's few cafés where adolescent girls and young women sit alone or chat with female or male friends. There are a few Eritreans and Ethiopians who work there, mostly young women, wearing trousers and no headscarf. As we were told, in this type of place the management requires waitresses to be well turned out, go to a hairdresser and to wear trousers. These gendered dress codes go against Sudanese laws, including the Public Order decree (see Chapter 3), which requires girls and women to cover their heads in public, wear 'proper' attire (no trousers) and forbids socializing with unrelated men. As a result, there are no young Sudanese women working in such cafés, which opens up a possibility for Eritreans to be employed as waitresses. It is mostly Eritreans who are recent arrivals in Sudan who work there, as those who were born in the country tend to conform more to the Sudan's conservative gender norms.

Helen was born in Asmara where she lived with her parents and her two sisters. Her older sister is 28 and has been living in Canada for the

K. Grabska et al., *Adolescent Girls' Migration in The Global South*, Palgrave Studies on Children and Development,
https://doi.org/10.1007/978-3-030-00093-6_4

past five or six years. She went to Ethiopia when she was 19, escaped from the military, stayed in a refugee camp and from there was resettled in Canada. Helen was not sure where her sister lived but told us that she took financial responsibility for her family. She has been working and studying at the same time and helping both her sisters and her parents in Eritrea. Her sister was not married and Helen felt that it was the time for her to find a husband and become a fully adult woman, as she described it: "She is older than me and the time is running [out] for her".

Helen's father ran a furniture store. When Helen was small, she wanted to be like him, a businesswoman. They were a happy family. Her mother was the homemaker and took care of the daughters. When Helen was 12, due to the tightening political and economic situation in Eritrea, her father could no longer make ends meet from the shop and decided to go to Angola and continue to run his business there. Once he earned enough money, he moved to Italy. He asked Helen's mother to join him, and she took the plane from Asmara. Helen explained that older people have no problems in leaving the country, because they have passed the military service age. "For the young ones, it is a big problem. They all have to go to the military service, and they are not allowed to leave the country until a certain age. This is the reason why so many people leave the country and look for chances of improving their lives somewhere else", she asserted. Her parents decided to leave their two daughters with some distant relatives in Eritrea. Helen was then 15 and her younger sister 13. They stayed together for the next three years and were supported by their sister in Canada. They both went to school, and Helen started university. After a year in Italy, her parents went to Norway where they sought asylum. They had been in a refugee camp for 18 months waiting for their interview by the time we met Helen.

When Helen first explained her decision to leave Eritrea, she focused on the narrative of escaping the pressures of the militarized authoritarian regime in Eritrea and the life-long national service obligation. Only later did she reveal how she had no chance to pursue her dreams back home. Subjected to multiple gendered obligations as a daughter and as a girl, she did not want to marry against her will and saw no chance to continue her education and having a meaningful life in Eritrea:

> In fact, I was engaged. My parents wanted me to marry a man, an Eritrean man, who lives in Dubai. You know, for young people there is no chance to have a life in Eritrea. This is the reason why they leave. They cannot

dream in Eritrea. The political situation affects the economic, and this in turn makes people leave. So many men left, and now there are not that many young men left in Eritrea. At the same time, these men who are abroad they want to get married. So, they look for girls in Eritrea (or in transit countries). These men are in their 30s or so. And they want to marry younger girls. So, they look for girls who are 17, 18 or 20. For Eritrean girls when they reach 25 or 26 it is already late to marry. So, the parents insist that the girls marry earlier.

This puts also a lot of pressure on the older girls. This is also the reason why they leave. Because they want to find husbands, they want to marry. In Eritrea there is something like 60 per cent women and 40 per cent men. This means there are not enough men for the girls to marry. This is one of the reasons why so many girls started migrating now.

But I did not want to marry. I had another plan. I wanted to study and find a good job and become independent. I believe that it is the turn of my older sister who is in Canada to marry. Till now she has had no chance because she had to migrate and then she had to support us. If you are the firstborn in the family you have a responsibility for the family. This is also the reason why girls migrate. In Eritrea it is impossible to find a good job, and to earn enough money to support the family. The girls who are the oldest in the family migrate so that they can help their families and the young siblings.

My younger sister and I decided to leave to Sudan and then to travel to Europe. Our parents opposed our decision, but we found a way through a friend and left Eritrea illegally, crossing the border on foot. When we were in Kasala (border town in Sudan), we called our parents and they had to pay the smugglers for our journey. It was a scary journey, but nothing happened to us. We then arrived by bus in Khartoum.

Helen's story reveals a more nuanced and complex scenario than the dominant discourse, which presents girls' motives to migrate in terms of helping the family, sacrificing themselves for their parents and siblings, and there being no choice other than migration (e.g. Montgomery 2016; Temin et al. 2013). It reveals girls' own aspirations and their capacity to act upon them. In the cases of Ethiopia and Bangladesh, as we saw in Chapter 3, the poverty discourse is dominant in discussions about the main reasons for migration while in the case of Eritrea the discourse on human rights violations is most visible. In Bangladesh, most studies locate migration to work in the garment industry in rural poverty (Amin et al. 1997; Kabeer and Mahmud 2004; Kibria 1995; Feldman 2001). In Ethiopia, poverty is also mentioned as the main reason for migration, caused by drought, conflict, and climate change (Atnafu et al. 2014; Carter and Rohwerder 2016; Comenetz and Caviedes 2002). For Eritrea, national service, authoritarian rule and human rights violations, combined with the dire economic situation, are seen as the major forces behind the exodus of refugees (see Andom 2015; Van Reisen 2017; Kibreab 2009). As a result, migrant girls are mainly presented as victims of structural forces. Notwithstanding the importance of poverty and human rights violations, the girls' narratives reveal more complex and multifaceted decision-making processes. They show elements of agency, as well as pressures, in the choice to migrate and in the way the decision to do so is taken. Individual decisions are made within very constrained options and can result from diverse factors: the struggle to survive versus pursuing aspirations and wishes. In this chapter, we present and analyze a number of (forced) migration stories and in doing so contribute to the theoretical debates on children and young people's mobility by showing the footprints of agency and their space for self-assertion.

Researching the Motives for Migration

Researching what motivates a person to migrate is problematic in several ways. First, the questions regarding the reasons to migrate are usually asked retrospectively, and hence the answers are given from a specific point in time and place that creates a personal distance from the initial reasons. It is more about how migrants and refugees *remember* their decision to migrate. There is thus a difference in the discursive and narrative way the reasons for movement are presented, and the actual experience of the gendered and generational decision-making process (see Willemse 2014). Second, the decision to migrate usually develops over a period of time at a given moment in the girl's life, and rarely completely independently but rather linked to what other family members are doing (see Gardner 2009). Thus, quantitative methods and one-time interviews are rather limited in uncovering the complex temporal and social relational factors in decision-making. Third, especially in the context of cross-border movement, with increasingly restricted access to regular migration channels, narratives of migration take place in a highly politicized context. At times narratives are twisted or presented only partially in order to fit the political and policy parameters of those with the right of access to legal status in the host country (either through access to asylum or labour migration). These elements, among others, pose major challenges for researchers interested in decision-making processes and motivations related to migration.

In our three country studies, we used several methods in order to better understand girls' circumstances and the research participants' motives for migrating (see Chapter 2). The qualitative surveys we carried out among the total of 168 respondents provided often simplified replies, fitting the dominant explanations of poverty and human rights violations that motivated girls to move within or across borders. The answers gave us general indications, but it was crucial to substantiate and to explain them through FGDs, in-depth and life-story interviews with girls and also, when possible, with their families. Insights from local co-researchers and their context-specific interpretations of answers given to the questionnaires provided a much more nuanced understanding of the complex decision-making motivations and strategies. While the questionnaires show the more simplified answers that emerged in the first encounters with the girls, the life stories reveal more complex and multifaceted decision-making processes.

Complexities of Migration Decision-Making

Narrating Reasons to Move Through Questionnaires

In the survey, the respondents were given a free choice to identify questions regarding their reasons for migration and could also identify more than one answer. Most of the respondents in the three countries identified several reasons and key turning points that led them to decide to leave their place of origin. The majority of Ethiopians and Eritreans in Sudan ticked boxes relating to the dire economic or political situation of their families back home and the desire to help them; 29 of the 48 respondents described their households as 'poor or 'very poor'. Similar answers were provided by Bangladeshi migrants, with 40 of the 60 citing poverty and 17 claiming they wanted to help their family members. In Ethiopia, only 20 of the 60 migrants mentioned poverty among the reasons for migration.

In the three countries, the majority of the migrants' households were described, according to the local perceptions of poverty and well-being, as either 'poor' or 'very poor', lacking both economic (land, livestock) and social resources (only one breadwinner in the family, no social networks to count on). In Bangladesh, a higher percentage of migrants came from 'very poor' households. According to the migrants' own evaluation of their family's socio-economic conditions, Bangladeshi-Bengali migrants tended to come from poorer households than Garo migrants, Ethiopians in Sudan from poorer families than Eritreans, and Ethiopian girls who went to the Middle East from poorer families than those who migrated internally.

In the migrants' words, 'poverty' itself is a condition of different situations and circumstances. In Bangladesh, most migrant girls talked of poverty as a situation of '*obhab*' (literally lack) that, as life stories later revealed, in the most severe cases was connected with the death or illness of the family breadwinner, the lack of support from brothers, some environmental disaster, or a sudden emergency, such as having to pay a large dowry for a daughter's marriage. In Sudan, Ethiopians and Eritreans who described their families as 'poor' or 'very poor' had often experienced some type of household crisis, with the death of one or both parents, severe health problems or a divorce. These were important events in order to understand the immediate trigger for the girls to move. Without the knowledge of the context and the life trajectory of the migrant and her household members, however, it was difficult to discern the importance of this particular event in the decision regarding migration. In other words, without knowing the background of a particular migrant, we were unable to understand why some who experienced a particular life event decided to move and others to stay.

In Ethiopia, the majority of the girls who declared they wanted to help their families came from rural households, mostly headed by a woman. The death of one or both parents was quoted as a reason for migration by a third of the internal migrants interviewed in Addis Ababa. In the interviews with returnees from the Middle East, poverty and the wish to help the family had also been the main reasons for migration: 24 out of 30 returnees had been going to school before migrating; some of them had been working but their income was not enough to sustain themselves and their family. Among these returnees, poverty was mentioned as the most important reason, and conflicts with parents and escaping restrictive social environments were mentioned much less.

In Sudan, political circumstances were given as the main reason for Eritreans to move to Khartoum. Eritrean refugee girls and young women often referred to the pressure of national service, the lack of work opportunities, and political and religious persecution. Ethiopian internal migrants also mentioned the wish to continue their education, the fear of abduction and early marriage and escaping the restrictive gender norms and values in the places of origin. Ethiopian and Eritrean adolescent girl migrants in Khartoum similarly mentioned gender and generational pressures from the family having played an important part in their decision-making as well as their desire to pursue education. As the survey revealed, Eritrean girls and young women tend to be better educated than Ethiopians and Bangladeshis. The majority of Eritreans finished class 6, and 19 out of 32 finished secondary school, eight reaching college or university level. Among the Ethiopians, the vast majority did not continue beyond class 5 and several had never gone to school. Among Bangladeshis, most did not continue beyond class 6. All of the girls stopped their education before migrating.

In Bangladesh, the migrants' emphasis on describing a situation of material hardship is consistent with older and more recent studies where poverty appears to be the driving force of migration to engage in the garment industry (Amin et al. 1997; Kabeer and Mahmud 2004; Kibria 1995; Feldman 2001). This motivation largely overshadows other reasons that a few girls mentioned: the desire to escape a difficult and in some cases abusive relationship with step-parents, to avoid an unwanted arranged marriage, a desire for more freedom, or because of a failed marriage. Only four Garo migrants mentioned the desire to continue studying as the main reason for moving to the capital.

There is an important methodological issue that also needs to be considered in interpreting girls' migration motives. Especially when replying to questionnaires, in a context where a relationship of trust between researcher and research is not yet established (usually questionnaires were administered during the first meeting with respondents) people tend to give socially acceptable answers, especially to sensitive questions. In all three case studies, the emphasis girls and young women put on wanting to help their families by migrating and contributing to their livelihoods could be the most socially acceptable answer, giving an image of girls as 'good and responsible daughters'. This is not to say that girls lied, but their explanation of their choice to leave the family had to be presented to others and perhaps sometimes to themselves in these socially acceptable ways, even if in reality, the decision might entail also more personal and individual hopes and aspirations.

Considering girls' often young age at migration, the dire economic situation of most of them in Bangladesh, Ethiopia and in Eritrea, and their experiences prior to migration, it is not surprising that they saw the choice to migrate almost completely in relation to their parents and family well-being. Their objectives and plans were linked in most cases to improving their family's livelihood, thus revealing the relational element of decision-making regarding migration (Huijsmans 2012) and its generational and gendered dynamics. The social aspect of the relational agency is key in understanding how relational agency emerges in the context of gender and generational relations.

A Life-Course Approach to Studying Migration Motivations and Decision-Making

Through a closer analysis of the life stories, paying particular attention to the life-course analysis collected among migrant and refugee girls, a more complex picture emerges of their motivations for and their expectations of migration. We developed this approach in order to explore the complexities of decision-making, but more importantly, the complexities of embedded intersectional inequalities that prompted the girls to move. We found it enriching to adopt a life-course approach to the study of decision-making, which seeks to describe the structures and sequences of events and transitions through an individual's life (Bailey 2009; Elder 1985; Hareven 2000).

Girls in each country had specific, frequently very personal, reasons for leaving their place of origin. Their decisions are located within often extremely precarious and dire economic or political situations, as well as oppressive gender regimes, and difficult or abusive family circumstances. There are, however, differences between countries and between different groups of migrants in the case studies. These allowed us to make a link between individual lives and biographies narrated through life stories (micro-level analysis) and how gendered life courses are shaped by culture, history and global economics, and how these articulate with various forms of movement and migration between different places. Linking the meso-level analysis of the household dynamics with the macro-level analysis of gendered labour markets, political regimes and migration policies allowed us to gain a deeper understanding of the relational nature of migration and its social relations embeddedness. Hence, rather than treating it as an 'event' at one point in time affecting a single decision-maker, migration is relational, linking lives over time and space (Bailey 2009; Findlay et al. 2015), and situating them in the web of gender as social relations.

Beyond Human Rights Discourses

As Helen's story at the beginning of this chapter illustrates, the usual narrative among Eritrean girls and young women in Khartoum located the decision to leave Eritrea in having 'no choice' (*mirchayaykonen*, which means I did not choose, or it was not my choice). The ethnographic fieldwork and life stories of Eritrean girls, young women, and their family members who joined them later in Khartoum pointed to the increasing number of young people leaving Eritrea in search for a 'choice and chance' somewhere else. Sanayit, aged 20, who had been in Khartoum for four years, said:

> In the evenings, we used to go out on the main street in Asmara, to have a walk, to find friends, to chat, to relax, to drink tea and go to bars. But now, when you go out especially on the weekends, almost no young people are there. You only see the old people, those who have health problems, everyone else is gone.

As was discussed in Chapter 3, in the last six years, there has been a significant rise in the number of young people migrating from Eritrea. Adolescence, as we have argued, is a particular phase in life when major decisions are made, but also when young people imagine what lives they want to lead. The transnational turn in youth studies has also identified how childhood and adolescence are no longer exclusively local, and how notions and aspirations of what it means to be a child, adolescent, or a young adult are influenced by the spread of global connectedness through increased communication, flows of goods and capital, travel and migration (e.g. Burman 1996; Huijsmans 2018). There is also a transnational dimension to the lives of young people who have the access to the internet, television and global communications, so that ideas of what it means to be young are being continuously renegotiated and influenced by global ideas (e.g. de Block and Buckingham 2007; Durham 2004). Even though access to the internet is highly regulated by the Eritrean government, communication still takes place. In addition, due to the emigration of Eritreans over the past 30 years and the resulting diaspora across the globe, most Eritrean families have relatives or household members who have left the country. It could therefore be argued that most young people in Eritrea are to some extent already living in transnational households.

Moreover, the role of the Eritrean diaspora's images of the outside possibilities, and the visible impact of social and financial (and to lesser extent political) remittances in the country, combined with a changing youth culture in Eritrea, contribute to young people's desire to migrate abroad. As most of research participants explained, 'we have no choice but to leave Eritrea'. Within the rhetoric of 'no choice', there are multiple scenarios, aspirations and hopes. Girls and young women (as well as young men) associate remaining in Eritrea with prolonged national service and badly paid jobs. While the liberation warriors' generation (*tegadelti*) was to a certain extent more easily influenced by the nationalist rhetoric of the ruling regime to offer their unremunerated efforts to build the state of Eritrea, the *warsay* (new generation) is increasingly unwilling to sacrifice itself for national ideals (see Bernal 2001). They see their parents and older siblings who gave up their lives for the ideas of freedom and national liberation who increasingly live in poverty, and in unending military service. At the same time, they see the new housing estates being built in cities and towns across Eritrea by those whose family members successfully emigrated. In Asmara, there are residential areas referred to as 'the Germans', or 'the Americans' as they are financed by members of the diaspora living in Germany and the United States. Moreover, social media and television create images about the potential of being young, being a girl, or a young woman. Just like young people elsewhere, young Eritreans have access to Facebook and Viber where their friends, neighbours and family members who made it to the desired locations post their success stories about their 'new selves'. These images become personal and immediate, and create a sense of a possibility that is urgent and likely.

In such a situation, where what is desired cannot be achieved and what is on offer seems completely inadequate, young girls and boys decide to seek a 'choice' somewhere else. In fact, they deliberately choose to escape in search of a better future for themselves, which points to the importance of individual aspirations and 'dreams', to quote Helen from the beginning of the chapter. Even if migration projects are framed within the collective responsibility for the family, personal aspirations play a central role in the decision-making process. As Bana, aged 21, who has been in Khartoum for three years explained:

> In fact, when I decided to leave Eritrea, I made a choice. I rejected the current situation in which I was living and lack of opportunities. So, you

> can say, that when people are leaving Eritrea they are making a choice. They usually say that they did not have a chance (*edil*) there, that's why they left.

The decision to leave is often justified in terms of having to help the family and the inability to 'have a (good) life' in Eritrea. As we saw, the survey responses confirmed that the predominant reason for leaving Eritrea was related to the need to evade military service, but life stories and in-depth discussions with adolescent girls and young women revealed more complex decision-making circumstances. Some said that they left because they wanted to pursue further education. Others because they wanted to get married, and argued that there is a declining choice of partners in Eritrea as so many young men are either in military service or have left the country. On the other hand, like Helen, some girls and young women went to Sudan to escape an arranged or failed marriage (often with Eritrean men in the diaspora). Belloni (2015), in her research among Eritreans in Asmara, found that some young women and adolescent girls were interested in migration in order to escape constraining gender norms and ideology in their communities. Thus, leaving Eritrea, as was case for Helen and others, was seen as a way to prolong the phase of being single—seeking an alternative experience of adolescence, and finding a new way of transition into womanhood and adulthood. It can be interpreted as a strategy for diversifying individual and collective strategies of survival, but more importantly, of enlarging the repertoire of personal and communal choice in terms of what life one imagines and wants to pursue and what type of gender identities one aspires to practise.

Underneath the 'Poverty' Discourse

The dominant discourse in the literature on migration in Bangladesh and in Ethiopia and out-migration from the country, focuses on poverty as a major driving factor (see Chapter 3). This was confirmed in interviews with the international and national migration experts, researchers and practitioners in Bangladesh, Ethiopia and Sudan as well as with employers of migrant Ethiopian girls and Ethiopian community representatives in Khartoum. Yet, under the layer of poverty and the need to assist their families, there are a myriad of other factors that influence adolescent girls' and young women's mobility. These have to be situated within the wider changes that have been taking place in Bangladesh (World Bank 2017) and Ethiopia in the past 20 or so years (Dom 2017). In Bangladesh, since the early 1990s there has been a steady increase in the number of girls enrolled in secondary and higher secondary education both in rural areas and in towns and cities. From 2005 there have been more girls than boys enrolled in grades 6–10 (Banbeis 2014). The growth of girls' education implies, among other things, that after puberty parents do not inevitably marry off their daughters. The girls' lives may follow different trajectories in the interlinked careers of education and marriage. There is a consensus, however, that this scenario has been significantly altered with the expansion of the garment manufacturing industry, which has become the first form of mass wage employment for women and girls outside the home. Migration from rural areas to industrial cities in order to work has become another possible life trajectory for girls.

In Ethiopia, according to the research carried out by the consortium WIDE[1] in 20 rural communities between 1995 and 2013, the following issues emerged from out-migration from them. In the early 2000s, seasonal male migration was an important element in livelihood strategies in some communities, often triggered by crisis or hardship. In 2010/13, the WIDE research team noted a striking diversification in out-migration. First, there was a decline in the importance of agricultural migration and an increase in the importance of urban and international migration. Second, there was the emergence of industrial migration, with a large increase in women's and young women's mobility. In general, the researchers observed a significant rise in the migration of young women and men compared to 1995 (Dom 2017). In some communities, more women than men were migrating. Urban and industrial migration was observed in most communities, and in 12 of them it was perceived as significant but mostly dominated by men. For women, international migration, especially to the Gulf, was more attractive. International migration included various directions, for example, in 15 communities it was mainly to the Gulf, in five to Sudan, and in one to South Africa. A significant change was the increased out-migration of ever younger people. While the local populations saw this as a concern, at the same

[1] Ethiopia WIDE is an on-going longitudinal study of 20 rural communities which began in 1994. Subsequent rounds of fieldwork were carried out in 2003 and in three stages between early 2010 and late 2013 (see http://ethiopiawide.net/).

time, children and adolescents' work and migration are perceived as 'normal' in both rural and urban Ethiopia. While statistics from Eritrea are impossible to acquire due to the government's secretive nature, the World Factbook reports the nation's GDP as US$8.7 billion, ranking Eritrea 162nd worldwide. Unemployment in the country is estimated at just 8.6%, but the poverty rate is estimated at 50%.[2]

The in-depth interviews and life stories with Bangladeshi, Ethiopian and Eritrean adolescent girls and young women revealed a more complex picture, including relational decision-making and obligations related to gender and generational order (daughters needing to help families), as suggested Helen's narrative about her sister's migration to Canada. There is an increasing importance of (imagined and at times realizable) potential to 'change one's life'. The tangible 'success' of migrants who have been supporting their families through remittances, constructing new homes and contributing to improvements in daily life, are attractive alternatives. In addition, the growing influence of social media and the global consumerist images of the 'good life' circulating on television, social media and smartphones, create new images of possible lives. For example, most of the Ethiopian girls and women interviewed in the research mentioned that they were attracted to Sudan because they had heard that it was easy to make money there. Some pointed out that their neighbours who had worked in Sudan were able to buy nice clothes, jewellery and build new houses. There is a new 'culture of migration', as some of the Ethiopian girls described it. Peer and community pressure (e.g. 'migration has become a competition' as one of the Ethiopian research participants mentioned) often stigmatizes those who decide to stay behind. This also came to the fore in the interviews with Ethiopian girls who had returned from the Middle East, as well as for Eritrean families. Eritrean family members who came for a visit to Khartoum[3] mentioned how proud they were of their daughters (and sons) who migrated from Eritrea. They usually referred to them as the 'successful ones', while children who were still in Eritrea did not have as many chances, in their view.

[2] https://www.cia.gov/library/publications/the-world-factbook/geos/er.html, accessed 12 March 2018.

[3] The family visits included those who could afford to pay for their travel, and thus represented the more successful migration experiences.

This positive, even romantic, image of the destination stood in sharp contrast with the ideas the majority of Bengali migrants had of Dhaka before migrating. Dhaka was far from representing 'the promised land' that would change their lives. Many of the Bengali girls interviewed said that they could not imagine what the actual work and living conditions would be like. While the decision is in part generated by a perceived lack of livelihood alternatives at home, the migrant girls' stories show that, after a deliberate evaluation of different possibilities, often discussed with the other family members, it comes to be seen as a chance to improve one's future prospects. Lamia, aged 22 at the time of interview, migrated to Dhaka when she was 15 (see Chapter 8). Initially, she mentioned leaving her village in Bogra district and then moving to Dhaka to work.

> We were four, my father, mother and two sisters, we were a happy family, father enrolled us in school, mum worked at home, father was a cultivator…then, when I was in class 5, father suddenly died. At that time for the family, hardship started, mum alone would work in people's houses, we two sisters were studying, we had very difficult times.

After her father's death, from the age of 12, Lamia worked as a domestic in the village. Her mother was also doing the same type of work and her sister was still at school. At some point Lamia realized that she would not be able to secure her living in this way: "I was only getting food three times a day and no money, nothing else…in this way my life wouldn't improve. One has to think at the future… there were two of us working there and the other girl said: 'I am going to Dhaka, are you coming?'" Thus, her move to Dhaka was linked to the prolonged impoverishment of the household, the specific event of the main breadwinner's (father's) death and being the oldest child. With a strong determination to help her family, Lamia also expressed a sense of gendered vulnerability and precariousness: "I am afraid that if something happens to me, if I fall ill, if I die, there will be nobody there to help my family. I don't have brothers, there is no male who could help us, we are only women". Thus, the fact that she had no brothers, the birth order and a specific event in her life were important elements in the family's decision to allow Lamia to go to Dhaka.

The interviews from Ethiopia, both among internal migrants as well as those who migrated internationally (whether to Sudan or to the Middle East), show that girls' migration is often perceived as a sacrifice for the well-being of their families. Migrating for one's own benefit is less acceptable, with a strong emphasis on the gendered and generational aspect of the household's life and collective subjectivities. Meseret lost her father when she was 10 years old, and first worked as a nanny before deciding to go to Addis Ababa. In the interview she emphasized that she migrated to support her mother, but she continued:

> I was so fed up with the life back home. I kept on nagging my mum that I want to leave to Addis Ababa. When my aunt came for a visit I insisted that I wanted to go with her. My mum didn't have any money so my aunt covered the expenses and brought me to Addis. It was a hard decision especially for my mum but I was more serious on the matter. The fact that we also see Addis as a bigger place fulfils people's needs. I was so eager. My mum said that she needed me by her side for good or for ill but I convinced her that I am not able to help her if we don't have money.

Sacrificing oneself for the family was also located within the restrictive gender labour markets and lack of work opportunities for young Ethiopian women and adolescent girls in Ethiopia. Yet, the sacrifice was not always narrated in terms of securing the family's basic survival. For a number of girls and young women, there was a strong incentive to help their siblings in pursuing their education (see Chapter 9). Girls often felt that their education was not going to benefit them, as there were limited work possibilities for educated women. In addition, they were under gendered social pressure to get married and assume the reproductive roles within the household. Instead, they argued, their work could help their siblings, usually brothers, to pursue a better life. Education was thus at times seen as offering little progress for girls who stayed behind, with minimal prospects of well-paid jobs afterwards locally. Landlessness and the very poor or poor status of their family was also a major factor driving girls to leave the country. Girls were also often running away from the gendered pressures and norms operating in their local communities. A number of girls mentioned that their parents or grandparents arranged for them to be married at an early age.

The story of Salam illustrates well these interlocking intersectional (gender, age, social class) tensions that led her to leave Ethiopia. Salam is a 23-year-old tea-seller working on the street in Amarat, a wealthy quarter of Khartoum. She was born in Shire town in Ethiopia. Her mother already had a child from another marriage. Her first husband had died. Then she married another man, but it turned out later that he had deceived her as he was already married and had nine children. Salam was born of this second marriage. Her father was an educated man and an administrator in the local government. Her mother was not educated. When Salam was a year old, her mother divorced her second husband, and married another man a year later. The third husband was apparently a drunkard and very domineering. She had two more children with him. When Salam was nine, she moved to Humera to live with her grandparents. The grandparents had several properties and lived off the rental income. Salam went to school up to grade 6. She was very good at school, and considered as one of the strongest in her class. She even skipped a class because of her outstanding performance. At the age of 13, the grandparents decided to marry her off. She mentioned:

> This was their culture. This is what they thought girls should do at that age. Girls who were 15 and not married, they were considered as old. Also, there were many girls who were raped at school and became pregnant. My grandparents most likely wanted to protect me in this way. They were afraid that I would get pregnant and then nobody would want to marry me.

Salam explained that one of her uncles, who was always protecting her and supporting her aspirations and ambitions to be educated, opposed her grandparents' idea. One of Salam's aunts came for a visit from Khartoum, and her grandparents gave the 13-year-old Salam three choices: to stop school, to get married or to go with her aunt to Khartoum. Salam decided to go to Khartoum with her aunt to avoid being pushed into marriage. She spent two years working in her aunt's small restaurant, for no pay. She missed her family very much, and life was difficult for her. She told her aunt that she wanted to visit her mother and returned to Ethiopia when she was 15 and stayed with her grandparents and her mother for a year. She opened a small tea stand and worked there for six months. "But once you have been outside of your place, you cannot return there, sit and do nothing. After a year, I decided to go back to Khartoum, but this time to work for myself". Salam's comment, similar to many other girls interviewed in Bangladesh, Ethiopia and Sudan, confirms that migration (within or across borders) often leads to further migration. This was not only linked to need for more income, but also due to the transformations that migration brought in girls' lives (see Chapters 9 and 10). Even though Salam opened up a small teashop, she considered the income to be so meagre that she felt she was doing nothing at home. "Although you work [in Ethiopia], the pay is so little, that you cannot even eat. Here, in Khartoum, when you work, you can at least eat", she explained.

Like Salam, a number of internal migrants in Ethiopia and Ethiopian and Eritrean girls in Sudan also left to avoid arranged marriages. Both Eritrea and Ethiopia have laws prohibiting marriage under the age of 18 and social norms about marriage are changing slowly. Even so, especially in rural Ethiopia (the Amhara region is, for example, infamous for abduction of girls for marriage)[4] and to a lesser extent in Eritrea, girls as young as 12 still face the danger of an arranged marriage. Early marriage and abuse by in-laws as well as by husbands were also reasons behind Bangladeshis' migration to Dhaka. Sharmeen's story, which will be presented in Chapter 5, shows how being married at 14 and exposed to abuse at the in-laws' house—but at the same time being unable to lead an independent life as divorced woman with a child and few resources at her parents' home—were behind her decision to move to Dhaka at the age of 17 and work in the garment industry.

Parental pressure, the failure of an arranged marriage, the violence experienced by the girls from their much older husbands or their parents-in-law, often accompanied by miscarriages or giving birth at a very early age, were mentioned as reasons for girls' movement. Girls often referred to their situation in Ethiopia as 'no hope' (*tesfaqoretewal*, literally 'hope is cut') (see Mains 2012). They often felt trapped between the lack of viable economic options, the lack of educational prospects, and constraining gender norms.

The stories of Ethiopian and Eritrean migrants both in Ethiopia and Sudan, and to a much lesser extent in Bangladesh, show that the desire to escape abusive family circumstances and oppressive gender regimes are important motivations for migration. In Ethiopia, among the internal

[4]The Amhara region in Ethiopia has the lowest median age at marriage in the country at 14.7 years—significantly below the national figure of 16.5 years—according to the Ethiopian Demographic and Health Survey of 2011. This region has one of the world's highest rates of child marriage though the Family Codes of the Region as well as the country provide that the minimum legal age of marriage is 18 for both sexes. Fifty-six per cent of Ethiopian girls marry before the legal age (see more at: http://www.unfpa.org/news/award-winning-programme-gives-ethiopian-girls-safer-transition-adulthood#sthash.MozypSMH.dpuf), accessed 29 March 2016.

migrants, there was a strong link between the decision to migrate and the negative role of step-parents, aunts and uncles, who abused the girls physically, sexually or psychologically. Rural girls who moved to Addis Ababa also described a situation where restrictive gender norms were limiting their mobility and their life choices. Parents fear that girls may start sexual relationships, be abducted and raped, or become pregnant, and therefore keep them at home and do not allow them to continue their education. Elsbieta, who grew up in the region of Menz (Amhara), said that she liked to play with boys and girls but her parents would punish her when she came home too late: "When this happened I would go to my brother or sister and they would let me in late at night after everyone had gone to bed". Her friendships were, however, innocent and she did not have any boyfriends:

> It's not common in our culture to have boyfriends. It's considered bad to have a boyfriend. You won't have a good image in the community. It would also mean that you won't be fit to be chosen to marry. It's mostly a brotherly friendship and nothing more. If a family finds out that someone's son touched their daughter, it can escalate to the level of killing people. It's the same if you're found drinking or going out at night.

And Meseret who came to Addis with her aunt said:

> Getting pregnant without wedlock is frowned upon and parents may ask children to leave their house for being a disgrace. In some instances, if other people didn't know about it they might keep her in the house until she gives birth.

At times, revealing personal decisions behind reasons for migration was hidden in narratives about 'other girls'' stories. For example, during the FGDs in Dhaka, migrant girls did not talk necessarily about themselves and referred mainly to other girls' stories when less socially acceptable motivations were mentioned. "Many came without telling their parents, many came to avoid getting married with someone they did not like. Girls don't like to get married at a very young age, so they came to escape the family pressure". Interestingly, when we visited some of the girls' villages, in three cases we found out that some of the migrants had been married and divorced before migrating. In such cases, migration had been an opportunity to escape the social stigma and shame attached to being divorced. In addition, being away from the family might increase their likelihood of remarrying, as girls in Dhaka could easily pretend never to have been married. While one of these three girls mentioned that she had migrated to Dhaka because of poverty, her parents' view was that she wanted to earn her own money to buy clothes and cosmetics and what "girls of that age like". The need to save money to pay the marriage dowry was also mentioned.

It was not only the girls' narratives that were hiding more of the personal gendered reasons for migration. Family members and their communities often presented girls' migration mainly as a response to poverty. For example, most of the Bengali respondents in Dhaka come from remote rural areas and from villages where young women's migration to seek work in the garment factories is now a widespread phenomenon. Migration was often interpreted by family members or neighbours as a response to rural poverty and lack of work opportunities locally. A neighbour of one migrant said:

> They cannot eat, they earn just enough to eat, they survive mainly on daily labour and they have no land. Educated people have no opportunity of employment because they cannot afford paying bribes. [...] Adolescent girls should be cared for by their parents. Nowadays the opposite happens, and this is not good.

Yet, girls' independent movement was also framed within gendered discourses of its dangers for women and girls. Some respondents expressed worries about girls' reputations and about the risks of traffickers (see Chapter 6). Intergenerational relationships are framed by a sense of hierarchical love[5] and respect due to parents (and elders) that certainly make it difficult for a young daughter to express individual preferences and desires and declare wanting to pursue more individual objectives.

[5] *Bhakti kora* (express devotion) is the Bengali term that best expresses the kind of respect and hierarchical love due to parents and elders by young people, and to her husband by his wife, while in return elders, parents and husbands are expected to provide guidance and economic support to their inferiors.

Gender Order and Age

Salam's and Lamia's stories point to some key gender and generational ideologies in Ethiopian and Bangladeshi communities, especially in rural areas and in smaller towns. Ethiopian, Eritrean and Bangladeshi societies are highly hierarchical with strong gender and generational inequalities. Gender norms regulate and influence the life of children from the very beginning, with girls being less valued than boys in the family as well as in the wider community. They are also highly influential in determining girls' and boys' aspirations and ambitions for the future. As in other patriarchal societies, boys are valued more highly than girls because they will continue the patrilineal family line. Children receive the father's family name, and traditionally boys would continue to live with their parents after marrying while girls move out. Numerous studies have shown that girls are at a disadvantage compared to boys in relation to education, health and basic human rights (Global Campaign for Education 2012; Plan International 2018).

In all three countries, governments have exerted pressure and made efforts to extend educational opportunities nationwide, and strengthened girls' access to education, as well as criminalizing underage marriages. The sexuality of adolescent girls, however, is still strictly controlled in all three contexts and premarital relationships are not accepted (Tadele 2006; Del Franco 2012; Amin 2015). As a girl's virginity is highly valued for securing a good marriage and respectability, parents and guardians often resort to 'protecting' girls from engaging in sexual relations. Adolescence is a key moment when girls are eager to experiment with their sexuality, but risk being perceived as sexual objects by boys and men. In Ethiopia, for example, parents and guardians often stop girls from going to school because they fear the negative consequences of mixed-sex education. They also are afraid of the potential abduction of girls into marriage, which is common in some areas. Parents and guardians also see arranged marriages at a younger age as a way to control girls' sexuality. A number of Ethiopian participants both in Ethiopia and in Sudan confirmed these concerns. Several girls were married from 13 to 15 years of age. Those who became pregnant by their boyfriends and were then rejected by them felt socially stigmatized. "The people do not see value in girls who got raped or pregnant from other men. They just ignore you. There is no way you can marry. You just stay alone. Even your family might reject you", explained Genet, an

18-year-old tea-seller in Sahafa neighbourhood in Khartoum. She was 14 when her parents got her married, and when she was abused by her husband and his family, she miscarried at the age of 15. Her husband was very jealous as she was a beautiful girl and many men were interested in her. He wanted to control her through the forced marriage and by beating her. She finally ran away from him, and being unable to stay with her family, she decided to come to Khartoum with an older woman whom she met at a local market in Ethiopia.

According to the report *Girls Not Brides* (2015), in Ethiopia, two in every five girls are married before their 18th birthday and nearly one in five girls marry before the age of 15. Rates vary greatly by region, with some higher than national figures. As mentioned above, early marriage is deeply rooted in many Ethiopian communities, perpetuated by poverty, a lack of educational and economic opportunities, and social customs that limit the rights of women and girls (Boyden et al. 2012; Emirie 2005; Erulkar 2013). Pregnancies out of wedlock are socially condemned. Unmarried mothers usually drop out from school. While the parents have to accept a child once it is born outside marriage, it is often perceived as an economic and social burden for them.

The situation for Eritrean girls is slightly better. Gender norms are similar in Eritrea with boys more highly valued in the family, and girls marrying out. There has, however, been some progress in terms of achieving gender equality during the struggle for national liberation, where women were very active in combat and in the liberation movement. As a result, early marriages have been illegal in Eritrea since the early 1990s. The Eritrean People's Liberation Front (EPLF) sought social transformation regarding women's issues and pushed for legislation that abolished forced marriages, child marriages and dowries. The Eritrean Civil Code (Articles 329 and 581) sets the minimum age of marriage at 18 years for both sexes. However, there is a lack of awareness about the legality of child marriage and its harmful impacts. A major difficulty in tackling child marriage is the conflicting nature of Eritrea's legal systems, as formal and customary laws are not harmonized. Customary law carries great weight in Eritrean society and provides for a minimum age of marriage of 15 for girls and 18 for boys (WHO 2016).

According to the UNFPA Child Marriage Profile: Eritrea (2012), limited access to education is associated with a high prevalence of child marriage. Sixty-four per cent of uneducated women aged between 20 and

24 years and 53% with primary education were married by the age of 18, compared to just 12% of women with secondary education or higher.

Among the research participants from Eritrea, only two were married before they were 18. One girl was married at the age of 12 and had her first child five years later. She eventually had a second child and followed her husband to Sudan at the age of 21. Her husband, however, secretly left for Libya and she lost contact with him. Another girl married at 17 and came to Sudan with two children aged two and four to find her husband, who had been missing for over a year. Generally, when asked about early marriages, girls and young women reported that they still happened in rural areas, and among uneducated families. Those from towns and cities and with access to education were more likely to delay marriage. Yet, gender norms regarding girls' purity and virginity were also strongly engrained in the Eritrean communities and the moral discourse about 'good girls'. Premarital relationships and extra-marital sex were not acceptable among Eritrean and Ethiopian communities, even in urban areas. Girls who had boyfriends were often referred to as 'loose girls' or 'bad girls'.

Another norm that has informed migration choice is the role of girls as the oldest sibling and their responsibility for the well-being of their families. Birth order played an important role in collective household decisions about who would migrate (see Gardner 2009 for discussion in Bangladesh); see Huijsmans 2014 on gender, seniority and migration. The eldest daughters in Bangladeshi, Ethiopian and Eritrean families felt responsible for supporting their kin. They often gave up their education and migrated in order to be able to support their siblings' education (usually boys, as discussed above), or taking care of their ageing or ill parents, or providing pathways of migration for their younger siblings. In fact, over the course of Katarzyna's research in Khartoum (two and a half years), most of the Eritrean girls and young women who participated in the research were joined by their siblings, who came to Khartoum to meet up with them and then continue their journey towards Europe. The girls were responsible for sponsoring their siblings' migration, which they often saw as a huge burden (see Chapter 9).

Family Circumstances: A Social Relational Approach to Decision-Making

Family circumstances had a decisive impact on girls' decision to migrate in all three country studies. The economic situation of the families has been discussed above. Here, we focus on family personal circumstances.

Among Bangladeshi, Eritrean and Ethiopian girls, the majority of those who migrated experienced some type of rupture, family crisis or violence within their households. Most of the girls came from families where divorce or the death of one or both parents was the main driving force. Like the case of Salam described above, girls suffered from the volatile and violent relations between their parents or guardians, often with stepmothers or stepfathers mistreating them. Tsedi is a domestic worker who is 23 years old. She lost her father at a young age and lived with her grandmother until her mother remarried. The relationship with her stepfather was not good: he abused her and did not want her to continue her education.

> After a while I could not stand his abuse anymore so I ran away and started living with other relatives. I continued my schooling and used to walk for an hour and a half to school. After a while my uncles arranged a marriage for me and I tried to talk to my mum saying that I did not want to get married, but she said it was beyond her power to stop it.

When Tsedi's godmother came from Addis Ababa she agreed to take her with her.

The stories of abuse and maltreatment girls experienced in their families, from their mothers, fathers, step-parents, and often uncles or aunts, were shocking, especially among the Ethiopian girls who were sex workers in Addis Ababa. This violence often took place in impoverished households, which had been marginalized due to a family crisis or economic circumstances. This also points to the general trend of increasing poverty, economic insecurity, and increased volatility in the lives of poor and very poor families. This dramatic situation can lead to violence and family breakdown, and interlocking inequalities.

Girls from households with a history of difficult circumstances did not usually maintain close contact with those who stayed behind. They also found it hard to recount memories of their childhood. Their silences were a reflection of a difficult past. Thus, the decision to move, even if taken individually and presented as such, has to be understood within wider gendered and generational family relations. Hence, a *social* relational approach to decision-making enables us to untangle the complex circumstances behind migration (see Huijsmans 2012, 2015).

Social Networks: Beyond Trafficking

While adolescent girls' movement is often framed within trafficking victimization discourses (Bastia 2005), the importance of smugglers and brokers is more visible in cross-border migration than in internal movement. Instead, social networks and long-standing destination ties all play a role in the decision to migrate and the intended destination. They enable migrants to have more positive migration experiences. The importance of friends or neighbours, or fictive 'kin' who had links to the city were visible in the life stories of Bangladeshi migrants and Ethiopians who came to Addis Ababa, although a number of Ethiopian and Eritrean girls who came to Sudan did not know anyone in the country. They were rather lured by friends or smugglers with the possibilities that the country was supposed to offer. These were usually the ones, particularly Ethiopians, who fell into the smugglers' trap. A number of Ethiopian research participants in Khartoum came on the basis of promises of work opportunities. A friend or a randomly met person, often a woman, would refer them to agents (*samsari*), who would facilitate their journey to Sudan and then place them in employment. The girls were told that they did not need to pay upfront but could repay once they started working in Sudan. On arriving in Khartoum, the agents would place girls as (usually live-in) domestics, in the homes of Sudanese employers and for the first months would collect the girls' salaries. The girls were controlled and could not escape their circumstances. They often had a day off at weekends, which they would spend in the smugglers' house together with other girls, where they were subjected to abuse, often rape, as well as having to do domestic work for the smugglers. The smugglers would also move the girls from one employer to another in order to control them as well as their salaries. A number of girls we interviewed related stories of how they managed to escape from the smugglers' trap. While smugglers do appear in girls' international migration, they are mainly portrayed in girls' narratives as the enablers rather than the causes of girls' migration.

Eritrean girls also described their experiences of being kidnapped by Rashaida groups operating on the borders between Sudan and Eritrea. They were often held captive, abused, raped for prolonged periods of time, before the ransom was paid by family members (see Van Reisen 2012). Several of the research participants suffered stress and depression, and their visions of being kidnapped haunted them. Some girls became pregnant as a result of forced sexual relations and had to take care of themselves as well as their children. As the children were of lighter complexion, girls were often stigmatized in their own communities. When we inquired whether they share their stories of rape and violence with their communities, all of the girls said no. Mona, a 23-year-old from Asmara, explained:

> You cannot do it. Once people (from your community) find out that you were held by Rashaida, you are finished. They will officially pity you, but no one will respect you. They will think that you are spoilt. No one will want to marry you. This is the reason why we do not tell our (real) stories to others, even our families.

The Ethiopian girls never refer to personal stories of abuse and violence, but rather talk about 'other girls' who have experienced this and how this has also driven 'the other girls' into sex work in Sudan.

While sometimes girls informed their families of their plans to leave, some families were reluctant whereas others were encouraging and supportive. Especially for Bangladeshi girls migrating internally and Ethiopian girls who moved to Addis Ababa to work as domestics, the decision was taken as part of household's attempt to diversify risks and enlarge collective livelihood strategies. Girls in three locations also often talked about planning the journey with some other friends or neighbours who were also interested in leaving. Ethiopians and Eritreans would then find *samsari*[6] (agents) who would help them to arrange travel across borders. Thus, the political situation in the country, the particular family situation, men being often incentives to and enablers of leaving (girls following boyfriends or escaping from arranged marriages) emerged from the research as the main influences on migratory decisions, rather than the brokers. This contradicts the dominant political and public discourse that locates adolescent girls and young women's migration as being coerced or trafficked by brokers.

[6]The term *samsara* (pl. *samsari*) in Arabic refers to agents, middlemen, but also middlewomen and intermediaries. The English version of samsara was used differently by research participants, and in the book, we use it interchangeably.

Escape, Vulnerability or Agency?

It comes as no surprise that the decision-making process is difficult to study. As mentioned earlier, this is where quantitative methods fail to show the complexity and relationality of decision-making, and its embeddedness in social relations of gender. By simply ticking a few prescribed boxes, one loses sight of the intense negotiations that take place within the families and by the individuals concerned. Decisions are never taken unilaterally and individually. They are rather taken in context-specific circumstances, usually with the direct or indirect influence of others, in a dialectic between agency and structural constraints and opportunities. The discourse associated with girls' and young women's migration which situates it directly in trafficking and exploitation is far too limiting, leaving too little room for the girls' own agency (Whitehead et al. 2007). The diverse and complex contexts in which girls take the decision to migrate, as presented above, show how there is no linear, one-dimensional causal dynamic of migration. Brokers and traffickers seem to play a much less influential role in girls' decisions than has hitherto been emphasized in the literature (see Termin et al. 2013; Erulkar et al. 2006; Fernandez 2013). Rather, the lack of opportunities and options, as well as constraining gender norms, are carefully considered, as well as girls' own aspirations to change their lives and the lives of their families. The desire to do 'something' about their situation points to the girls' agency who, by deciding to leave, take control of their lives.

Life stories, long-term follow-up ethnographic fieldwork with girls, and in-depth interviews revealed how each decision resulted from mixed factors, survival versus aspirations, and agency versus pressure. So, how to interpret adolescent migrant and refugee girls' agency and how they manifest it through their actions and choices regarding the decision to migrate? The idea of the agency of children on the move has been taken up in a few key theoretical studies, in notions of "thicker and thinner" agency (Klocker 2007) or "tactical" agency (Honwana 2005). In her research with child domestic workers in Tanzania who work long hours and face various forms of abuse, Klocker offers the idea of thick and thin agency to understand the continuum of children and young people's constrained agency in different contexts. She argues that:

> … "thin" agency refers to decisions and everyday actions that are carried out within highly restrictive contexts, characterized by few viable

> alternatives. "Thick" agency is having the latitude to act within a broad range of options. (Klocker 2007, p. 85)

Over time and space, as well as across different relationships, a person's agency can be "thicker" or "thinner". The concept of "tactical" agency developed by Honwana in her research among child soldiers in Mozambique emphasizes the coping with the concrete and immediate conditions of children's lives. "Their actions, however, come from a position of weakness" (Honwana 2005, p. 49). The analysis demonstrates that child soldiers occupy an in-between position of both being victims and perpetrators, innocent and guilty, showing that "tactical" agency includes vulnerability that enables one to cope, even in the situation of being "weak". In this way, the agency of children and young people in difficult circumstances is often referred to as "an agency of the weak".

The relational nature of agency of children and young people is an important element in understanding the interconnectedness of their ability to act. Others (White and Choudhury 2010; Punch 2001, 2015) have shown that far from being autonomous, children's agency needs to be negotiated, and often supported by adults. In this way, it is more of a collective agency (White and Choudhury 2010) than an individual one. Punch's long-term research among children in Bolivia elucidates the need to understand children's agency in relation to negotiated and constrained interdependencies within (between and among siblings) and across generations (children–parents) (Punch 2016). Our findings show the importance of the social relations. Here, as we explained in Chapter 1, the *social* relations are key to understand how relational agency of children is affected by gender norms, gender identities, gender institutions and gender ideologies.

The narratives of Bangladeshi, Ethiopian and Eritrean girls and young women demonstrate that agency and resilience can be found in many aspects before migration and during the time of decision-making about moving. As mentioned above, most of the girls who migrated were facing extremely difficult circumstances at home, within their community, or in their country of origin. They left with the hope of improving their livelihoods, their own and their families' security, and their own or their siblings' education. While it is difficult to assess how the decision to migrate came into being, most of the girls in Bangladesh, Ethiopia and Eritrea mentioned that they took the decision to migrate themselves. The decisions for Eritreans were taken in secret, without any family members or friends being informed, in order not to expose them to the risk of arrest and imprisonment. Due to the strict rules of the police state, evading national service and leaving without permission might lead to long-term imprisonment. In this case, the decision can be interpreted more as an individual one yet linked to the wider social, economic, and political circumstances and the needs of the family and the country. This decision is often negotiated from a position of weakness. For the Ethiopians and Bangladeshis, on the other hand, the decisions were taken both against the parents' will as well as with the blessing of the family, individually, or often collectively. They often felt trapped between lack of viable economic options, lack of educational prospects, and constraining gender norms. Within these constraining circumstances, girls' decision to migrate can be interpreted as a sign of a "thin" agency, an agency of "the weak", an example of girls' ability to act.

The more complex qualitative material from our migrant and refugee respondents shows how there are elements of agency, as well as pressure, in the motivations for migration and in the way the decision to migrate is taken. Individual decisions are made within a very constrained range of options and can result from contrasting (diverse) factors: the struggle to survive versus pursuing aspirations and desires. These factors are dependent on the girl's age, previous experiences, level of education, marital status and socio-economic condition of her birth family and the socio-political context of the country.

The Journey and the Movement as Relational

One element that is emblematic in becoming a migrant or refugee is the aspect of the spatial move from one place to another and the actual experience of the physical journey. This was evident in the girls' and women's discourses about their experiences of moving from rural areas to the capital, or crossing borders. Space plays a major role through gender systems, the structure of educational markets and opportunities, and structural relations of poverty and inequality. The journey from one place to another and through different spaces allows us to better articulate the gendered importance of migration as part of the transitions from childhood to adolescence and adulthood. We will come back to these issues in the concluding chapter of this book.

Second, narrating decision-making processes and their migration experiences also became a way for adolescent girls and young women to realize that they have acquired a different status in the community. This method of life story, with particular points in the life course as turning moments, was also evident in Hallah Ghorashi's work with Iranian refugees (2008). Similarly, the narration of migratory decision-making and trajectories became part of becoming a migrant or a refugee for Bangladeshi, Ethiopian and Eritreans in our study. "I had no idea about migration before, I know people are travelling, but I knew nothing about migration. It is only because I am talking about it, and you [researcher] are asking questions, I have realized that I am a migrant, I am a refugee", explained Hebret, a 24-year-old Eritrean co-researcher and research participant in the study in Khartoum. In this way, narration was giving silence a chance, was creating a site of co-creation of knowledge and subjectivities.

Third, by employing a life-course approach in our research methods and in our analysis, we were able to establish, what Katy Gardner calls, "the relationship between the embodied journey through time" (2009, p. 229). Our focus on transitions in the life course allowed us to look at migration not as a single 'event' affecting a single decision-maker, but rather to analyse the movement as relational, linking (individual) lives over time and space (Bailey 2009; Findlay et al. 2015), and regulated by social relations and gender relations in particular. By doing this, we were able to discern the gendered and generational dynamics of the decision-making process. By looking at a specific phase (in this case adolescence) of life over migrants' longer life course, we are able to identify the particular circumstances of decision-making regarding migration. Moreover, transitions between childhood, adolescence and adulthood weave together the spheres of production and social reproduction, and movement from one place to another allows us to identify how such transitions are experienced and perceived. As King et al. (2004) assert, "the relevance to migration is immediately apparent: the life course framework contextualises not only individual and group decisions about the timing of migrations but also about the formative influences and outcomes" (2004, p. 19). We will come back to these issues in the following chapters.

The attention to the life-course analysis allows us to focus on the social aspects relational agency of children and young people as embedded in a set of social gender relations within and beyond the household. The life stories of the research participants as well as ethnographic methods and secondary data allowed us to establish a link between individual lives and biographies (micro-level analysis) and how gendered life courses are shaped by culture, history and global economics, how these articulate with various forms of movement and migration between different places. Moreover, the individual biographies, as we have shown here, are articulated with 'meso'-level formations (household other social networks), and then linked to the wider national and global conditions. As a result, the interconnectedness of levels of analysis unveils the complexities of decision-making beyond oversimplified discourses of poverty and human rights violations. It reveals also interconnectedness of lives, and places migration squarely within global and transnational dynamics. As Gardner argues describing the life-course analytical approach among Bangladeshi male migrants:

> from the young man (or woman) in the village, to the social networks that assist him (or her) in moving, and to the global histories and economic structures that have helped create the 'transnational habitus' (Vertovec 2004) of his (or her) community, in which movement abroad (or within the country) is seen not only as the only way to go about life, but has become the expected part of his life course. (Gardner 2009, p. 229)

Here, the idea of travelling becomes an integral part of transition from adolescence to adulthood, similarly to what Treiber has called "becoming by moving" (2014).

References

Amin, S., Diamond, I., Naved, R. T., & Newby, M. (1997). *Transition to Adulthood of Female Factory Workers: Some Evidence from Bangladesh* (Population Council Paper No. 102). New York: Population Council.

Amin, S. (Ed.). (2015). *Urban Adolescents Needs Assessment Survey in Bangladesh.* Dhaka: BIED, BRACU, and Population Council.

Andom, N. (2015, November). Demystifying Irregular Youth Hemorrhage from Post-2000s Eritrea: Driven by Politics or Economics. In *Conference Paper for Migration and Exile in the Horn of Africa: State of Knowledge and Current Debates* (pp. 16–18). Khartoum: CEDEJ.

Atnafu, A., Oucho, L., & Zeitlyn, B. (2014). *Poverty, Youth and Rural-Urban Migration in Ethiopia* (Migration out of Poverty Working Paper No. 17). Brighton: University of Sussex.

Bailey, Adrian. (2009). Population Geography: Life Course Matters. *Progress in Human Geography, 33*(3), 407–418.

Banbeis. (2014). Bangladesh Educational Statistics 2014.
Bastia, T. (2005). Child Trafficking or Teenage Migration? Bolivian Migrants in Argentina. *International Migration, 43*(4), 57–87.
Belloni, M. (2015). *Cosmologies of Destinations: Routes and Routes of Eritrean Forced Migration to Europe*. Ph.D. thesis, University of Trento.
Bernal, V. (2001). From Warriors to Wives: Contradictions of Liberation and Development in Eritrea. *Northeast African Studies, 8*(3), 129–154.
Boyden, J., Pankhurst, A., & Tafere, Y. (2012). Child Protection and Harmful Traditional Practices: Female Early Marriage and Genital Modification in Ethiopia. *Development in Practice, 22*(4), 510–522.
Burman, E. (1996). Local, Global, or Globalised: Child Development and International Child Rights Legislation. *Childhood, 3*(1), 45–66.
Carter, B., & Rohwerder, B. (2016). *Rapid Fragility and Migration Assessment for Ethiopia* (Rapid Literature Review). Birmingham: GSDRC, University of Birmingham.
Comenetz, J., & Caviedes, C. (2002). Climate Variability, Political Crises, and Historical Population Displacements in Ethiopia. *Environmental Hazards, 4*(4), 113–127.
de Block, L., & Buckingham, D. (2007). *Global Children, Global Media: Migration, Media and Childhood*. Basingstoke: Palgrave Macmillan.
Del Franco, N. (2012). *Negotiating Adolescence in Rural Bangladesh: A Journey through School, Love and Marriage*. New Delhi: Zubaan Books.
Dom, C. (2017). Migrating for Work from Rural Communities (2010–2013). In A. Pankhurst (Ed.), *Change and Transformation in 20 Rural Communities in Ethiopia: Selected Aspects and Implications for Policy*. WIDE: Addis Ababa.
Durham, M. G. (2004). Constructing the "New Ethnicities": Media, Sexuality, and Diaspora Identity in the Lives of South Asian Immigrant Girls. *Critical Studies in Media Communication, 21*(2), 140–161.
Elder, G. H. (1985). Perspectives on the Life Course. In Elder, Jr., G. H. (Ed.), *Life Course Dynamics: Trajectories and Transitions, 1968–1980* (pp. 23–49). Ithaca, NY: Cornell University Press.
Emirie, G. (2005). *Early Marriage and Its Effects on Girls' Education in Rural Ethiopia: The Case of Mecha Woreda in West Gojjam, North-Western Ethiopia*. Ph.D. thesis, University of Göttingen.
Erulkar, A. (2013). Early Marriage, Marital Relations and Intimate Partner Violence in Ethiopia. *International Perspectives on Sexual and Reproductive Health, 39*(1), 6–13.
Erulkar, A., Mekbib, T., Simie, N., & Gulema, T. (2006). Migration and Vulnerability Among Adolescents in Slum Areas of Addis Ababa. *Ethiopia. Journal of Youth Studies, 9*(3), 361–374.
Feldman, S. (2001). Exploring Theories of Patriarchy: A Perspective from Contemporary Bangladesh. *Signs: Journal of Women in Culture and Society, 26*(4), 1097–1127.

Fernandez, B. (2013). Traffickers, Brokers, Employment Agents, and Social Networks: The Regulation of Intermediaries in the Migration of Ethiopian Domestic Workers to the Middle East. *International Migration Review, 47*(4), 814–843.

Findlay, A., McCollum, D., Coulter, R., & Gayl, V. (2015). New Mobilities Across the Life Course: A Framework for Analysing Demographically Linked Drivers of Migration. *Population, Space and Place, 21*(4), 390–402.

Gardner, K. (2009). Lives in Motion: The Life-Course, Movement and Migration in Bangladesh. *Journal of South Asian Development, 4*(2), 229–251.

Ghorashi, H. (2008). Giving Silence a Chance: The Importance of Life Stories for Research on Refugees. *Journal of Refugee Studies, 21*(1), 117–132.

Girls Not Brides. (2015). *Fact Sheet: Ethiopia's National Strategy and Action Plan on Harmful Traditional Practices.*

Global Campaign for Education. (2012). *Gender Discrimination in Education: The Violation of Right of Women and Girls.* A Report Submitted to the Committee on the Elimination of Discrimination against Women (CEDAW).

Hareven, T. K. (2000). *Families, History, and Social Change: Life Course and Cross-Cultural Perspectives.* Boulder, CO: Westview Press.

Honwana, A. (2005). Innocent and Guilty: Child Soldiers as Interstitial and Tactical Agents. In A. Honwana & F. de Boeck (Eds.), *Makers and Breakers: Children and Youth in Post-colonial Africa* (31–52). Oxford: James Currey.

Huijsmans, R. (2012). Beyond Compartmentalization: A Relational Approach Towards Agency and Vulnerability of Young Migrants. *New Directions for Child and Adolescent Development, 136,* 29–45.

Huijsmans, R. (2014). Becoming a Young Migrant or Stayer Seen Through the Lens of 'Householding': Households 'in Flux' and the Intersection of Relations of Gender and Seniority. *Geoforum, 51,* 294–304.

Huijsmans, R. (2015). Children and Young People in Migration: A Relational Approach. In C. Ní Laoire, A. White, & T. Skelton (Eds.), *Movement, Mobilities and Journeys.* Singapore: Springer.

Huijsmans, R. (2018). Transnational Childhoods. In H. Montgomery & M. Robb (Eds.), *Children and Young People's Worlds.* Cambridge: Policy Press & Open University.

Kabeer, N., & Mahmud, S. (2004). Globalization, Gender and Poverty: Bangladeshi Women Workers in Export and Local Markets. *Journal of International Development, 16*(1), 93–109.

Kibreab, G. (2009). Forced Labour in Eritrea. *Journal of Modern African Studies, 47*(1), 41–72.

Kibria, N. (1995). Culture, Social Class and Income Control in the Lives of Women Garment Workers in Bangladesh. *Gender and Society, 9*(3), 289–309.

Klocker, N. (2007). An Example of "Thin" Agency: Child Domestic Workers in Tanzania. In R. Panelli, S. Punch, & E. Robson (Eds.), *Global Perspectives on*

Rural Childhood and Youth: Young Rural Lives (pp. 83–94). New York and London: Routledge.

King, R., Thomson, M., Fielding, T., & Warnes, T. (2004). *Gender, Age and Generations* (State of the Art Report Cluster 8), IMESCO, Sussex Centre for Migration and Population Studies, University of Sussex.

Mains, D. (2012). *Hope Is Cut: Youth, Unemployment and the Future in Urban Ethiopia*. Philadelphia, PA: Temple University Press.

Montgomery, M. R., Balk, D., Liu, Z., Agarwal, S., Jones, E., Adamo, S. (2016). Urban Migration of Adolescent Girls: Quantitative Results from Developing Countries. In J. Michael (Ed.), International Handbook of Migration and Population Distribution (573–604). Dordrecht: Springer.

Plan International. (2018). *Girls' Rights Are Human Rights: An In-depth Study of the Status of Girls in the International Human Rights Framework* (Report Girls' Rights Platform). Woking, UK: Plan International.

Punch, S. (2001). Negotiating Autonomy: Childhoods in Rural Bolivia. In L. Alanen & B. Mayall (Eds.), *Conceptualising Child-adult Relations* (23–36). London: Routledge Falmer.

Punch, S. (2015). Possibilities for Learning Between Childhoods and Youth in the Minority and Majority Worlds: Youth Transitions as an Example of Cross-world Dialogue. In J. Wyn & H. Cahill (Eds.). *Handbook of Children and Youth Studies* (689–701). Singapore: Springer.

Punch, S. (2016). Exploring Children's Agency Across Majority and Minority World Contexts. In F. Esser, Meike S. Baader, T. Betz, & B. Hunderland (Eds.), *Reconceptualising Agency and Childhood: New Perspectives in Childhood Studies* (183–196). London: Routledge.

Tadele, G. (2006). *Bleak Prospects: Young Men, Sexuality and HIV/AIDS in an Ethiopian Town*. Leiden: African Studies Center.

Temin, M., Montgomery, M. R., Engebretsen, S., & Barker, K. M. (2013). *Girls on the Move: Adolescent Girls and Migration in the Developing World. A Girls Count Report on Adolescent Girls*. New York: Population Council.

Treiber, M. (2014). Becoming by Moving: Khartoum and Addis Ababa as Migratory Stages Between Eritrea and 'Something'. In M. Abdalla, D. Dias Barros, & M. Berthet Ribeiro (Eds.), *Spaces in Movement: New Perspectives on Migration in African Settings* (pp. 189–205). Köln: Rüdiger Köppe Verlag.

UNFPA. (2012). *Child Marriage Profile: Eritrea, Report*. New York: United Nations Populations Fund, UNFPA.

Van Reisen, M. (2012). *Human Trafficking: Sinai and Beyond*. European External Policy Advisors. Tilburg: Tilburg University.

Van Reisen, M., Mawere, M. (Eds.). (2017). *Human Trafficking and Trauma in the Digital Era: The Ongoing Tragedy of the Trade in Refugees from Eritrea*. Bamenda: Langaa RPCIG.

Vertovec, S. (2004). Trends and Impacts of Migrant Transnationalism. *Centre on Migration, Policy and Society* (Working Paper No. 3). University of Oxford.

WHO. (2016). *Eritrea Launched Campaign to End Child Marriage* (Report). Asmara: WHO.

White, S., & Choudhury, S. (2010). Children's Participation in Bangladesh: Issues of Agency and Structures of Violence. In B. Percy-Smith & N. Thomas (Eds.), *A Handbook of Children and Young People's Participation* (39–50). London: Routledge.

Whitehead, A., Hashim, I., & Iversen, V. (2007). *Child Migration, Child Agency and Intergenerational Relations in Africa and South Asia*. Development Research Centre on Migration, Globalisation and Poverty (Working Paper). Brighton: University of Sussex.

Willemse, K. (2014). "Everything I Told You Was True": The Biographic Narrative as a Method of Critical Feminist Knowledge Production. *Women's Studies International Forum, 43,* 38–49.

World Bank. (2017). *Export Competitiveness for Jobs (P156113).* Combined Project Information Documents /Integrated Safeguards Datasheet (PID/ISDS). Washington, DC: World Bank.

CHAPTER 5

Life in the Cities

"*Here There Are Things Going on All the Time*": Sharmeen's Encounters with the City

Sharmeen came to Dhaka when she was 17 years old. The first time we met her was in February 2014, through her host and friend Baby apa.[1] Sharmeen was very shy and serious at the beginning but started smiling when she told us how she enjoyed hanging around with friends in Dhaka: "Before coming to Dhaka, I knew nothing about the work in a garment factory. I did not understand how it works here. In the beginning, I felt very bad, I was crying all the time because I could not see my son". Sharmeen was married at the age of 14 but divorced after having been abused by her husband and in-laws. She had one son, whom she left with her parents when she moved to Dhaka. The first months were thus very difficult:

> I did not like Dhaka. I was standing up from 8 a.m. to 11 p.m., spinning thread (*suta kata*) and doing other tasks. Then I would go to my cousin's home. I would help my cousin with cooking and doing household chores. I stayed with my cousin for seven months. [...] I gave money to my cousin for food, the rest of the money I spent on soap and oil. I couldn't save

[1] Apa means older sister, and is used as a term of respect for older women.

K. Grabska et al., *Adolescent Girls' Migration in The Global South*, Palgrave Studies on Children and Development,
https://doi.org/10.1007/978-3-030-00093-6_5

a single penny for myself. Then I got sick with jaundice and I went back home for some time.

Sharmeen returned to Dhaka after a few months. She moved in with Baby apa's family in the same slum where she lived before. Despite the initial difficulties, the long working hours and badly missing her son, Sharmeen adjusted to life in Dhaka and started appreciating some aspects of it. She said:

I am better than before, when I was in the village. I am better here because I earn money. In the village, there was *obhab* (lack, nothing to do to earn a living), there was no freedom. Even speaking to someone on the road could be a problem. Here you can be outside any time of the night and day. In the village when it gets dark people go to sleep. Here there are things going on all the time. Here I can hang around. I have also been to the cinema with some people who work with me. I have been to the airport and to the zoo and I go to my friends' places. We talk and then I go back home. What I like most is to walk around.

Thus, the initial loneliness, strangeness, and missing her son were slowly replaced by finding ways to enjoy the city and the relative freedom it offered. Being also economically autonomous gave Sharmeen a sense of greater scope to make her own decisions. Four months after our initial meeting, we saw Sharmeen again. Her situation had changed. She was still living and working in Dhaka but her former husband had joined her. Her parents had been insisting for months that she should re-marry and they had been actively looking for a new husband. She rejected this possibility because she was afraid of losing her son and so decided to go back to his father. Her former husband's move to Dhaka also changed Sharmeen's encounter with the city, including losing some of the freedom she had enjoyed to explore the opportunities in the capital.

Most of the times I go to my 'office' by motor rickshaw, but sometimes I walk and it can take more than 30 minutes to reach the house, then I have to cook for the next day. If it takes more time to reach the home than usual, he asks me why I am late. Now, I pass most of the days off in the house because I have to do too many household chores, but when I was single, I enjoyed every Friday with my friends visiting many places. Now, I have to think about money. But he spends most of the Fridays outside, like today, he has not come yet, if he comes he will call me and lunch should

> be ready. Now I listen to my husband's words; I do everything according to his will. Now my freedom is curtailed, I cannot do whatever I like.

Sharmeen's story opens up several important points of the girls' first encounters with the city: their initial feeling of isolation, loneliness and strangeness, and missing their family. At the same time, the city also offered chances to explore new possibilities that marked migrants' experiences. There is not much literature on the experiences of young migrant girls once they reach an urban destination (Heissler 2015; Montgomery et al. 2016). Despite the growing presence of young migrant girls in sub-Saharan Africa, for example, research has until recently mainly focused on the labour migration of boys and young men (Gardner 2009; Thorsen 2007; Vigh 2009). As mentioned in Chapter 1, young women's experiences of migration are mostly interpreted through the lens of risks and vulnerabilities rather than by looking at the strategies they employ to achieve their objectives (Clark and Cotton 2013; Erulkar 2006; Luke et al. 2012; Magadi 2013). This chapter sheds light on migrant girls' processes of settling in and situating themselves in the city (see Buhr and McGarrigle 2017; Grabska 2014; Pardue 2017), how they navigate the new environments (see Vigh 2009), and their daily encounters and disappointments (Derks 2008; Mills 1997). We follow the girls through their place-making projects (see Turton 2005; Grabska 2014) in the city, their search for accommodation, jobs and livelihoods, their working life and their disappointments. In all three of the case studies, adolescent girls are subjected to strong systems of social control, and often experience stigmatization, discrimination and harassment. Gender, age, social class, ethnicity and migration status intersect in such ways that migrant and refugee girls are extremely vulnerable and at great risk (see Chapter 6). At the same time, the cities also offer chances to pursue different choices, increase girls' options in terms of lives that they desire and aspire to, and enlarge their view of themselves in the world.

First Impressions and Experiences

Sharmeen's account of her initial experiences and feelings in Dhaka is consistent with that of most of the other Bangladeshi migrants we interviewed. For almost all of them, relatives, neighbours and acquaintances living in Dhaka had been essential in providing the opportunities to move. They facilitated the journey, in some cases by helping them find a job and providing accommodation. The majority of the girls mentioned a *khala* (aunt) or a *bon* (cousin) who either travelled with them or provided accommodation on arrival. Often, despite the use of kinship terminology, these aunts and cousins were not related by blood or marriage. The migrants explained that they were *attyoswajan* (one's own people).[2] All the Bengali and Garo migrant girls we interviewed had moved from their rural homes directly to Dhaka. In their narratives, once the decision to migrate had been taken, the journey to reach the capital, mostly by bus, was quite a smooth experience. Only a few had left without their parents' knowledge, but even in these cases the presence of some *attyoswajan* at the destination made it easier to find shelter.

The situation was different for Ethiopian and Eritrean girls, who sometimes had moved to another town before arriving in Addis Ababa or Khartoum, and whose parents were not always aware of their migration plans (see Chapter 4). In addition, the journey was full of obstacles for Eritrean girls and sometimes also for Ethiopian girls migrating to Sudan. They travelled in trucks with many other migrants, crossed the border illegally, and were sometimes abused and even raped by the smugglers (see Chapter 4).

Most of the girls did not know what to expect in the city and their initial impressions and reactions were sometimes rather negative. In Bangladesh, feelings of loneliness and loss prevailed, especially among the youngest, who had never been married and who left a situation where they felt protected and secure. They missed their family, their parents' support and their siblings. Lamia (see Chapter 8), for example, who had been in Dhaka since 2007, was working as quality controller in a factory in Mirpur, in the north-west of the city. In her first months in Dhaka, she lived in a *mess*, or shared accommodation where girls live with a family and pay a fixed monthly rent that includes food and accommodation. She explained:

> At first I felt very bad after coming to Dhaka, I was crying for home and for my mum, arriving here was very stressful. I had a lot of problems with

[2]This term is also commonly used in rural Bangladesh (Del Franco 2012). An individual's *attiyoswajan* can include not only people related by blood or by marriage but also neighbours, people living in the same or a different village, people attending the same school or working in the same office and even people of a different caste or religion. All members of an *attiyoswajan* group are addressed in kinship terms.

> food, I could not eat the rice they were cooking [in the *mess*], the vegetable and the lentils were just water… so I ate only bread for two months… Now in Bhola *bustee* there is one toilet for eight rooms. This makes life very difficult, you always have to wait. Those, like me who work in a factory are lucky because they can use the toilet there.

Jamila, who is 17 years of age, commented in an FGD: "It is very painful to stay here without my parents, I must say. We talk on the phone. When I was in the village, I could run to my parents and they would cuddle me. Here there is no one to cuddle me. I work all day long and still they reproach me". This resonates with the studies by Agarwal et al. (2016) and Derks (2008), who show the girls' difficulties in adjusting to city life, especially during the first months. Initially, they find the city is a strange and dangerous place.

Garo migrant girls always joined relatives who had been living in the capital for a long time and were therefore in a better situation. Similarly, most of the adolescent girls arriving in Khartoum from Ethiopia and Eritrea used their personal family or friends' networks to find initial accommodation. After a long and exhausting trip, arriving in the dusty city of Khartoum was usually met with both excitement and relief. Salam, from Humera in northern Ethiopia, moved to Khartoum with an aunt when she was 13 years old. When we met her, she was 23 and a street tea-seller in Amarat, a wealthy quarter of Khartoum. She and others who came to Sudan with their family members found it easier to adjust. Salam said: "Khartoum was very different from my town in Ethiopia. It was a big city, with women and girls having to cover up and dress very differently. But, I was with my auntie, so it was fine. I just went and stayed with her the first couple of years". For those who had no connections in the city, however, the arrival had been an overwhelming and threatening experience. Kibra was only 17 when she arrived from an Eritrean refugee camp in Ethiopia. She migrated with the help of a smuggler (*samsara*) and because she had no money to pay him for the journey, he made her work for him.

> I was locked in a house in Omdurman, had to cook for the *samsara* and his family, and also for all the Eritreans who were passing through the house. These were the ones who were going to be smuggled to Libya and then to Europe. The *samsara* would gather them there, and then they would wait a few days before being transported on trucks through the

> desert to Libya. I was not allowed to go out, and only one day, when he did not show up, and there were no people in the house, I took courage and escaped. I did not even know which part of the city I was in.

Kibra was pregnant, possibly from being raped or of doing sex work in Ethiopia before coming to Khartoum. Some Eritreans tried to help her, but because she could not work and contribute to the household, they threw her out. She ended up living on the streets for many months when finally a Sudanese man escorted her to an Eritrean Pentecostal church near to where she slept. When we met her, she was deeply traumatized and disturbed. The Pentecostal church helped her with accommodation, food and clothes for the new baby.

In the interviews with girls who migrated to Addis Ababa a few told us about their first impressions and experiences. The harsh reality in which they were living may have overshadowed their memories of the first days of excitement, or perhaps keeping silent was a way to cope with bad experiences. Those who did share their first impressions were often positive. They had high expectations of their life in the city. Addis Ababa was considered a symbol of modernity and progress, and migration was seen as a way to become a more modern person, in the words of some of the girls. Meseret, who was invited by her aunt to come to Addis when she was 15 years old, remembered:

> As soon as I got here, I was amazed by the colourfulness of the city. My hopes and dreams of being educated and becoming a better person got brighter with the city lights and I was extremely happy of what was waiting for me. I saw myself finishing school; getting a well-paid job and helping my mother out of the life that she led.

Elsa, who came from a small town north of Addis Ababa, said: "I like the people, the light is bright and different from us, the cafeterias, hotels, the style of the people, the way they dress, the buildings are different from the countryside". The city's attraction as a place of modernity, where one can become a modern person, not only through education and employment but also through access to consumer goods and a different lifestyle, is well known (Hannerz 1980; Ferguson 1992; Appadurai 1996). These aspirations of becoming modern are highly gendered (see Derks 2008; Mills 1997; Rofel 1999). For adolescent girls and young women, migration to the city is often double-edged: on the one hand they look forward to changing their lives, and moving out of restrictive gender regimes, but on the other hand migrating means that they are for the first time in their lives on their own, without the protection of immediate relatives, which can lead to feelings of anxiety, despair and loneliness.

While the girls who migrated to Addis Ababa had high expectations, those who went to Dhaka or Khartoum did not see these cities as 'the promised land' where they would fulfil all their hopes. They had vaguely heard about the possibilities of earning money, which was often the main reason for their migration, and all of them looked forward to a better future, in which they could help their families and improve their own lives. Their expectations often turned quickly into disappointments, however, faced with the reality of poor living conditions, a heavy workload, low pay and various forms of abuse.

Place-Making Projects in the City

While the city was often supposed to be a temporary destination, for a large number of research participants it became a longer-term reality. Although most maintained strong links with their place of origin and/or their families and friends scattered across the globe, as in the case of Eritreans, they also sought to carve out a space for themselves in the city. Turton (2005) argues in his article on place-making among the Mursi in southern Ethiopia that to "understand how people experience place, and how it becomes 'inextricably bound up' with their social and personal identity, we must treat it, not as a stage upon which social activity is carried out, but as a product of social activity" (2005, p. 275). He builds on Appadurai's notion of the production of locality (1996, pp. 178–179), in which a locality is a 'dimension' of social life, in contrast with geographical places such as neighbourhoods. People are continuously constructing and producing localities in relation to others, and in doing so are engaged in place-making. Migrant girls in Addis Ababa, Dhaka and Khartoum were involved in such processes, even if in their narratives they emphasized the temporary nature of their stay in the city.

Place-making is strongly related to gender and other axes of differentiation such as ethnicity, class and age (Massey 1991, 1994). The settling in and place-making of migrant girls become part of the (re)negotiation of gender and generational identities linked to carving out a space for themselves in a new community (see Grabska 2014). Here the concept of emplacement as used by Grabska in her study among refugees and

Fig. 5.1 A room in the Bhola slum, Mirpur, Dhaka, Bangladesh

returnees to South Sudan might be useful. Grabska sees "emplacement as a dialectic and negotiation between the 'stayees' and the displaced that is influenced by the latter's capacities to put themselves and others into a place and the power relations that unequally distribute this capacity" (Grabska 2014, p. 11; see also Jansen and Löfving 2009, p. 13). In the case of migrant girls in Dhaka, Addis Ababa and Khartoum, their settling in and emplacement in the city was influenced by their social capital, their social networks, and the dialectic and negotiation between them and other city residents. Place-making projects involved settling in, finding accommodation, finding work, and establishing a social life (Figs. 5.1, 5.2 and 5.3).

Settling in and Housing Arrangements

Settling in is a process that takes time—to get to know the city, to establish new contacts and relations, and to gain some social and financial

Fig. 5.2 Accommodation in Addis Ababa, Ethiopia

capital. While the nexus between urban mobility and migrant integration has been widely studied, Buhr and McGarrigle (2017, p. 227) argue that not "enough attention has been paid to the link between migrants' urban mobilities and the material urgencies of settlement, such as finding accommodation, work and simply learning to navigate a still unfamiliar territory". In addition, this is also a highly context-specific and gendered process (see Grabska 2014) in which the opportunities and expectations of settling in and making a place for oneself are often different for women and men. Relatively few studies have paid attention to these gendered differences in place-making, especially regarding young women who have migrated independently.

The living conditions of migrant and refugee communities vary depending on their financial situation, social status, access to social capital and networks of support. Garau et al. (2005) show that in terms of accommodation the situation of recent migrants to the cities does not always correspond to the common assumption that they all end up living in slums. While most of our research participants lived in rather miserable conditions, both in slums as well as in relatively impoverished areas of

Fig. 5.3 Accommodation in Khartoum, Sudan

the city, there were substantial differences between slum areas and poor neighbourhoods, the latter being more developed and with better facilities than the former. In addition, there are differences in the living patterns among migrants in the cities. In Dhaka, migrant girls tended to conglomerate in slum areas and share similar living conditions whereas those in Khartoum and Addis Ababa were scattered throughout these cities and their living conditions could vary.

Many girls shared their accommodation either with family, or other girls or women, often from their places of origin. Sharing is not only to minimize living costs, it is also a strategy, as the Eritrean girls in Khartoum reported, to overcome loneliness and harassment from Sudanese neighbours and landlords who consider it inappropriate for young girls and women to live alone. In Sudan, young girls and women are usually not allowed to share accommodation with (unrelated) men. In some cases, when brothers of some of the respondents arrived in the city, the girls had to look for different accommodation and landlords who would allow them to share with their male relatives. Most often sharing among relatives and friends is arranged according to their place of origin, religious beliefs or new social networks developed during their migration journeys. For example, people from the Bilen[3] ethnic group in Eritrea tend to live close to each other mainly in the Jereif area, which is arranged by nationalities and ethnic origins. Next to 'Nigerian' and 'Genubeen' (South Sudanese) houses, there are 'Ethiopians' and 'Eritreans'. The Eritrean households are also divided by places of origin, with groups of relatives or people of the same ethnic origin sharing the same spaces. These housing arrangements are an attempt to accumulate their scarce social capital. Such arrangements allow migrants and refugees to cooperate, reciprocate moral and financial obligations, as well as for protection, and to jointly survive on scarce resources. Garo migrants in Dhaka had similar housing arrangements.

The following extract from Katarzyna's field notes describes the living conditions of a group of Eritrean adolescent girls and young women living together in Khartoum.

> Salha, a 23-year-old from Halimente in Eritrea, in Khartoum since 6 years, met us on the main Jereifroad. We took a small alley leading to enormous villas, many of them still under construction. We passed new colourful expensive villas with cars parked in front of them. We crossed a small square (*midan*) with garbage piled up everywhere, but not in front of the expensive homes. And then we turned to the left and entered a small gate leading to a... shack... a falling apart mud shack, with a zinc and grass

[3]It was explained to us that the Bilen group tends to be very mutually supportive, as it is one of the smallest ethnic groups in Eritrea but with one of the highest proportion of members in the diaspora. Thus, they keep close kin and ethnic relations.

> roof. Everything looked dilapidated, dirty, and in the most precarious condition. In front of the gate, there were two young Eritrean men sitting on the ground and looking at their mobile phones. When we entered the compound, to the right, there was a hole in the ground used as a toilet, and three separate rooms without doors. There were several groups of people living in this place. The room that we entered had two beds. It was very small without windows, and some basic amenities. There was no running water, no electricity, no proper toilet. There was a strong smell of sewage and urine everywhere. It was one of the poorest places, and dirtiest places we have seen in Khartoum, just next to the expensive villas with well-functioning amenities. The worlds apart, the worlds next to each other, adjacent and yet divided by the deep inequalities and injustices, as in some other neighbourhoods in Khartoum.

This description could easily be used to portray the so-called 'Bhola *bustee*', one of the slum areas where some of the Bengali migrants lived in Mirpur, a suburb of Dhaka. The migrants who were living there complained about the lack of clean water and toilet facilities and were concerned about the frequent health problems. In fact, many girls reported having fallen ill after a few months of moving to Dhaka, for instance with jaundice, hepatitis, food poisoning or diarrhoea. Nurjajan, a 19-year-old from Bhola District, and Jamila, a 16-year-old from Netrakona district, complained: "We don't like the electricity blackouts, we have problems with the water…in the slum sometimes we can't get water. In summer, it is very hot because of the tin roofs. Our biggest problem is that we don't have water. Sometimes we have water in the morning and no water for the rest of the day. We don't boil water because gas is expensive". Slightly better were the living conditions in Bauniabandh, the other slum area where Bengali migrants were living. The Garo migrants in Dhaka were much better off in terms of accommodation. Most of those we interviewed were sharing flats in areas of the city where many Garo were living, although those who had no acquaintances in the city had to spend the period of apprenticeship secluded in the parlour premises. As Raitapuro and Bal (2016) underline in their study on Garo migrants, having some sort of a social network in the city greatly facilities not only the decision to move but also the quality of life at the destination.

In all three cities, rents are very high given the money migrant girls earn. In Khartoum, most girls spend between 250 SDG and 750 SDG (US$34–85) per person for a shared room. During the two and a half years of the research, and with the devaluation of the Sudanese Pound, rents steadily increased. This led to volatile living conditions, with girls having often to move from one place to another in search of cheaper and better living conditions. A high degree of housing mobility also characterizes the lives of sex workers in Addis Ababa. Finding cheap and good accommodation close to where they work is a challenge. At the time of the research, the monthly rent was between 600 Birr and 1200 Birr (US$30–60). The fact that they have to travel back home late at night or early in the morning makes living in remote parts of the city very inconvenient. It is not only expensive because they have to take private taxis and *bajaj* (small taxis) to get home but it also puts them in vulnerable situations, travelling at times when there are very few people around. Another reason why sex workers often move house is that they do not want their neighbours to know what type of work they are doing. Sex workers are thus highly mobile in the city, moving from house to house, and from area to area. Tigist, for example (Chapter 6), first lived with a friend in an apartment in CMC, a new neighbourhood on the outskirts of Addis Ababa. The apartment was small but affordable, but very far from the city centre. After a row with her friend Tigist rented a room by herself closer to the area where she worked, but was unable to pay the rent and a few months later she moved to a cheaper place in a slum area. The shed was made of corrugated iron, had no windows and the bathroom was shared with 14 others. As soon as her income improved Tigist moved to a better place, but again was unable to pay the rent and moved out a few months later. Finding affordable housing is a huge problem in Addis Ababa, and the neoliberal housing policies have worsened the situation (see Chapter 3).

Many Bengali migrants also moved house after an initial period in which they lived with those who had facilitated their journey. Sharmeen, for example, like many other Bangladeshis, had changed accommodation three times in three years but had not moved out of Pallabi area where Bauniabandh slum is located. However, most of those we interviewed in Dhaka were still residing in the slum area where they had first arrived, two to six years earlier (the period that most of them had been living in Dhaka) but not always with the same people. Only a few girls, some of those who married after migrating, and some of the older migrants, have managed to move to a better area in Pallabi neighbourhood.

Those whose migration was facilitated by 'relatives' often moved in with them, which had the advantage of not having to find their own accommodation. The disadvantage was that they often felt very much constrained in terms of mobility, especially when they were living with married sisters and brothers-in-law or uncles and aunts. Elsa commented about her experiences in Addis Ababa: "She [her aunt] did not want me to approach people. I was not allowed to talk with anyone else". Salma, a 15-year-old who had been in Dhaka for a year, stated in a group discussion:

> If someone touches a girl it is a question of honour, [thus] I could not go anywhere on my own. My aunt would not allow me. I could not even go to buy something. My aunt was saying that I had to behave like I was in the village. In the village, I could not talk to anyone. I could not go anywhere alone. I was always under surveillance. My aunt wanted me to behave the same in Dhaka.

This confirms Heissler's findings (2013) in her study on the role of social networks in child labour migration in Bangladesh, which showed that family networks, while protecting the young migrants, especially on arrival, may become a source of social control that the girls perceive as constraining once they gain more self-confidence. Domestic workers in Addis Ababa who were living with relatives and not treated well often ran away and started living on their own or with friends. Through these attempts to find a place for themselves, girls were establishing new or maintaining old social networks, and engaging with the urban space and its residential neighbourhoods.

Working and Earning

Another element in place-making projects was access to work and securing a living. The daily lives of migrant and refugee girls and young women revolve mainly around work as they struggle to earn enough to provide for themselves and sometimes for those left behind. In Khartoum, 19-year-old Salam from Ethiopia spends the whole day on the street selling tea from her little cart. She wakes at around 8 a.m. and goes to her workplace an hour later, continuing until 7 p.m. Back home at around 9 p.m., she cooks some food and then goes to her friends to chat. She goes to bed at around 11 p.m. On Friday, her day off, she sometimes goes to the Ethiopian church, and after that she sits with her friends in her compound. They drink coffee, watch television and talk. Girls' routines are similar in Dhaka. Lamia, who is a garment worker, gets up at 5 a.m., cooks, takes a shower and does the dishes. At about 7.30 a.m. she goes to the factory, where she has a lunch break after five hours. She goes home at 1 p.m., and then goes back to the factory until 5 p.m. If she needs money she works overtime, which means that she works until 10 p.m. She spends her days off with friends, in the slum area or elsewhere in the city.

Migrant girls who are domestic workers in Addis Ababa often live with the employer's family and have no regular working hours. They start their work in the early morning; around 5 a.m., preparing breakfast and cleaning the house, and end in the evening, after the last meal and the kitchen and house have been cleaned, which can be as late as 10 p.m. If they are responsible for children they may even have to work at night, attending to them when they wake up.

Sex workers in Addis Ababa start their work around 10 p.m. and stop in the early hours of the morning, depending on what they have earned. When they have many clients or are well paid they may return home at 2 a.m., but when there is less work they stay up till 5 a.m. They sleep until the early afternoon, and start their day around 2 p.m.

Most employment is exploitative and the salaries too low to compensate for the high costs of living in big cities. In Khartoum, for example, most of the migrant and refugee girls were juggling two or three jobs. They complained about different aspects of their working conditions: the long working hours, the mistreatment and harassment they are subjected to at work, the low earnings and the lack of time off. Those who worked as live-in domestics in Khartoum had usually only one day a week to spend with their friends or family. Sometimes, like 17-year-old Feven, they would ask for time off to participate in religious celebrations as a strategy to get away from their employer's house and have some freedom. Domestic work in Sudanese families is very poorly paid (between 250 and 800 SDG per month, equivalent to US$30–100), and girls often suffer sexual advances and abuse from male members of the family, and harassment and maltreatment from the women. Ruta, a brilliant young Eritrean girl, who had been a university student in Asmara, could not speak any Arabic when she first arrived and had limited networks. With a neighbour's help, she finally got a job as a cleaner with a Sudanese family. She commented:

> They treated me very badly. The woman would call me from another part of the house just because she wanted me to bring her a glass of water that

was standing almost in front of her. They would give me leftovers from the fridge that stayed there for a long time. Once I got so sick, that until now I have problems with my stomach. I also had to sleep on the floor in the kitchen, and at night, the father of the family, and then one of his sons, tried to have sex with me. This is when I decided to leave without even taking my salary.

Working as domestics for Sudanese families is seen as the lowest in the hierarchy of employment options available for the migrant girls and young women in Khartoum. It was also usually the first work that the girls would find through the *samsari* (middlemen, agents), neighbours and friends. The recently arrived girls and young women had little knowledge of Arabic, low skills, and a limited network of support and contacts. They had little power in negotiating employment, and so resorted to such jobs. Once they learned some skills and Arabic, and acquired some small capital, they usually moved to other jobs, including setting up their own tea stalls. For Eritreans, however, it was rather rare to work as tea-sellers as they perceived this type of work as dangerous, dirty and subject to police and other harassment. Ethiopian adolescent girls and young women, on the contrary, are highly visible on the streets of Khartoum as tea-sellers. They are subjected to verbal harassment, abuse, often physical and sexual, especially when they work at nights, and the constant threat of police raids, the so-called *kasha*. Salam, quoted above, also mentioned that she does not like working as a tea-seller.

It is a hard job, you have to sit all day long in the heat on a dusty street, men abuse you, some of them try to sleep with you. But nothing has happened to me so far. Also, I only do this job because of money. Until recently, I had to support my younger brother. Thanks to the money I was sending he finished school and graduated from nursing college. He now works as a nurse and earns money. Now, I have to help my mum, but it is better now.

Ethiopians and sometimes Eritrean girls also work in tea places or so-called cafeterias run by Sudanese and Ethiopians, or Eritreans, and located in different parts of the city, usually in the migrant neighbourhoods. Officially, they sell coffee and tea, but there are also water pipes (shisha), music and television rooms. There are also some backrooms where other services are offered, sometimes including sexual intercourse.

These places are frequented exclusively by men, and thus it was almost impossible for a woman to do fieldwork. The need for money and a lack of other viable work opportunities makes girls accept harsh working conditions. As street tea-sellers or working in the cafés the girls would earn about 2000–2500 SDG (US$220–240) a month, working 12 hours a day with just one day off.

In Dhaka, most of those who migrated with the intention of working in a garment factory soon managed to find a job with the help of acquaintances. Some who arrived in Dhaka in their early teens had to wait longer before being employed because they were underage, and so worked as domestics in the meantime. Some managed to be employed even if visibly underage and reported that they had to hide in the bathrooms if visitors came to the factory. The newly arrived, completely unskilled, are employed as 'helpers'. After a while they are promoted to 'sewing machine operator' and after some years' experience they become 'quality controllers'. The work conditions vary from factory to factory in terms of regularity and punctuality in receiving the salary, working hours and overtime pay, the possibility of taking leave and other benefits.

Sharmeen, whose story opened this chapter, was earning only 1260 taka (US$16)[4] as a helper, hardly enough for her daily needs. Nurjahan said that in some respects her living conditions had worsened after migrating: "My health got much worse than before. We have to work a lot, from morning to night. Sometimes we have to do night shifts. We don't sleep enough. At work, there is a lot of pressure and no time to relax, not even to go to the toilet. We have one-hour lunch break from 1 to 2 p.m. We are insulted badly all the time. If I knew I wouldn't have come". After some years, having acquired some skills and being promoted from helper to machine operator, workers earn more and their working and living conditions improve. They can afford to send money home but they still have to make sacrifices in terms of their own expenditure. According to the research respondents, without doing overtime, the salary of a machine operator amounts to about 6000 taka (US$72) of which 2500 taka to 3000 taka (US$30–36) have to be spent on food and accommodation. Those who send remittances manage to send 2000–3000 taka (US$24–36) monthly. This does not leave much for

[4]All the exchange rates for taka (Bangladesh), Sudanese pounds (SDG) and Birr (Ethiopia) are from 2015. Due to inflation in each of the countries, they change rapidly and are volatile.

themselves or for savings. Many girls complain of often being mistreated and reprimanded and are aware that because of the huge labour supply in the sector, they can lose their job any time if they do not comply with their work environment and conditions. The working conditions of Garo girls employed in beauty parlours are also variable, depending mainly on the owner and the size of the parlour. Big, more structured parlours provide better working conditions. In the small parlours, where most of the girls we interviewed work, they can be asked to give up the weekly day off or Christmas leave if there are very big jobs, such as a wedding, or any sudden need on the part of friends of the owner.

In Addis Ababa, domestic workers' salaries are very low; they earn around 200 Birr (US$7) a month and sometimes are only paid in kind (food and lodging), particularly among those who work for relatives, who invited the girls to live with them and who promised to send them to school. Sex workers earn between 50 to 200 Birr (US$2.50–10) for a short job and 600 to 1000 Birr (US$30–50) for a whole night. Sex workers who work in hotels are more restricted in their mobility. They have to drink and chew *chat*[5] and smoke cigarettes in the hotel bar in order to pick up clients. Street workers can start and stop working whenever they like. Most migrant girls said that they would prefer to leave sex work. They complained about how clients treat them, the hardship of their lives at night, the fact that they were unable to attend school because they work at night and sleep during the day, and their addictions to *chat*, cigarettes and alcohol. Hayat phrased it as follows:

> I just wish that I could get a job that pays well enough for me to have a normal life. By this I mean a life that will allow me to work all day and be able to sleep at night and not the other way around. I wouldn't mind working as a waitress or a cleaner. I also wish that I could get a job that will not make me a victim of all my drug addictions.

Some of them said that the money that they earned was "bad money"[6] because they obtained it by doing sinful things, and that they were therefore unable to save it. It disappeared as soon as it was in their

[5] *Chat* (Catha Edulis) is a shrub whose leaves have a mildly stimulant effect when chewed. Chat is widely used in the Horn of Africa and Yemen, mainly by men but sometimes by women.

[6] In the interviews girls called it the devil's money (*teshetangenzab*).

hands. They spent it on make-up, clothes, shoes, *chat*, cigarettes and alcohol. In their view, if it had been good money, they would have been able to invest it in a better future, but it is very difficult to find another job with a relatively good salary. The salaries for jobs suitable for young women who have not finished their education, such as waitressing and working in shops, are very low (around 1500 Birr, or US$77 a month). Most of the sex workers said that they could not live on such a salary, as the rent just for their room was 1500 Birr. Only women who share housing, or who live with relatives, can afford to take up such jobs.

These findings show that there are very few options in the labour market for adolescent girls and young women who have migrated to the city. They are forced into paid work that is often marginalized and stigmatized. They also point to the highly structured and gendered labour markets, which push girls into work that is often devalued, dangerous and degrading. Yet, through manoeuvring these workplaces, adolescent girl migrants establish new connections, acquire new work experiences, and improve their knowledge of the city. They try to carve out more secure places to work and earn money, as they move from one employer to another, or negotiate working hours at the garment factories.

Social Life

"Whenever I wanted I could go to the market. When I felt bad I could go to the cinema hall to watch movies with my friends. That means there was no one to impose restrictions upon me. At home, my parents were saying: 'you can't go here or you can't go there', but here in Dhaka I can go to the cinema hall to watch movies and I walk to the factory with my friends. I like it", Sharmeen explained when asked about the benefits of living alone in Dhaka. Similarly, other migrant girls in the three cities appreciated aspects of their social life in the city compared to their life at home. They underlined the advantage of being able to buy all kinds of goods every day in town, as opposed to having to wait for the weekly *bazar* in the most remote villages. On the other hand, in the village they could eat fresh fruit and vegetables, which they could pick directly. Some were missing the open fields and nature while others appreciated precisely the opposite—the crowds and the ability to mix and meet different kinds of people. Cities thus opened up new possibilities for their personal place-making projects, for their growth as individuals, and for their enhanced views of the world around them, and their place within it. These opportunities are, however, often beset with risks, so adolescent girl migrants needed to carefully navigate this unstable terrain (see Vigh 2010). We borrow the term of social navigation from Henrik Vigh in his research among Guinea-Bissau youth in the context of war. As he argues, "the concept of social navigation makes it possible to focus on the way we move within changing social environments" (2010, p. 140). In each of the three cities, migrant and refugee girls use their unstable terrain to open up possibilities for themselves and those close to them.

Like Addis Ababa, Dhaka is seen as a place where there are multiple chances to meet, where different kind of goods are easily accessible, where it is possible to enjoy more freedom of movement because parents are not there to control and forbid. On the other hand, especially for those who have just arrived and are at the lowest level of the pay scale in the factory, the salary is just enough to cover basic expenses and send remittances. As Jamila powerfully said: "Sometimes I would like to eat something nice but I can't. If I spend money for myself I will not be able to send money home, so I think that here I can eat in one way or the other but at home if I don't send money they would starve". The reality is that most of them spend their time between the 'office', as they call the factory, and their room in the slum, because of the long working hours and the lack of free time, because they are tired, or because they cannot afford to go anywhere.

In all three cities, friendships are one of the girls' main navigation tactics. Friendships easily develop between girls who work in the same place, live together, attend the same church, or share their commute. They visit each other and, despite the limitations, those who can spare some money enjoy going with friends to buy cosmetics and clothes. Profound affective relationships may also become sources of support in times of need. In Dhaka, Lamia, for example, acknowledged with gratitude Suma's economic help during her sister's illness. The two friends migrated together to Oman in 2015, after sharing a room in the Bhola *bustee* for five years. In Addis Ababa, Tigist and Worku are also very close friends who met when they both had just started sex work and share their daily lives. "Friendship is important in our life. We share money for transport, we invite each other for dinner, we must have money all the time and if we don't have clients, the one who has money shares it. We visit each other if someone is ill". Sex workers mainly spend their leisure time with friends, making coffee, chewing *chat*, smoking *shisha*, listening to music or watching television. Some of them go to church.

For migrant and refugee girls in Khartoum, spending time with neighbours, relatives and friends were also their major social events. On Fridays, their day off, most girls and young women went to church and afterwards would visit friends and relatives in the city. Sharing food and preparing coffee with popcorn and biscuits were the favourite and the safest leisure activities for the young migrants and refugees. Members of the Pentecostal church usually had very elaborate services for which they would prepare during the week. The Pentecostals are a very tight community, uniting around specific churches and chapels. The choir members rehearsed twice a week in a private home in Amarat, another up-market neighbourhood in Khartoum. This is one of the favourite times for one of our Eritrean co-researchers, who belonged to the church. She said: "When I can go and meet my friends and sing with them, this is when I feel free, this is when I feel happy. This is what I always wanted to do, singing. And here in Khartoum I can do that". The Pentecostal church was banned in Eritrea in 2001 and since then its members have been prosecuted, imprisoned and tortured. Several of our respondents spent some years in prison as young girls in Eritrea for belonging to the church. Churches, mosques and other places of worship often play an important role in the lives of migrants worldwide. They not only provide spiritual help but also access to resources and a social network (see Buhr and McGarrigle 2017; Constable 2007; Liebelt 2011).

Weddings are another popular way to socialize and visit friends in Khartoum. Our Eritrean co-researchers who were Pentecostals usually attended weddings on Thursdays and Fridays. These events were very elaborate, with big halls rented to host up to 500 or 800 people, with music, food and traditional dance. This was also an opportunity for girls and unmarried young women to meet potential husbands and partners. Thus, they always looked impeccable, with beautifully braided hair, stunning jewellery and shiny dresses, despite their difficult financial situations. For very special occasions, the young women would save up money to have an evening out at one of the two malls in Khartoum, usually the Afra Mall. This bright, modern architectural structure with all its fast-food outlets, Indian cinema, bowling alley, and expensive clothing and jewellery shops was a place where girls felt in a different world. They enjoyed the freedom of not having to wear the hijab, and of eating greasy fast food served by Filipinos or other Eritreans. The place has little to do with the rest of Khartoum, or with the rest of Sudan. It is reminiscent for the migrants of 'Dubai' and 'the West'.

Derks (2008, p. 155) shows how young migrant women in Phnom Penh navigate the thin line between being modern and being seen as too modern, attempting to conform to different and sometimes opposing gender ideologies. This is in line with the experiences of young migrant girls in Dhaka, Addis Ababa and Khartoum. They too "explore the new opportunities open to them and thereby shape their self-representations as modern women" (Derks 2008, p. 142). Derks does not refer to the importance of digital technologies, which are now accessible all over the world and play a major role in migrants' lives, mobile phones in particular (Bunmak 2012; Grabska 2016; Lin and Tong 2008; Ngan and Ma 2008). Migrant girls in the three cities dress up for social events such as visits to shopping malls, weddings and religious celebrations, and post their photos on Facebook or update their profile pictures on other social media, including Viber and Skype. Digital technologies and social media have become an important aspect of the ways in which migrant girls are practising place-making and community-making. These technologies enlarge and solidify the translocal dynamics of place-making projects, with connections to the places of origin, cities of migration, other possible or imagined destinations, and places where family and friends are scattered.

Despite the pressures and social control, the city also provides an opportunity to experiment with friendships with people of the other sex, and thus question dominant gender norms for socializing. For example, friendships and relationships with boys are also potentially 'easier' in Dhaka than in the villages. Jamila commented:

> In Dhaka we have more opportunities to mix with boys. There is more freedom since our parents are not here. We have occasions to talk to boys. For example, say that I am a helper (unskilled worker) in a factory and next to me there is a boy who also works as a helper. Then there are machine operators, input officers, all of them are boys. We talk freely to them…we can also flirt with them.

In the countries and places of origin, it is usually seen as inappropriate and sanctioned by social norms and strict gender codes to associate with unrelated people of the other sex. Yet, in the city, girls and boys have more occasions and spaces for encounter than in the villages and the use of mobile phones is an important means for getting in touch and starting a relationship. However, for the Bangladeshi migrants in Dhaka, the apparent ease with which is possible to entertain phone conversations is counterbalanced by the strong social control in the slums, albeit in forms that differ from those in rural villages. The control that adults exert over young people's behaviour, especially young women's, occurs in the context of widespread parental concerns for the sexual security of girls and the predatory behaviour of men. Parents express these as powerful motivations to get their daughters married when they are very young (Rashid 2011). This resonates with research conducted by Terre des Hommes Italy and Aparajeyo Bangladesh (2010) in the slums where they work. Poverty and the lack of security are the main reasons parents give for withdrawing their daughters from school as early as 11–12 years of age and for trying to either to get them employed as domestics or in garment factories, or to give them in marriage. In the families living in the slums, both parents usually work and when they are not at school, girls remain at home without protection and control. Parents fear that they may enter into '*prem*' (love) relationships or be forced into sexual relationships. These relationships will seriously jeopardize their future marriage prospects. According to teachers and parents, young boys and girls are particularly 'prone to emotions' and 'easily fall in love', in which case they may get married without their parents' consent. There is also a common perception that so-called 'love marriages' are on the rise, with an increasing number of very young couples eloping, hoping to force their parents' consent through a *fait accompli*. Teachers and other adults also report that, in their experience, these marriages are unstable.

Thus, it is very difficult to develop and live friendships with those of the other sex since every contact between unrelated boys and girls is seen as potentially leading to sexual relationships and so must be censored. The fear of losing one's face and reputation with behaviour that challenges the recognized social norms is quite strong, as well as a preoccupation with keeping intact one's good name among relatives and villagers back home. Some do engage in more or less secret contacts and intimacies. Some 'love stories' have all the characteristics of a secret, romantic engagement like those seen in romantic movies and comedies which, along with popular songs, provide teenagers with the language of 'romantic love' to voice their feelings and give meaning to their clandestine meetings.

Both on- and offline social networks are thus of utmost importance for migrant girls. Sex workers in Addis Ababa mentioned the expansion of their social network as one of the positive sides of their migration.

Hiwot, who had migrated first to Beirut than to Kuwait and then back to Beirut, said: "Previously I was not good at approaching people. But now the work itself has changed me, it forces me to communicate with people, it makes you meet people and it makes you free". They were also very positive about the fact that their mobility was not restricted and they were free to move around in Addis Ababa. Other girls, however, mentioned that freedom is relative. Meseret evaluated the freedom in Addis differently:

> I don't think my life is freer here than back home. I sell my body to make an income. I have the same routine life which involves working at night, coming home in the morning, sleeping all day, waking up at a certain hour to eat followed with multiple drugs to stay up all night. It is a vicious circle and cannot be compared with the freedom and real fun that I had with my friends and family back home. I just wished I could continue school, but I think it is too late now and will probably not happen.

While the importance of social networks for migrants has been analysed in many cases (see Hagan 1998; Ryan et al. 2008; Williams 2006), we argue that for migrant girls they are a way in which they "tame" the city. These social networks can be linked to their places and countries of origin or to their family back home, but can also be independent of their former relations. Settling in and emplacing themselves, even if only temporarily, is strongly linked to their position as girls, as migrants, as being of a certain age, and in the case of Eritreans and Ethiopians in Khartoum, of a certain ethnicity and nationality. The intersection of these different identities affected the ways in which they practise place-making.

Expectations and Disappointments

Expectations of migration to cities and the accompanying disappointments are part and parcel of the migrants' place-making projects and their attempts to secure a better life for themselves and their loved-ones. Meseret, who expressed her high hopes for the future, was very disappointed with life in Addis Ababa. Her father died when she was little and her mother had difficulties in making ends meet. She neglected her children, which affected Meseret very much, and she was excited when she got the chance to move to Addis to join her aunt, who promised to send her to school. But her aunt did not keep her promise; she had to do household chores instead, and when her uncle raped her she decided to run away. When we met her, Meseret was doing sex work and upset with the turn her life had taken. She was angry and sad that she had not been able to continue her education. "The longer I stay in this business,[7] the more I see that my dreams are not being realized". Frehiwot was also very disappointed. She had come to Addis Ababa knowing that she would be doing sex work, and had hoped to quickly earn a lot of money:

> To be honest, I wasn't afraid when I came to Addis; I was rather optimistic and surprised to be in Addis. It was like arriving in America. But I thought I will be rich and collect a lot of money. The woman who brought me here shared the same feeling: 'You will help your aunt let alone yourself, you will succeed financially'. Ambitiously she told us: 'In the worst-case scenario, you can change your life just working for two months.' When I earned 2000 Birr (US$73) in the first business, I started to think my dream was coming true. But when days passed the reality changed upside down... nothing to show for two years.

The majority of Ethiopian and Eritreans girls in Khartoum also strongly expressed a sense of disappointment in realizing that their initial expectations and hopes had met with a quite different reality. When a lack of opportunities becomes protracted, uncertainty and precariousness prevail. Some Ethiopians in Khartoum, for example, felt 'stuck' because they didn't expect that it would have been so difficult to achieve their aim to make money and go back to Ethiopia relatively soon, while Eritreans felt frustrated in their initial plans to move on from Sudan. This contributes to putting migrants and refugees in a situation of liminality, well captured by the literature (Agier 2011; Horst 2006; Malkki 1995), and in which hope and waiting play central roles (Horst and Grabska 2015, p. 2). We will develop this important aspect in Chapter 8 where we discuss more extensively Eritrean girls' perceptions and aspirations for the future. The lack of imagining possibilities in the city, however, affects the processes of emplacement and place-making in the city.

In addition to earning money, one of the girls' most important expectations was related to the potentially greater opportunities to pursue education. The study by Montgomery et al. (2016) shows that about

[7] Business is the word used for sex work in Amharic.

30–40% of urban migrant girls manage to continue their schooling. Our data show a different picture as we consider only adolescent girls who have migrated on their own. Education is among the motives for migration mentioned by the migrants and ranked high among their aspirations and hopes for the future (see Chapter 4). Many of the migrant girls interviewed in Addis Ababa had come with the intention to continue their education, as did many of the Garo in Dhaka. Domestic workers in Addis Ababa hoped to be able to leave domestic work and find a better-paid job by attending evening classes. Sex workers also aspired to continue their education but no longer saw any likelihood of going back to school because of their lifestyle. Ethiopians in Khartoum had somewhat ruled out the possibility of attending school because of the lack of time. For Eritreans, education remained a distant plan as part of their journey towards better destinations in Europe or North America. None of the Bengali girls we interviewed in Dhaka was attending any kind of formal or informal schooling and some of them, like the Ethiopians, regretted having had to leave their villages where they could have continued going to school. Garo girls' hope of continuing to study while working was also, in most cases, unmet.

There is thus a strong discourse about the value of education, especially for girls, in the three countries. These discourses are inspired by global ideas about gender and education, which are built on the notion that girls' education is crucial for the development of the nation. "When you educate a girl, you educate a nation" is a slogan[8] used by many development organizations. Girls' education is seen as a route to development, and a way to curb migration. Notwithstanding the importance of girls' education, it does not guarantee a brighter future in the absence of structural changes in the economy. The Ethiopian government has, for example, made considerable efforts to expand educational opportunities in the country but has done very little to improve the labour market (see Chapter 3). Young and educated people are therefore unemployed and still hope to migrate. The girls' disappointments and unmet aspirations with regard to their education should therefore also be understood as idealizing its possible benefits. Many migrant girls, in particular in Ethiopia, believed that their peers in the villages who had continued

[8]The proverb "If you educate a man, you educate an individual, but when you educate a woman, you educate a nation" is attributed to the Ghanaian scholar James Emmanuel Kwegyir-Aggrey (1875–1927).

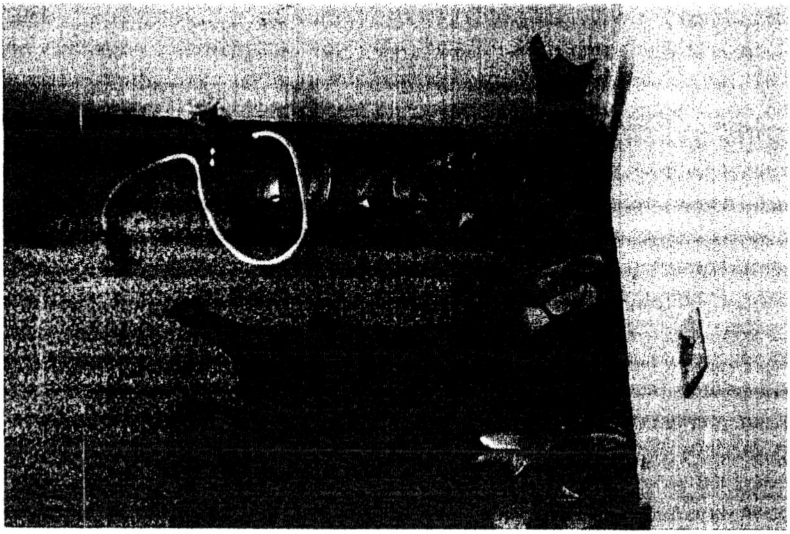

Fig. 5.4 Smoking shisha and socializing in Addis Ababa, Ethiopia

their schooling were better off, yet whether their lives also improved as a result remains an open question (Fig. 5.4).

Carving Out a Space for Herself in the City

Initial migrant and refugee girls' encounters with the cities were a mixture of enthusiasm and disappointment, new opportunities and threatening social spaces. The lives of girls in Dhaka, Khartoum and Addis Ababa show similarities and differences. Their daily life is dominated by work, which leaves them with few other opportunities for socialization and encounters, while their low earnings limit their mobility and their chance to enjoy what the cities can offer in terms of products and services. In addition, the majority of the girls live in unhealthy and overcrowded accommodation, although sharing a room or a small apartment with other migrants can favour the development of friendships and lasting relationships that can become an important source of support. This is even more evident in the case of Eritreans and Ethiopians in Khartoum and Garo migrants in Dhaka, who tend to share accommodation with friends and relatives according to their place of origin or ethnic identity. Despite the initial difficulties of having to deal with an unfamiliar and strange environment, by building social capital girls are able to improve their living and working conditions. They also actively, if not consciously, engage in place-making projects in the cities, by carving out a space that is familiar, safe and less threatening. While paying attention to their actions and practice of navigating an unstable terrain, we emphasize their active engagement with the cities, even if in their narratives they emphasized the temporary nature of their planned stays.

Migrant girls in Dhaka and Addis Ababa, especially sex workers and garment workers, emphasized the positive aspects of living in a city, their increased mobility compared to the areas they come from. This was much less so for the domestic workers whose lives are confined to their employer's house. Those who are unmarried, divorced or unaccompanied by their husband lack the kind of social protection that a husband can provide but also have more opportunities to be mobile, deepen their knowledge of the cities and potentially to pursue their own aspirations (see Montgomery et al. 2016). On the other hand, Ethiopians and Eritreans in Khartoum had to adjust to more restrictive gender norms than in their own countries. In all three cities, the place-making projects of adolescent migrant and refugee girls occur within systems of strong social control, which are highly regulated by gender norms. Hence, these processes are gendered yet, they also intersect with girls' age, social class, family situation, nationality, ethnic background and legal status. The use of mobile phones, choice of residence in certain areas of the city, or choice of work, are often strategies in the social navigation of the obstacles facing migrant girls in these cities.

At times, girls have to make difficult choices. Sharmeen's story shows that despite her initial difficulties, she was able to settle and feel at home in Dhaka. She had also progressed in her job but, as for the majority of women garment workers, the work was not enough for her to feel economically and socially secure. She consciously decided to give up the *shadinota* (independence, freedom) she had gained through working to acquire the much more valued position that marriage can provide. This decision allowed her to make a different place for herself in the city, with the protection of her status as a married woman, but at the same time, within the gendered constraints attached to such position. In the next chapters, we will consider how other migrants in the three cities made different choices in this respect, and how they navigate different vulnerabilities and risks and use a range of economic and social resources.

The cities offer chances to pursue new place-making projects, in which girls negotiate their place, their status, their belonging, their livelihoods and their security through a range of social navigation strategies. This dialectic takes place between migrant girls and their hosts in the cities, but also with their families across translocal spaces (both in the place of origin and other places of migration). Thus, cities offer chances to pursue different choices and increase girls' options in terms of lives that they desire. Working and earning contribute to strengthening their self-esteem and their position in their household and the wider society. Our findings show that for girls no less than for boys, work is central to the migration experience. Working and earning have the potential to challenge gendered roles and responsibilities and the way in which these change for boys and girls during their life course.

References

Agarwal, S., Jones, E., & Verma, S. (2016). Migrant Adolescent Girls in Urban Slums in India: Aspirations, Opportunities and Challenges. *Indian Journal of Youth and Adolescent Health, 3*(4), 8–21.

Agier, M. (2011). *Managing the Undesirables: Refugee Camps and Humanitarian Government*. Cambridge: Polity Press.

Aparajeyo Bangladesh. (2010). *Youth-Led Survey on the Commercial and Sexual Exploitation of Vulnerable Children and Youth in Dhaka Slum Areas*. Dhaka: Aparajeyo Bangladesh.

Appadurai, A. (1996). *Modernity at Large: Cultural Dimensions of Globalization*. Minneapolis, MN: University of Minnesota Press.

Buhr, F., & McGarrigle, J. (2017). Navigating Urban Life in Lisbon: A Study of Migrants' Mobilities and Use of Space. *Social Inclusion, 5*(4), 226–234.

Bunmak, S. (2012). Cell Phone Networks and Migrant Networks: The Case of Nayu Migrant Workers in Malaysia. *Malaysian Journal of Society and Space, 8*(1), 38–49.

Clark, S., & Cotton, C. (2013). Transitions to Adulthood in Urban Kenya: A Focus on Adolescent Migrants. *Demographic Research, 28*(37), 1053–1092.

Constable, N. (2007). *Maid to Order in Hong Kong. Stories of Migrant Workers*. Ithaca, NY: Cornell University Press.

Del Franco, N. (2012). *Negotiating Adolescence in Rural Bangladesh: A Journey Through School, Love and Marriage*. New Delhi: Zubaan Books.

Derks, A. (2008). *Khmer Women on the Move: Exploring Work and Life in Urban Cambodia*. Honolulu, HI: University of Hawai'i Press.

Erulkar, A. (2006). Migration and Vulnerability Among Adolescents in Slum Areas of Addis Ababa, Ethiopia. *Journal of Youth Studies, 9*(3), 361–374.

Ferguson, J. (1992). The Country and the City on the Copperbelt. *Cultural Anthropology, 7*(1), 80–92.

Garau, P., Sclar, E. D., & Carolini, G. Y. (Eds.). (2005). *A Home in the City: UN Millennium Project Task Force on Improving the Lives of Slum Dwellers*. London: Earthscan.

Gardner, K. (2009). Lives in motion: The life-course, movement and migration in Bangladesh. *Journal of South Asian Development, 4*, 229–251.

Grabska, K. (2014). *Gender, Home and Identity: Nuer Repatriation to Southern Sudan*. Oxford: James Currey.

Grabska, K. (2016). Eritrean Migratory Trajectories of Adolescence in Khartoum: (Im)Mobility, Identities, and Social Media. In S. Hale & G. Kadoda (Eds.), *Networks of Knowledge Production in Sudan: Identities, Motilities, and Technology*. Lanham, MD: Lexington Books.

Hagan, J. (1998). Social Networks, Gender and Immigrant Incorporation: Resources and Constraints. *American Sociological Review, 63*(1), 55–67.

Hannerz. (1980). *Exploring the City: Inquiries Toward an Urban Anthropology*. New York: Columbia University Press.

Heissler, K. A. (2013). Rethinking 'Trafficking' in Children's Migratory Processes: The Role of Social Networks in Child Labour Migration in Bangladesh. *Children's Geographies, 11*(1), 89–101.

Heissler, K. A. (2015). Migration and the Spaces of Labouring and Learning for Children and Young People in Asian Contexts. In T. Skelton, T. Abebe, & J. Waters (Eds.), *Laboring and Learning. Geographies of Children and Young People*. Singapore: Springer.

Horst, C. (2006). *Transnational Nomads: How Somalis Cope with Refugee Life in the Dadaab Refugee Camps of Kenya*. New York and Oxford: Berghahn Books.

Horst, C., & Grabska, K. (2015). Flight and Exile: Uncertainty in the Context of Conflict-Induced Displacement. *Social Analysis, 59*(1), 1–18.

Jansen, S., & Löfving, S. (2009). *Struggles for Home: Violence, Hope and the Movement of People*. New York and Oxford: Berghahn Books.

Liebelt, C. (2011). *Caring for the 'Holy Land': Filipina Domestic Workers in Israel*. New York/Oxford: Berghahn Books.

Lin, A., & Tong, A. (2008). Mobile Cultures of Migrant Workers in Southern China: Informal Literacies in the Negotiation of (New) Social Relations of the New Working Women. *Knowledge, Technology, and Policy, 21*, 73–81.

Luke, N., Xu, H., Mberu, B. U., & Goldberg, R. E. (2012). Migration Experience and Premarital Sexual Initiation in Urban Kenya: An Event History Analysis. *Studies in Family Planning, 43*(2), 115–126.

Magadi, M. A. (2013). Migration as a risk factor for HIV infection among youths in Sub-Saharan Africa: Evidence from the DHS. *The Annals of the American Association for Political and Social Science, 648*(1), 136–158.
Malkki, L. (1995). Refugees and Exile: From 'Refugee Studies' to the National Order of Things. *Annual Review of Anthropology, 24*, 495–523.
Massey, D. (1991). A Global Sense of Place. *Marxism Today, 38*, 24–29.
Massey, D. (1994). *Space, Place and Gender*. Cambridge: Polity Press.
Mills, M. B. (1997). Contesting the Margins of Modernity: Women, Migration, and Consumption in Thailand. *American Ethnologist, 24*(1), 37–61.
Montgomery, M. R., Balk, D., Liu, Z., Agarwal, S., Jones E., & Adamo, S. (2016). Urban Migration of Adolescent Girls: Quantitative Results from Developing Countries. In J. Michael (Ed.), *International Handbook of Migration and Population Distribution* (pp. 573–604). Dordrecht: Springer.
Ngan, R., & Ma, S. (2008). The Relationship of Mobile Telephony to Job Mobility in China's Pearl River Delta. *Knowledge, Technology, and Policy, 21*, 55–63.
Pardue, D. (2017). Cities as Migrant Emplacement, *Anthropology News*.
Raitapuro, M., & Bal, E. (2016). 'Talking About Mobility': Garos' Aspiring Migration and Mobility in an 'Insecure' Bangladesh. *South Asian History and Culture, 7*(4), 386–400.
Rashid, S. F. (2011). Human Rights and Reproductive Health: Political Realities and Pragmatic Choices for Married Adolescent Women Living in Urban Slums, Bangladesh. *BMC International and Human Rights, 11*(3), 1–10.
Rofel, L. (1999). *Other Modernities: Gendered Yearnings in China after Socialism*. Berkeley, Los Angeles, London: University of California Press.
Ryan, L., Sales, R., Tilki, M., & Siara, B. (2008). Social Networks, Social Support and Social Capital: The Experiences of Recent Polish Migrants in London. *Sociology, 42*(4), 672–690.
Thorsen, D. (2007). Junior-Senior Linkages in Migration: Youngsters' Perceptions of Migration in Rural Burkina Faso. In H. P. Hahn & G. Klute (Eds.), *Cultures of Migration : African Perspectives* (pp. 175–199). Berlin: LiT Verlag.
Turton, D. (2005). The Meaning of Place in a World of Movement: Lessons from Long-Term Field Research in Southern Ethiopia. *Journal of Refugee Studies, 18*, 258–280.
Vigh, H. (2009). Wayward Migration: On Imagined Futures and Technological Voids. *Ethnos, 74*(1), 91–109.
Vigh, H. (2010). Youth Mobilisation as Social Navigation. Reflections on the Concept of Dubriagem. *Cadernos de Estudos Africanos, 18–19*, 140–164.
Williams, L. (2006). Social Networks of Refugees in the UK. *Journal of Ethnic and Migration Studies, 32*(5), 865–879.

CHAPTER 6

Risks, Threats and Setbacks

"*They Used to Call Us Cursed*": Tigist's Story

Tigist was 24 years old when we interviewed her in early 2014. She had been living in Addis Ababa since she was 16 and was an active member of NIKAT.[1] Tigist spoke English. She finished 10th grade but never obtained her certificate as she was forced to leave her home town, Dire Dawa, in eastern Ethiopia. Tigist was willing to work as a research assistant and introduced us to many other girls who had left their places of origin as adolescents and were living in Addis Ababa. Tigist's parents were both teachers but because they were working in another area she spent the first years of her life with her grandmother. "I still have a good memory of her; she used to take care of me in a special way. I started going to school when I was living with her". After her grandmother died she lived with her parents until they both died in a car accident. "I lost my parents without having spent much time with them. I only spent one and a half years with them before they died", she repeated twice during the interview.

Tigist and her younger brother started living with their aunt, their mother's sister, but the situation soon deteriorated. Tigist recalled:

[1] NIKAT is a sex-workers' organization in Addis Ababa (see Chapter 2).

K. Grabska et al., *Adolescent Girls' Migration in The Global South*, Palgrave Studies on Children and Development,
https://doi.org/10.1007/978-3-030-00093-6_6

> She started to do things to us that not even a stranger would do to someone (…). When I came back from school I would only get a loaf of bread and half *injera* (Ethiopian bread), while her children were eating meat, we were eating *shuro* (chickpea paste) that was not cooked well. My aunt used to buy clothes for her children, but not for us. I went to school wearing my worn-out slippers, sewing and mending them with pins and cords. (…). They [her relatives] used to call us cursed, they used to discriminate [against] us, they also beat us.

Tigist and her brother were already suffering but the situation became worse when Tigist obtained higher marks than her cousin in the national exam. Her aunt was furious and locked her up in a small room and punished her by giving her only a loaf of bread each day. She also burned her hand with a knife. The situation was so bad that Tigist decided to run away. She jumped out of a window and started living on the street. These were the most horrific months in her life. She tearfully recalled:

> There were old people and young gangsters living in the street. (…). The young boys tried to rape me many times but I was protected by the older people. (…) There was no clean water, my body was very dirty, everything was bad, I was hungry and started eating food that was full of garbage.

When she fell sick, she was taken to the hospital and then got in touch with the mother of an old school friend, who took her in. Thanks to her, Tigist went back to school and started selling vegetables. She planned to help her brother, who was still living with her aunt. At one point she met a young man, who said that he knew her from before, and befriended him. He took her for a short trip to Jijiga. Tigist remembered:

> He promised to reserve separate rooms but when we arrived he got me drunk and the next morning I found out that I was raped. (…) I was very disappointed and told my friend's mother. She said that my only chance was that I would live with him and try to love him. (…) I was 16 years old when he took me to Addis.

Tigist and her boyfriend started living together but his parents did not approve of the relationship because she was much younger than he and did not have a family. One day when she came home from working as a cashier she found that he had disappeared and taken all his belongings with him. Desperate, she started working as a waitress to make more money. "My customers were mostly women; they used to ask me to change my job because I was young and not paid enough". Through these young women, Tigist found a job in a hotel. "It was my first time to work in a hotel. I knew nothing about it. (…) I had only had sex with my boyfriend. I had no idea how many times I had to have sex[there]".

At the time of the interview, Tigist had been living in Addis Ababa for eight years, and experienced the many risks of being a young migrant sex worker. She was working on the street and no longer in a hotel, and living with a close friend, who also did sex work. She had benefited from the activities of NIKAT; she had followed computer classes and was an active peer educator. Although she was outspoken about the rights of sex workers, she wanted to leave sex work. Her dream was to open a small shop or have a job in which she could use her computer skills. When we were able to help her open a coffee shop[2] she was very excited. She hoped that she would finally be able to leave sex work. It was, however, a major challenge to overcome her addiction to *chat* and *shisha* and the money that she was earning was not enough to pay the rent. Four months after opening the shop, she closed it again. She moved to a house where friends were living, and soon went back to sex work.

Tigist's story is a powerful illustration of the risks, threats and setbacks migrant girls experience in Ethiopia, as well as in Bangladesh and in Sudan. Tigist lost her parents at a young age, was abused by her aunt, lived on the street, migrated to Addis Ababa with a male friend, was raped and later abandoned by him, and entered sex work, which in itself entails many risks. Similar to stories of migrant and refugee girls from Dhaka and Khartoum, her story also shows the volatility of her life, with dramatic turning points that influenced her life deeply. In this chapter, we discuss first the various risks, threats and setbacks in the lives of migrant girls. We then turn to an analysis of vulnerabilities and volatilities. The sources of vulnerability for migrant and refugee girls and young women are multiple and intersectional: their position as girls and young women from a specific ethnic and national background, their legal situation as foreigners, and the absence of parents, guardians or relatives. In

[2]Tigist played a major role in the documentaries made on the basis of the research (see Chapter 2). We collected donations in order to help Tigist realize her dream of opening a coffeeshop. Drinking coffee is a favourite pastime in Ethiopia and preparing coffee a national custom. People drink coffee in many different places, including in front of small coffeeshops.

addition, the nature of their work, their level of education and the almost non-existent support from international, national and community organizations increase their vulnerability. We argue that the lives of migrant girls are overwhelmingly volatile, which becomes especially clear when one takes a long-term perspective on the lives of adolescent migrant girls and refugees. Their lives are marked by protracted uncertainty and precariousness (see Horst and Grabska 2015). Their stories demonstrate how the experiences of risk, vulnerability and volatility are gendered and potentially limit or affect any changes in gender relations. At the same time, some of these risks and vulnerabilities might be mitigated both by the available institutional support system, and also by the girls' own agency in expanding their social capital (see Chapter 7).

Risks and Threats

"Risk shapes and is shaped by migration", state Williams and Baláž (2012, p. 167) in their article on migration, risk and uncertainty. They also argue that the role of risk in migration has not been theorized sufficiently. Migration can be informed by risk and uncertainty in the place of origin and can both generate and ameliorate risk (ibid.). Risks can be understood as known uncertainties or known likelihoods. According to Williams and Baláž (2012, p. 168) uncertainty has two sources: first, imperfect knowledge about the conditions both in the place of origin and in the possible destinations; and second, the unpredictability of the future. All future changes involve some uncertainty and individuals therefore act on the basis of expectations. Migrants face specific challenges in forming future expectations because they often have limited knowledge of the situation in their intended destination. Williams and Baláž argue that migration is more associated with uncertainty than with risk, and that is more useful to see knowledge and uncertainty as a fluid continuum, along which individuals move in both directions as decisions are never made in complete ignorance. Horst and Grabska build on this arguing that "the concept of risk is based on a full understanding of possible outcomes and of the likelihood of those outcomes occurring—without knowing which outcome will occur in each individual instance" (2015, p. 2). As such, the concept of risk can be understood as "a framing device which conceptually translates uncertainty from being an open-ended field of unpredicted possibilities into a bounded set of possible consequences" (Boholm 2003, p. 167). Whereas much of the research on risk as calculated uncertainty comes from economics, a socio-cultural approach towards risk "acknowledges the fact that risk knowledge is seen as historical and local, as constantly contested and as a subject to disputes and debates over their nature, their control and who is to blame for their creation" (Zinn 2006, p. 278). In the following sections, we discuss the main sources of risks and threats in the lives of migrant girls, first in their place of origin and then at the destination.

Men and Women as Threats

As described in Chapter 4, girls are subject to predatory male behaviour at home, during the journey and at their destination. Some experience physical and psychological violence perpetrated by their father, step-father, or other men in the family. Some decide to leave because of marital violence, both from the husband and the parents-in-law. The story of Sharmeen from Bangladesh (Chapter 5) reveals the risks facing girls when they are married at an early age without having a more secure position in their family. Rahel, who was 18 years of age at the time of the interview, escaped her home in Eritrea when she was 15. She followed her older brother who was already in Khartoum. This was in the aftermath of her father's death and her mother marrying a violent man who abused her and her children. Rahel did not mention any direct sexual violence against her, but she often talked about the man's brutality and what he had done to her. Her older brother escaped first, and then paid for his sister's journey to Khartoum. He was very worried about her and wanted to protect her. This illustrates that although parents and relatives can be a source of protection, they can also present risks.

Abusive and violent behaviour is not exclusively perpetrated by men—women can also present risks and threats for girls. Some girls had been abused by women in their family members, as Tigist's story shows. Tigist had positive memories of her childhood before her parents' death, after which she became the victim of an abusive aunt. The loss of a parent and especially both parents can expose Ethiopian girls to great risk. Poverty increases the possibilities of neglect, abuse and exploitation. According to Abebe and Skovdal (2010, p. 574):

> [O]rphan care is influenced by complex and interdependent familial, economic, cultural, geographical, social and personal factors. For example, the gender and age of orphans seem to influence who families wish to provide

care for. Older boys who can carry out labour-intensive agricultural work in rural areas and younger girls who can help with domestic chores generally tend to be favoured when it comes to receiving care because of the nature of work they perform.

The previous bond between the deceased and adoptive parents also affects the quality of care given to orphans (ibid.). Aunts, as our research found, especially among Ethiopian adolescent girls and young women in Addis Ababa, seem to pose a particular risk in the country. Hewan, a 21-year-old sex worker in Addis Ababa, grew up with her aunt, thinking that she was her mother. She was constantly abused and exploited. "I used to ask myself 'Why would my mum do that?'. […] When I asked people why she was beating me so much, they told me that she was not my mother". Hewan's mother had died when she was a baby and her mother's sister took her in. When Hewan found out that her aunt was not her biological mother, the abuse intensified and she decided to run away with her boyfriend. She took the risk of migrating to Addis Ababa because she could no longer stand the level of abuse.

One of the potential outcomes of abuse by family members is that girls (and boys) risk becoming homeless and start living on the street. Tigist said that the three months that she lived on the street were the worst in her life. She slept outside, ate food from dustbins, and was at risk of being raped by young men who were also living on the street. As Paula Heinonen describes in her ethnography of youth gangs and street children in Ethiopia (2011), life on the street increased risks of gender-based violence for girls, including verbal and physical abuse and sometimes even gang rapes. All of the girls in her study had run away from home because of the abuse they had experienced there (Heinonen 2011, p. 132). Those who joined the gangs had been raped and were too ashamed to return home. As will be discussed below, for girls to have premarital sex and hence no longer be virgin is strongly condemned in Ethiopia, Bangladesh and Eritrea, and many of the risks girls ran were related to their gender and sexuality.

Gender and Sexuality as Sources of Risks

In all three case studies, adolescent girls were subject to pressuring and constraining gender norms, both at home and in the place of migration (see Chapter 3). Many of these gender norms are related to girls' sexuality and the assumed dangers involved. In Bangladesh, when a girl has started menstruating people say that she has come of age (*'boyos hoece'*), and from then on her mobility is limited by the observance of *purdah* (see Chapter 5). Adults and parents try to restrict any interaction between boys and girls. They view adolescence as a problematic period, and puberty is commonly viewed as a phase of particularly strong emotions. Adolescent girls and boys are considered to be even more *abeg probon* (prone to passion) than adults. They are said to be exceptionally *gorom* (hot) and to have hot blood,[3] which is deemed to depend on their sexual maturation. The word *probon* can also be translated as 'addicted' and the expression *abeg probon* conveys also a sense of weakness, dependence and lack of control. Every form of interaction before marriage with people of the other sex is considered very dangerous because of the strength of young people's sexuality. Every kind of interaction between boys and girls is presumed to have illicit sexual overtones. The fear that a daughter may lose her chastity or acquire a bad reputation and lose her honour by engaging in premarital relationships is one of the reasons why parents tend to arrange a daughter's marriage as soon as possible. The strength of the dominant views of sexuality, honour and gender in Bangladesh circumscribes the risks and the vulnerabilities that girls face.

There are also strong social pressures to marry on girls who have reached puberty in Ethiopia and Eritrea (see Chapter 4). Although government campaigns have enhanced girls' access to education and criminalized early marriage, the sexuality of adolescent girls is still strictly controlled and premarital relationships are not accepted (Kebede et al. 2014; Tadele 2006). A girl's virginity is valued highly in order to secure a good marriage and respectability, so parents and guardians often seek to 'protect' girls from engaging in sexual relations. Adolescence is a period when girls are eager to experiment with their sexuality, but there is the risk of boys and men perceiving them as sexual objects. Parents and guardians thus often stop girls from going to school because they fear the negative consequences of mixed education and potential abduction of girls into marriage (see Chapter 4). Based on qualitative and

[3]Osella and Osella (2002, p. 119) note that in Kerala, body heat and strong sexual desire are an attribute of young people of both sexes, in contrast to other anthropological sources, where women are depicted as more prone to it.

quantitative data collected in the Young Lives[4] study, Boyden, Pankhurst and Tafere state:

> …in safeguarding family interests and girls' social standing and transition to adulthood, genital modification and early marriage are seen by many as protecting females against social and economic risks such as abandonment, stigma, and destitution. Also, by limiting extramarital sex, insofar as this is feasible, many believe that these practices reduce health risks, even though global standards perceive them as major health concerns. (2012, p. 519)

Girls' sexuality is not only related to the risk of early marriage or abduction but adolescent girls are also exposed to sexual harassment or abuse by boys and men in their surroundings. Tigist successfully avoided being raped when she was living on the streets but had non-consensual sexual relations when she joined a male friend on a weekend trip. Gender-based violence is very common in Ethiopia. According to a study conducted by Save the Children (2008), 49% of Ethiopian women had experienced physical violence and 59% had been the victim of intimate partner violence. Unmarried adolescent girls are also exposed to sexual violence, including rape, especially in rural areas (Worku and Addissie 2002). Girls may have consensual sex with their boyfriends before they are married, but this is socially strongly condemned. Girls are expected to remain virgin until they marry. Research has, however, shown that many girls and young women are in fact sexually active before marriage, in particular in Addis Ababa (Both 2017). Unmarried women who become pregnant are socially marginalized and are seen to bring shame to the family. The concept of *yilunta* (Heinonen 2011, p. 32) is extremely important in Ethiopian society, referring to a "heightened perception of what others may say or even think about what one does in private or in public". Adults and children alike have a strong sense of *yilunta* and the gender-based values attached to it. While boys and men have to conform to dominant notions of masculinity, such as financially providing for their family, girls and women have to appear respectable, which mainly means that they must protect their sexuality.

[4]Young Lives study is a large-scale research programme at the University of Oxford. Their groundbreaking longitudinal research with 12,000 children growing up in 4 different countries has enabled the researchers to create new approaches to the study of children's growing up and transitions. See https://www.younglives.org.uk/.

This is similar for adolescent girls in Eritrea and Bangladesh, but they spoke less than Ethiopian girls about sexual harassment in their place of origin. Some Eritreans, however, talked about the sexual harassment and violence that they or 'others' experienced in the national service. Respectability is also gendered and for adolescent girls and women is linked to virginity before marriage. This was also one of the main reasons why adolescent girls and young women who were raped during their journey to Sudan kept this secret in order not to lose their reputation in their communities. It has also been widely reported by NGOs and UNHCR that many young Eritrean women were raped on the way to Europe, either by smugglers, fellow migrants, or border guards. Some young Eritreans would take contraceptive measures before embarking on the trip across Sahara from Khartoum.

Access to Education and Work at Risk

As mentioned in Chapters 3 and 4, access to education and paid work is both highly gendered and strongly related to age. Adolescent girls drop out of school more often than adolescent boys, despite the increased educational opportunities for girls in rural and urban areas in Bangladesh, Ethiopia and Eritrea. There is a real risk of girls being forced to give up their education in order to help out their families. In Ethiopia and in Eritrea, first-born girls in particular tend to leave school in order to help their families by earning a living. They often contribute to the costs of educating their younger (male) siblings. While girls' education is now more widely available and more acceptable, many girls still face constraints and obstacles in gaining access to and continuing with education. The likelihood that girls will drop out of school are related to a wide range of factors including prioritizing boys' over girls' education, the distance to the school, the absence of female teachers, and the risks of sexual harassment and abduction. A number of studies have shown that girls' drop-out rates increase in secondary school. Completing the first cycle of secondary school, and obtaining a Secondary School Certificate, is expensive and not perceived to lead to any desirable form of employment for girls in Ethiopia and in Bangladesh. If there is no return on investing in education, for poor parents daughter's marriage is the best way to secure her future.

These findings on girls' schooling may be related to the extremely limited scope for wage employment for women and girls in rural areas.

In all three countries, women from the poorest landless families may work as poorly paid agricultural day labourers, or more often as domestics in neighbouring houses, where they are most likely to be paid in kind. In Bangladesh, as well as being poorly paid these jobs are perceived as contrary to *purdah* norms, and women who have to take them are held in very low esteem. In Ethiopia, employment options for young women with little education are also very limited. They may work as domestics, in agriculture, in the service sector and trade, and in factories, such as the cut-flower industry and the garment sector. The labour market is highly gendered, with young and uneducated women tending to take up low-paid, low-status work. Low-status work is often characterized by poor working conditions, such as heavy workloads, low pay, no fixed working hours, no labour protection, and no secondary labour rights. These jobs expose the young women to exploitation and abuse. In Ethiopia and in Bangladesh, a few educated women may find employment in NGOs, or as teachers, but the supply for such jobs far outstrips the demand. In Eritrea, women's employment situation is similar despite the emphasis on equal rights in the labour market and the revolutionary promises to women that they are on an equal standing with men in all aspects of life. The payment is extremely low, and the prices of commodities very high. A pair of jeans, as one of the respondents commented, is equal to three months of salary in public administration. Serving in the national service is obligatory also for young women or those who do not perform well at school.

The Risk of Migration: Travelling, Working, Socializing

Gender and sexuality also significantly affect the risks and threats experienced by migrant girls during the journey and in their destination. While Bangladeshi girls and Ethiopian internal migrants spoke little about their journeys, which may indicate that they travelled in relatively secure ways, girls who migrated to Khartoum had lengthy stories to tell (see also Chapter 4). They encountered numerous risks and threats, largely from men. They were likely to have experienced sexual violence and rape at the hands of smugglers, fellow migrants, Sudanese security personnel, or Rashaida kidnappers. Letina, for example, left Keren in a group of nine people. She was the only girl. The journey to the Sudanese border took 13 days, mainly walking. Letina told us:

> I did not sleep the entire journey. At some point, one of the boys from the group wanted to play with me [have sex]. I was so afraid, but I could not tell anyone in the group because I could not trust them. I did not know any of them. (...) At some point, my feet hurt a lot. They were bleeding from all the walking. The *samsara* (middleman) helped me; he even waited for me and shared with me his water. Thank God nothing happened to me. Most girls get into trouble. (...) [At the border] ... we were stopped by the Rashaida group and each of us had to pay ransom. I was afraid that the Rashaida would rape me. This is what they do to girls to force their families to pay ransom. But somehow I was lucky. I contacted my English teacher who was already in the UK and he paid for me. I then spent three months in Shegerab, the UN refugee camp near Kassala town. Other girls took care of me.

Most of the Eritrean girls left with the support of *samsari* (see Chapters 4 and 7). Sometimes, they left in a group of friends, or alone with strangers, as was the case of Ruta. They usually walked or had arranged transport, if this was possible. Once having crossed the border into Sudan, and with any luck not falling into the hands of Rashaida or Sudanese security forces, they would contact either their parents in Eritrea or relatives or friends abroad to ask for money to pay the *samsari*. These were the phone calls that family members dreaded. They seldom had enough money to support their daughters and so would sell their valuables, or ask family members and friends in the diaspora to help out with paying the ransom. Mona was held by Rashaida for several weeks until her neighbour in Asmara sold his car and sent the money for the ransom. The *samsari* (agents) do not release the migrants until the money is paid. When they arrive at their destination, the girls run the risk of abuse, deceit and exploitation by those who enabled their journey to the cities or abroad (see Chapter 5).

Another set of risks is related to the type of work. Domestic workers in Ethiopia, Sudan and the Middle East are exposed to sexual harassment as they work in the privacy of the home (Esim and Smith 2004; Erulkar and Mekbib 2007; Fernandez and de Regt 2014). A strong stigmatization of Ethiopian and Eritrean adolescent girls and women in Sudan is often located in the moral notions of *Habesha* (see Chapter 3). Ethiopian and Eritrean migrant women are perceived as 'prostitutes' and sexual violence committed against them is justified within moral norms operating in the Sudanese society. For domestic workers in Ethiopia, the situation is also not much better. Meseret (see Chapter 5) was raped repeatedly by her uncle in Addis Ababa but did not dare to say anything about it because of the fear of losing her job and incurring her aunt's anger. Many other domestic workers experienced verbal, physical and sexual abuse by their employers. While Bangladeshi girls spoke less about sexual harassment, in particular at work, it is a reality both in factories and in the slums. Making a proposal of marriage is usually a way to have sex with adolescent girls and young women. Sex workers in Addis Ababa told us in detail about the risks they experience at work. In hotels (brothels) they were better protected than on the street, but the dependence and working environment was often a reason to shift to working on the street. Feven came to Addis two years ago, knowing that she would be doing sex work and hoping to earn more than she did in her hometown (see Chapter 5). She had experienced many forms of abuse during her work:

> Many men beat us when the position and way they want [sex] is difficult for us, and I don't want people to beat me. Most of them want us when they get drunk and they don't care about us. Life consists of ups and downs and people pass through it, but many men don't understand this fact and see us like dolls. When I face such harassment, I can't do anything, it is just my fate to accept the punch. I feel powerless and empty because I put myself there with my own consent.

In addition to sexual violence, both domestic workers and sex workers are at risk of becoming HIV-positive; the number of adolescent sex workers with HIV and AIDS is on the rise in Ethiopia (Erulkar 2014). None of the migrant girls interviewed told us about their HIV status, even those who knew, which points to the strong stigma attached to people with HIV and AIDS in Ethiopia (Tadele 2006; Erulkar 2014).[5] Our personal contacts with sex workers revealed that some of them were HIV-positive. Girls and young women were ashamed of their HIV status, and worried about the future, in particular those with children. They were afraid that they would die and leave their children behind alone. There is widespread awareness about HIV and AIDS in Ethiopia, and condoms are available free of charge, yet there are still men who prefer unprotected sex. Organizations that support sex workers, such as NIKAT

[5] It is also very likely that even if the girls knew, they did not feel it was appropriate to mention it in the interviews.

and Timret Le Hiwot, play an important role in raising the awareness of sex workers about the importance of their clients using a condom. Sex workers who are HIV-positive can get free medication in a number of hospitals in the city. During one FGD with sex workers in the area of Katanga, a poor slum in Addis Ababa, one participant summed up the risks in the lives of migrant girls very poignantly:

> When people know that you are not from here, they consider you innocent and someone can take advantage of you during or outside of work. The times are better now as women's rights are better respected than the times when we first came. Then men would try to rape us in groups. Even not knowing directions and the area properly can lead someone to be taken advantage of as they can tell us the wrong direction to trap us. We could easily become victims of many diseases. We can also fall [into a] trap in unplanned pregnancies. Overall, we enter a life that we didn't expect. Not a bad life, but not a life as good as you had imagined.

Girls are at greater risk of sexual violence than other migrants in the cities. In this regard, our research concurs with other studies conducted in slums in Bangladesh that show that while there is a higher prevalence and social acceptance of gender-based violence in the slums compared to other urban areas (NIPORT et al. 2008; García-Moreno et al. 2005), migrant women and girls who live away from familiar social networks are more vulnerable to violence and to imposed early marriage than those who were born in the slums, or who migrated with parents or husbands (Camellia et al. 2012). In her study on Ukrainian domestic workers in Warsaw, Kindler (2011) argues that the intersection of gender, legal status and the nature of the work influences how migrant women evaluate risk in addition to their exposure and response to risk (ibid., p. 25). The women she interviewed were all aware of the risks of working as domestics in Poland but they still opted for it. She identified three types of migrant women: risk bearers, risk sharers and opportunity seekers (ibid., pp. 182–184). Risk bearers were women who saw no alternative to migrating abroad even though they were aware of the risks; risk sharers were those who considered their migration to entail a high level of risk and tried to minimize it; and opportunity seekers were hoping their lives would be better after migration, and were not afraid of the risks. This typology is also applicable to the migrant girls and young women we interviewed, even though we did not ask them specifically about how they assessed the risks of migration. Many of the girls who migrated to Sudan and to the Middle East knew the risks entailed in becoming a migrant domestic worker, but hoped that they would be "lucky" (*edil*) and not fall prey to abuse and exploitation.

In the interviews, many girls also spoke also about risks associated with developing relations with boys and men in the place of destination. In Khartoum, most of the girls talked about the risks of being cheated and taken advantage of by men. Tsirite (see Chapter 7), a 22-year-old from Ethiopia working as a tea-seller in Khartoum said:

> We do not trust Ethiopian men, and neither the Sudanese. They want to make friends with you, but what they really want is to control you and your income. They want to take your money and then also expect you to work for them doing domestic work while they are relaxing on their beds. It is better not to have boyfriends here. This is not a good place for boyfriends.

In Bangladesh, most of the girls we talked to said that the main reason they came to Dhaka was to work to help their families and that they were not interested in any form of entertainment. They smiled and giggled when we asked if they had a boyfriend, but most admitted to having phone conversations with someone. There is also widespread mistrust in boys and men and fears of being cheated by young and older suitors. This is often justified by experience. As Lamia said:

> In Dhaka ... relationships with boys...there is a different 'system'. Actually they don't have relationships...they just pass their time. After sometime you will realize that they are married and they have children at home, but they flirt—just to enjoy.

Nurjahan, a 19-year-old woman, who had been married before migrating and was living in the Bhola slum in Dhaka, said that boys run after girls who have money and that they don't consider those who live in the slums:

> The bad thing is that this is a slum environment, the good thing is that boys would not disturb girls who live in the slum because they would think that these girls are dirty and that there is no advantage in mixing with slum people.

As a consequence, most of the migrant girls we talked to in Bangladesh do not openly take advantage of any potential opportunities that Dhaka might offer and tend to be very restrained. During one FGD, a girl said that she was looking forward to going back home because in Dhaka "there is too much freedom" (*shadinota*). We were told the same by Halima, who repeatedly said that she was spending her days between her room and the factory, with no interest and trust in colleagues and neighbours.

> Life in the village was good. Here people don't talk to each other. Nobody would say anything to a girl who goes home at 10–11 in the night. In the village it's not like this, it doesn't work like this. In the village there are people who check on you, here there aren't.

The situation for migrant girls in Addis Ababa and in Khartoum is similar. They usually keep a low profile, tend to spend most of their time between work and home, and have no other activities. In Khartoum, the only social activities in which the girls and young women participate are to go to church, and occasionally visit friends and attend weddings (see Chapters 5 and 7).

These stories make clear that most of the risks migrant girls experience are gendered and are related to being adolescents. As adolescent girls, they are confronted with dominant notions of femininity in which their sexuality is perceived as being endangered and therefore needs to be protected. These notions are related to a particular phase in the course of their life. As migrant girls, they miss the protection of immediate family members and especially male relatives such as fathers and brothers who could protect them from unwelcome sexual advances, even though their presence is no guarantee. Often from lower socio-economic backgrounds, from rural areas, and sometimes from particular ethnic groups are factors in the risks to which adolescent girls are exposed. The types of risk that the adolescent girls and young women experienced at home, during their journeys, and at the place of destination are linked to their vulnerabilities. The risks of abuse, early marriage, sexual violence, and exploitation undermine their ability to cope with their experiences of migration. We turn to this discussion next.

Vulnerabilities

According to Robert Chambers:

> Vulnerability refers to exposure to contingencies and stress, and difficulty in coping with them. Vulnerability has thus two sides: an external side of risks, shocks, and stress to which an individual or household is subject; and an internal side which is defencelessness, meaning a lack of means to cope without damaging loss. Loss can take many forms—becoming or being physically weaker, economically impoverished, socially dependent, humiliated or psychologically harmed. (Chambers 1989, p. 1)

There are multiple sources of vulnerabilities for migrant and refugee girls and young women: their position as girls and women, from a specific ethnic and national background, their legal situation as foreigners, the absence of parents, guardians or relatives who could provide support, the nature of their work, their level of education, and the almost non-existent support from international, national and community organizations. These vulnerabilities constitute risks, shocks and stress that girls and their families experience and contribute to their lack of inner defences. As Moser and Holland argue, a social element of vulnerability includes "the insecurity of the wellbeing of individuals, households, or communities in the face of a changing environment" (1997, p. 5). These make migrant girls more vulnerable than their local peers, who were born and grew up in the places of destination. In the following section, we discuss the most important sources of vulnerability, which are closely related to the risks described in the first half of this chapter.

Being Alone

One of the main sources of vulnerability of migrant girls and young women is their limited network of community relations, especially during the first years of their arrival in the city. Tsedi, a sex worker in Addis Ababa, said:

> Life in in Addis is challenging. You can only cope with the city if you are a fast learner, or if you have a good family who gives you directions. But I didn't have anyone to give me advice and I did things as they came. This led me in the wrong direction.

As mentioned above, one of the main sources of vulnerability for migrant girls is the absence of their parents, or other close relatives, who can provide for and support them. Family relations are of utmost importance in Bangladeshi, Ethiopian and Eritrean societies and form the main source of an individual's support, both psychological and financial. Girls who have left, or lost, their parents in their places of origin are therefore extremely vulnerable to abuse and exploitation. Tigist's case is a good example. The absence of any male relatives is an added source of vulnerability. Girls who do not have a father or brothers are more vulnerable than girls who have male relatives in their place of origin. Ethiopia, Bangladesh, Eritrea and Sudan are patriarchal societies in which the status and living conditions of women and girls largely depends on the presence of men. Women and girls without male protection face numerous challenges, and those who have migrated to a city are even more vulnerable. The alternative support networks migrant girls create are very fragile. At the same time, it is important to recognize that not all families are sources of support, certainly not for those girls who were subject to abuse at home and for whom migration was an escape.

This paradox emerged clearly in Bangladesh, where protection also implies control. In Bangladesh, young female migrants often initially moved to be with an older sister or distant relatives, who may not treat them as well as their parents would. However, migrant girls can incur further risks if they live alone and lack 'an umbrella over their heads', as one neighbour said referring to a migrant girl: Jamila. In Jamila's case, the symbolic umbrella was the presence of her uncle with whose family she lived for a few months after arriving in Dhaka. Sharmeen (Chapter 5) went back to her ex-husband because she needed male social protection. As a divorced woman living independently in Dhaka, her social status was at stake. This was common for most of the young migrants we interviewed and distinguishes them from other adolescents who were born in the slum or had migrated and live with relatives. As the girls' stories show, living with close relatives is a source of support as well of as control and limitations. By leaving her uncle's house after a few months in Dhaka, Jamila became more independent but was far more exposed to different kinds of danger. Even more vulnerable are those migrants who do not have any male relatives or a reliable neighbour in their village who can take care of their female relatives. These relatives also sometimes travel to Dhaka to intervene in the lives of the migrant girls. The younger migrants felt helpless and insecure because of the absence of their parents and the lack of emotional support. Their situation had changed overnight from depending on their parents to one of *shadinota* (freedom). This brought some of them to regret their situation in the village where they felt controlled but also cared for. Some older migrants were in a more secure and stable situation. This was the case of those who had been living in Dhaka for longer and were earning more, and who felt self-confident enough to try to migrate further afield. This was also the case of some young women who became married in their place of destination, and had also been able to move from the *bustee* to better accommodation.

In some respects, migrant and local girls share similar sources of vulnerability and constraints due to their age and gender. For example, they share the same constraints in terms of mobility, possibility of interaction with boys and men, the same risks in terms of physical and sexual violence and ultimately the same social sanctions if and when they do not conform to the social norms, which regulate the transition to adulthood, sexuality and marriage. In all three case studies, these norms deny and repress premarital attraction and intimacy and limit the possibilities of girls and boys experiencing friendly relationships and getting to know each other before marriage. In Bangladesh, the social gender norms and the sanctions for breaking them seem to be more severe than in Ethiopia and Eritrea. For migrant girls living in the Middle East or in Sudan, an additional layer of gender norms operating in the host society places them in a lower social bracket than local girls. As mentioned in Chapter 4, Ethiopians and Eritreans are often seen as 'loose' and sexually available, which seems to the host society to justify the abuse towards them. This discrimination and stigmatization of migrant girls is another source of vulnerability. The fact that migrant girls are doing low-status jobs and are living without the protection of their family damages their social status. If they have problems, neighbours or other local people rarely support them. According to the girls interviewed in Addis Ababa, people turn their heads away and do not want to get involved in the case of conflicts. More importantly, law-enforcing bodies, such as the police, do not support migrant girls when they are the victims of crime. Sex workers in Addis Ababa in particular complained about the lack of respect for them and the various ways in which they are discriminated against and stigmatized. When their clients are violent, the police often turn a blind eye. In Khartoum, migrant girls and young women face the constant fear of arrest and imprisonment because of their lack of residence permits, or their perceived breaking of moral codes. This brings us to the specific vulnerabilities girls face as migrants, in particular outside their own countries.

Being a Migrant Girl

One of the key sources of vulnerability of girls who migrated abroad was their legal status in the country. The often irregular status of adolescent girls' and young women migrants in Khartoum significantly affects their vulnerability. While Sudan has been hosting refugees and migrants for decades, according to official policies, refugees are supposed to stay in refugee camps, not in cities. Those who move to Khartoum are often subjected to arbitrary arrests, police harassment, detention or even deportation. While most migrants and refugees are subject to such treatment, young girls and women are at a greater risk of sexual violence. Several girls shared their stories of random pick-ups by police or other Sudanese men who then raped them. Stories of harassment, both verbal and physical, was prominent in young women's narratives. In Khartoum, we witnessed several round-ups near the Ethiopian church in Khartoum 2 just after Sunday prayers. As 21-year-old Meseret from Ethiopia explained: "You know, these security people come in civil clothes, they sit with us, drink tea and chat, and then, they start rounding up people and put them to jail. They pretend they are our brothers, but they cheat us". Ruta commented: "I wish I could tell Sudanese that we, Habasha, are also human beings. They treat us like rubbish. But we have our humanity, we have our culture, we deserve respect".

As part of the research in Ethiopia, we interviewed 30 young women who had migrated to the Middle East when they were below the age of 18. They had changed their birth certificates in order to be allowed to migrate, but many of them became undocumented after having run away from their employers. Running away is one of the few possibilities of leaving a situation of abuse and exploitation and could be considered an act of resistance. Undocumented migrants run the risk of being arrested and deported, and are very vulnerable to violence and abuse. The stories of those who were deported from Saudi Arabia during the large-scale deportation campaign in 2013 and 2014 were particularly shocking. More than 160,000 Ethiopians were deported in a period of four months after the end of an amnesty period (see De Regt and Tafesse 2017; Lecadet and Tafesse 2018). The interviewed girls who were deported experienced violent arrest, imprisonment, sexual harassment and rape. Zemzem was 19 years old when we interviewed her. She first migrated from Debre Birhan, in Amhara region, to Addis Ababa, escaping the threat of early marriage. She lived for a while with her sister but left her after constant quarrels and became a domestic. At a certain point she decided to go abroad, aspiring to change her life structurally. She went to Saudi Arabia through a recruitment agent, on a two-year contract, but ran away. She was arrested when she was in the street:

> It was so bad, the police caught me when I went to a shop to buy oil. They put me in a car and took me to prison. In the prison I saw many Ethiopians, some of them were dying. The Saudi police put drugs in our bread to make us sleep because many people were having mental breakdowns.

For some migrant girls, their particular ethnic origin is the main source of vulnerability. The discrimination experienced by the ethnic minority Garo is reflected in the great obstacles migrant Garo girls encounter in owning and running their own beauty parlours, owing partly to the lack of financial capital for the initial investment and also to the lack of social capital in terms of connections (*jogajog*) with influential people. Ethiopian and Eritrean girls in Khartoum also experienced discrimination and stigmatization because of their ethnic background. Their physical appearance makes them stand out and be vulnerable to verbal and physical abuse. Several girls shared their stories of random pick-ups by police or by other Sudanese men who then raped them. One story was particularly dramatic. A 22-year-old mother of a three-year-old boy was lured by a group of three Sudanese men who then held her hostage for three days raping her in turn. Afterwards, they left her naked in the middle of a square in one of the popular neighbourhoods. She managed to find her way home, with strangers lending her clothes. She was greeted by a large group of Eritrean rickshaw drivers who were searching for her. Girls adopted a variety of strategies to remain invisible in the city, often by wearing black *abayas* (black robes worn in some Arab countries) and headscarves, an outfit seen as the appropriate attire for a Muslim girl in Sudan (see Chapter 7). Similar strategies are used by Ethiopian girls and women working in the Middle East, where they also face discrimination on the basis of their ethnic background (see Fernandez 2010; de Regt 2009). Ethiopian and Eritrean girls are seen as 'loose' and 'bad girls', who are sexually available, in particular when they live independently and so transgress the moral codes of *adab* (morality and proper behaviour).

This brings us to another important source of vulnerability, which is that migrant girls in Dhaka, Addis Ababa and Khartoum, with the exception of live-in domestic workers, live in rented housing. As a result, and also because they have not been living in the city for a long time, they occupy a lower layer in the power hierarchy of the residential areas. In the slums of Dhaka, informal power is wielded to the '*istanio*', and newcomers, especially migrant girls, can easily become homeless, for example, if they do not conform to the unwritten rules that govern the slum.

All of the girls interviewed said that one of the most important improvements in their situation would be to have their 'own place' to live. For Ethiopians and Eritreans living in Khartoum, the insecurity rental situation, high inflation and increasingly difficult economic context make them subject to pressures from and potential exploitation by the property owners. Young migrants and refugees tended to change their housing quite frequently, and as they were also in rather insecure working situations, they often lacked money for the rent and thus needed to move frequently. As mentioned in Chapter 4, sex workers in Addis Ababa also move house frequently because of the high rent, but also because they did not want to become known as sex workers in the area where they were living.

In all three case studies, limited support from community organizations, international and national organizations, the national government, or embassies abroad further marginalizes migrant and refugee adolescent girls and young women (see Chapter 7). These vulnerabilities of the migrant girls and young women expose the multifaceted aspect of vulnerability: political, economic and social. At times, the sources of vulnerability are individual risk factors while at others they are structural or institutional norms and regulations and gender norms. Chambers draws attention to the distinction between vulnerability and poverty. Vulnerability as we have presented here, "means not lack or want, but defencelessness, insecurity, and exposure to risk, shocks and stress" (Chambers 1989, p. 1). Our examples point to individual, household and structural characteristics and outcomes. They also show that vulnerability is multilayered, changing across time and space. In this way, they show the links between vulnerability to access and ownership of assets, and the role of social ties and institutional arrangements, as well as particular social relations operating in different geographical contexts. An important further structural aspect of vulnerability is volatility, which as demonstrated in our research, is omnipresent in the lives of adolescent migrant girls and young women.

Intersecting Vulnerabilities: Gender, Age and Migration

Gender, age and migration intersect in such ways that migrant girls are extremely vulnerable and face major risks; the mere fact that they are living in the cities without the protection of their parents and in particular without male relatives, and hence do not conform to the dominant gender order, has a great impact on their social status and consequently on their vulnerability. A longer perspective on the lives of adolescent girl migrants and refugees demonstrates that their lives are overwhelmingly volatile. We follow the metaphor and approach developed by Room (2000) in particular, who emphasizes one key dimension of vulnerability. 'Snakes and ladders' refers to expected and unexpected variability that can lead to advance (ladder) or decline (snake) in well-being. Due to the extreme volatility that marks the everyday experiences of migrant adolescent girls, the girls and young women find it difficult to carry out their plans or even to make other than very short-term ones. Their lives are thus marked by protracted uncertainty and precariousness (Horst and Grabska 2015). In Chapter 5 we showed that most of the migrant girls had little knowledge of what they could expect in the cities. They took a risk by migrating and were often ill-prepared and so were confronted with various challenges. These challenges were in many cases related to being girls of a particular age, who migrated on their own to the city. Even when they had been prepared, however, the conditions of their migration were uncertain. As Williams and Baláž (2012, p. 169) argue, migration can better be associated with uncertainty than with risk.

The stories of the girls presented in this chapter vividly illustrate how volatility and vulnerability are part of everyday experience. In Khartoum, for example, throughout the fieldwork, girls' and young women's circumstances were changing very rapidly. Losing and changing jobs and housing was a common, almost daily, experience. Ruptures and crises in the families who stayed behind, perhaps leading to unpredicted arrivals of siblings, often put pressure on the young women.

In Dhaka, the whole garment industry is characterized by insecurity and precariousness. A factory may suddenly close down and jobs be lost; hours and wages may be reduced. The girls themselves may have to leave because of a health emergency and after returning home for treatment, they lose their jobs. Like all those who live in the *bustee*, but more likely than most, migrant girls are at risk of eviction. As we observed by following some of the migrants over more than a year, their situations, as well as those of their families, are also quite volatile. The fate and well-being of a girl migrant and those of her family can change overnight. They are affected by many different factors and events: the sudden death of parents or siblings at home, for example, the illness of children, getting married or divorced, the intrusive surveillance of neighbours, can completely modify the migrant's opportunities and obligations. In Ethiopia, financial volatility was constant in the lives of sex workers who always ran short of money and whose income was unstable and unpredictable. Other financial difficulties arose when they had to change their accommodation, which happened often. Ever-present volatility in their lives affects migrant girls' ability to make longer-term plans and undermines their ability to respond to sudden changes in their situations and to withstand shocks. Being out of their protective environment exacerbates these difficulties and the additional penalties of being adolescent or young, of being girls or women, and being migrants, reinforce the fragility and precariousness of their lives.

In all three countries, the risks, vulnerabilities and volatilities that are associated with being migrant girls are very acute and often more so than those of girls and women who have not migrated. They are certainly different and often more severe than those of young men. Their stories demonstrate how the experience of risk, vulnerability and volatility is gendered and potentially limits or affects the course of changes in gender relations. Some of these risks and vulnerabilities might be mitigated by the available institutional support system, but also by the girls' own agency in expanding their social capital. We will turn to this discussion in the next chapter.

References

Abebe, T., & Skovdal, M. (2010). Livelihoods, Care and the Familial Relations of Orphans in Eastern Africa. *AIDS Care, 22*(5), 570–576.

Boholm, Å. (2003). The Cultural Nature of Risk: Can There Be an Anthropology of Uncertainty? *Ethnos, 68*(2), 159–178.

Both, R. (2017). *Sex, Tensions and Pills: Young People's Use of Contemporary Reproductive and Sexual Health Technologies in Addis Ababa, Ethiopia*. Ph.D. dissertation, University of Amsterdam.

Boyden, J., Pankhurst, A., & Tafere, A. (2012). Child Protection and Harmful Traditional Practices: Female Early Marriage and Genital Modification in Ethiopia. *Development in Practice, 22*(4), 510–522.

Camellia, S., Khan, N. N., & Naved R. T. (2012). Violence Against Unmarried Adolescent Girls. In R. T. Naved & S. Amin (Eds.), *Growing Up Safe and Healthy (SAFE): Baseline Report on Sexual and Reproductive Health and Rights and Violence Against Women and Girls in Dhaka Slums*. Dhaka: Icddr,b.

Chambers, R. (Ed.). (1989). Vulnerability: How the Poor Cope. *IDS Bulletin, 20*(2), 1–7.

de Regt, M. (2009). Preferences and Prejudices: Employers' Views on Domestic Workers in the Republic of Yemen. *Signs: Journal of Women in Culture and Society, 34*(3), 559–582.

De Regt, M., & Tafesse, M. (2017). "Deported Before Experiencing the Good Sides of Migration": Ethiopians Returning from Saudi Arabia. In F. Demissie (Ed.), *Ethiopians in an Era of Migration: Scattered Beyond Borders* (pp. 104–118). London: Routledge.

Erulkar, A. (2014). *Building the Assets to Thrive: Addressing the HIV-Related Vulnerabilities of Adolescent Girls in Ethiopia*. New York: Population Council.

Erulkar, A., & Mekbib, T. (2007). Invisible and Vulnerable: Adolescent Domestic Workers in Addis Ababa. *Ethiopia. Vulnerable Children and Youth Studies, 2*(3), 246–256.

Esim, S., & Smith, M. (2004). *Gender and Migration in Arab States: The Case of Domestic Workers*. Beirut: International Labour Organization.

Fernandez, B. (2010). Cheap and Disposable? The Impact of the Global Economic Crisis on the Migration of Ethiopian Women Domestic Workers to the Gulf. *Gender & Development, 18*(2), 249–262.

Fernandez, B., & de Regt, M. (2014). *Making a Home in the World: Migrant Domestic Workers in the Middle East*. New York: Palgrave Macmillan.

García-Moreno, C., et al. (2005). Public Health Violence Against Women. *Science, 310*, 1282–1283.

Heinonen, P. (2011). *Youth Gangs and Street Children: Culture, Nurture and Masculinity in Ethiopia*. New York and Oxford: Berghahn.

Horst, C., & Grabska, K. (2015). Flight and Exile: Uncertainty in the Context of Conflict-Induced Displacement. *Social Analysis, 59*(1), 1–18.

Kebede, M. T., Hilden, P. K., & Middelthon, A. (2014). Negotiated Silence: The Management of Self as a Moral Subject in Young Ethiopian Women's Discourse about Sexuality. *Sex Education, 14*(6), 666–678.

Kindler, M. (2011). *A Risky Business? Ukranian Migrant Women in Warsaw's Domestic Work Sector*. Amsterdam: University of Amsterdam Press.

Lecadet, C., & Tafesse, M. (2018). The Expulsion of Ethiopian Workers from Saudi Arabia (2013–2014): The Management of a Humanitarian and Political Crisis. *Annales d'Ethiopie 2016–2017, 31*, 225–243.

Moser, C., & Holland, J. (1997). *Urban Poverty and Violence in Jamaica.* Washington, DC: World Bank.

National Institute of Population Research and Training (NIPORT)., et al. (2008). *2006 Bangladesh Demographic and Health Survey.* Dhaka: NIPORT.

Osella, C., & Osella, F. (2002). Contextualising Sexuality: Young Men in Kerala, South India. In L. Rice Pranee & L. Manderson (Eds.). *Coming of Age in South and Southeast Asia: Youth, Courtship and Sexuality* (113–131). Richmond, UK: Curzon.

Room, G. (2000). Trajectories of Social Exclusion: The Wider Context for the Third and First Worlds. In D. Gordon & P. Townsend (Eds.), *Breadline Europe: The Measurement of Poverty* (pp. 407–440). Bristol: Policy Press.

Save the Children. (2008). A Study on Violence against Girls in Primary Schools and Its Impact on Girls' Education in Ethiopia. Addis Ababa: Save the Children Denmark, Ministry of Education and Ministry of Women's Affairs.

Tadele, G. (2006). *Bleak Prospects: Young Men, Sexuality and HIV/AIDS in an Ethiopian Town.* Leiden: African Studies Centre.

Williams, A. M., & Baláž, V. (2012). Migration, Risk, and Uncertainty: Theoretical Perspectives. *Population, Space and Place, 18,* 167–180.

Worku, A., & Addissie, M. (2002). Sexual Violence Among Female High School Students in Debark, Northwest Ethiopia. *East Africa Medical Journal, 97*(2), 96–99.

Zinn, J. (2006). Risk, Affect and Emotion. *Forum: Qualitative Social Research, 7*(1), art. 29.

CHAPTER 7

Being Protected and Protecting Yourself

"*You Have to Learn How to Protect Yourself*": Tsirite's Quest for Protection

"No one protects you here, you are on your own. You have to learn how to protect yourself". This was the usual response of the girls and young women interviewed in the three cities. Learning to protect oneself was also often seen as a positive consequence of migration in their narratives. "If I go home now, even if I have not made a lot of money, I have seen many things in my life, I have faced many hardships. I learned how to take care of myself", said Tsirite, a 22-year-old from Axum in Ethiopia. She arrived in Khartoum when she was 17 years old with her best friend Mashou, who was then aged 16. They used an Ethiopian agent (smuggler) to bring them to Sudan, but they both ended up working without pay as live-in domestics for Sudanese families. She described how she learned to rely on herself:

> When I arrived in Khartoum, the agent (*samsara*) made me work as a cleaner for a Sudanese woman for 200 SDG [US$25 a month at that time]. After one month she did not pay my salary. I argued with the woman and told her that if she wanted me to work there, she has to pay me. She threatened me with the police, but I said to her, although I could not communicate well in Arabic, that I did not care. The police would do nothing to me, or nothing worse than I was already experiencing. I took

K. Grabska et al., *Adolescent Girls' Migration in The Global South*, Palgrave Studies on Children and Development,
https://doi.org/10.1007/978-3-030-00093-6_7

> some salt and put it in the water and told her: 'I am not like salt, I will not melt and dissolve in water'. I called some friends and told them to come and take me. I told the woman, 'If you want me to work for you, you have to pay my salary'. And then I left. I told her that I was going to a house in Bahri [one of the three main parts of Khartoum], but I went to another place so that she could not find me. After some time, the woman came and begged me to come back to work. She agreed to pay me 340 SDG.

We met Tsirite in the main Ethiopian Orthodox Church in Khartoum, while she was attending an Easter prayer. Dressed in her traditional Ethiopian *zoraya* dress and with her head covered, Tsirite looked very tall. She invited us to her place, a small room in a compound shared by several Ethiopians, Eritreans and a Sudanese family. Sitting around a little table in the shared living room and drinking coffee, Tsirite was laughing while telling us the story. She was so confident and so proud of her inner strength and the fact that she does not allow anyone to abuse her.

> I worked since I was 13 years old. I know how to survive and take care of myself. I am not afraid of anybody, nobody can scare me. I was good at work and the woman liked me. The Sudanese do not care if you are very tired. You are working, and they are sitting, dressing up, putting on make-up. Even if you are in the other corner of the house, and they want a glass of water that is next to them, they will call you to make you come and get it for them. Sudanese just sit and watch us work. And we, *Habesha*, we like to work. I worked for nine months for this woman, and then I told her that I would go back to my country. I did not tell her where I live [the house of the broker] and I gave her a wrong address. This is how I finished working for her.

The narratives of adolescent girls and young women migrants and refugees in Addis Ababa, Dhaka and Khartoum were filled with similar stories of resistance and resilience. In the absence of official protection, and facing numerous risks, setbacks and vulnerabilities (see Chapter 6), migrant girls needed to build up a social network and protect themselves. These insights of resistance, resilience and of enacting protection for themselves and for their household members, friends and often fellow migrants contribute to wider debates about social protection in the context of migration (see Levitt et al. 2016; Levitt et al. 2015; Faist 2013, 2014). There has been much written about remittances, both financial and social, and on social protection for migrants, especially those in developed countries. Yet little is known about how young migrants and refugees, and especially adolescent girls and young women, deal with issues of protection, and social protection in particular, in the context of migration, especially in countries of destination or transit in the Global South, where institutionalized forms of (social) protection are limited or non-existent. Moreover, the remittances they send home fund health, education and social services which migrant-sending governments do not provide or households cannot afford, and "the social remittances, or the knowledge, practices, and skills which migration also introduces, transform social and economic life in positive and negative ways" (Levitt et al. 2016, p. 2; see Chapter 9).

In this chapter, we analyze how young people on the move are protected and provided for in contemporary global contexts. We look at the sources of protection and support on which migrant and refugee girls can rely on the three countries. The first section examines institutionalized (social) protection and support and argues that while adolescent migrant girls are clearly visible in the three capital cities, they are largely invisible for those planning and implementing development interventions. Girls, like Tsirite, rely mostly on informal sources of support such as those offered by social and religious networks. This will be discussed in the second section. In the third section, we examine how girls build social capital by supporting each other and sharing resources, housing, money and food. These self-protection strategies also extend to providing social and economic protection for families, friends and loved-ones both in places of origin as well as in other migration destinations where relatives and friends are scattered. These transnational and trans-local networks of (social) protection created by adolescent girls and young women point to their resourcefulness and ability to take action in response to their vulnerabilities. In addition, they show how the failure of governments to provide social protection to the country's citizens, especially those who are marginalized, has consequences for deepening gender inequalities and placing a burden on young people.

Governmental and Organizational Support and Protection

In global development policy discourses, adolescent girls have been identified as a major focus group (see Chapters 1 and 3). Migrant and refugee girls have, however, been given much less attention at the national level in terms of protection and support. Despite the large numbers of adolescent migrant girls and the presence of many international and local organizations in Dhaka, Addis Ababa and Khartoum, there is a lack of institutional support networks that could protect them. Government institutions have no particular policies regarding migrant girls and national and international organizations rarely treat them as a specific group for projects and programmes. In our interviews with representatives of these organizations and government institutions in the three cities, we often heard that migrant and refugee girls are their "interest and priority", although there were scant references to specific programmes and projects. All three countries are the signatories to the United Nations Convention on the Rights of the Child, and Ethiopia and Sudan of the African Charter and a number of other international declarations, which include clauses referring to the rights of children and the rights of migrants and refugees. The fact that these do not translate into policies to protect children and migrants is the main problem.

In Bangladesh, policy and development interventions have focused on adolescent girls mainly in relation to and as possible victims of child marriage. Most of these interventions are framed in the language of human rights and identify the expansion of secondary education as the main means to postpone girls' marriage and tackle its negative consequences: early child-bearing and the consequent health risks for the mother and child, domestic violence and the intergenerational transmission of poverty. Some projects also try to postpone girls' marriage by providing opportunities for training and involvement in income-generating activities. The Population Council Bangladesh has been running a project called Bangladeshi Association for Life Skills, Income, and Knowledge for Adolescents (BALIKA) to evaluate the effectiveness of different approaches to prevent child marriage. The project has several components. Education support offers in-school girls tuition in mathematics and English and computing or financial skill training for out-of-school girls. In the life-skills component, girls receive training on gender issues, women rights and negotiation, critical thinking and decision-making; and in relation to livelihoods, girls are trained in entrepreneurship, mobile-phone servicing, photography and basic first aid.

In a similar vein, the Kishori Abhijan (literally 'adolescent journey') project is an example of a comprehensive attempt to postpone marriage for girls and promote "girls' empowerment". A pilot phase of Kishori Abhijan ran from 2001 to 2005 and a second phase, funded by the

European Union Delegation to Bangladesh, from 2006 to 2011. The project was jointly implemented by Unicef Bangladesh and the Ministry of Women and Children Affairs (MoWCA) and some local NGOs. The project's main objectives are "to empower adolescents, especially girls, to participate meaningfully in decisions that affect their lives (including education, livelihood strategies and increasing age at marriage) and to become active agents of social change and to create and sustain a supportive environment for adolescent girl development at the household and community level" (Sood and Shuaib 2011, p. iv). Another major area of interventions in Bangladesh seeks to improve the working conditions of garment workers, but there is no particular focus on adolescent migrant girls. A recent three-year project funded by the Europe Aid and implemented by three local NGOs focused on children's rural–urban migration and involves mostly child domestic workers. It entails interventions in some districts of southern Bangladesh to identify the poorest households that would be more likely to send children to towns to work as domestics in order to 'prevent' their migration and/or register them so that they could be followed up in their migratory trajectories.

In Ethiopia, the migration of children, including adolescents, has only recently become an area for interventions by local and international organizations. For example, the Population Council, in cooperation with the OAK Foundation and Save the Children has conducted studies and initiated interventions to protect and support "children on the move". Save the Children is a partner of Terre des Hommes and in that capacity was involved in the "Destination Unknown" campaign. Local organizations such as CHADET (the Organization for Child Development and Transformation) and OPRIFS (the Organization for the Prevention, Rehabilitation and Integration of Female Street Children) have launched programmes aimed at independent migrant children. The main goal of these interventions is to prevent children from migrating and to rehabilitate children that have run into problems. More recently, projects are being developed that focus on ensuring safer migration of children rather than seeking to prevent children from migrating. The Bureau of the Ministry of Women, Children and Youth is involved in protecting and rehabilitating children who migrate independently and takes its responsibility very seriously. There are, however, no interventions or support mechanisms that specifically focus on migrant adolescent girls. Adolescent girls are mainly the focus of development interventions in the field of education, campaigns against early marriage, and HIV and

AIDS.[1] Most of the migrant-specific activities are directed at migrant children outside Addis Ababa, and migrant girls in Addis Ababa do not benefit from them. In Addis Ababa, the most important sources of protection for migrant girls are organizations that support sex workers such as NIKAT Charitable Society (see Chapter 6) and Timret Le Hiwot, and organizations such as OPRIFS, which supports girls who live on the streets, often after having run away from abusive employment. While a considerable number of sex workers are under 18 years of age, and many have a migrant background, adolescent migrant girls are not distinguished as a group that needs special interventions. These organizations do, however, provide important support for migrant girls, and those who are involved and benefit from their activities are often very positive about them.

In Khartoum, international organizations are abundant but none of them focuses specifically on adolescent migrant girls. The United Nations High Commissioner for Refugees (UNHCR) offers financial, legal and psychosocial referrals for registered refugees. With its commitment to gender equality and focus on diversity (with specific mentioning of youth), UNHCR has special focal points for dealing with children, trafficked persons, and those who have suffered gender-based and sexual violence. However, none of the Eritrean girls and young women who participated in the research was aware of the presence of UNHCR in Khartoum. Some, through our research and outreach activities, subsequently learned about and sought UNHCR's protection services. A couple of girls who had been traumatized by their experiences of being kidnapped by Rashaida (see Chapters 4 and 6), or by spending months in an Egyptian jail while attempting to cross through Egypt and eventually Europe, were given psychological assistance. Three were referred for resettlement to third countries due to their vulnerabilities and particular protection needs, but eventually only one was resettled in Germany, with UNHCR's assistance.

Other organizations, such as Unicef and Save the Children focus on the Sudanese population, even though they argue that their mandate includes anyone residing in Sudan. International Organisation for Migration (IOM) has a large presence in Khartoum and in Sudan more

[1]For examples of the projects of the Population Council, see Ferede and Erulkar (2009), Girma and Erulkar (2009); and Girl Effect Ethiopia (https://www.girleffect.org/where-we-work/africa/ethiopia/).

generally. However, they offer very general support to migrants, mainly in terms of information campaigns and medical checks for those who are being resettled and support for returning migrants. A newly created information centre for migrants was launched in 2016. Representatives of IOM in an interview admitted that they have never recorded an adolescent migrant or a young woman who approached the office, and more generally, there were only a handful of migrants who visited the office in the previous year. None of the Sudanese government institutions has any specific programmes or projects addressing young migrants or refugees. Most local NGO programmes are focused on women and girls in general and are not specifically aimed at migrants. One of the few local organizations that assist migrant and refugee girls is SEEMA, a centre for training and protection on gender-based violence. It provides psychosocial and legal assistance, capacity building of service providers and expanding the network of NGOs working with internally displaced persons (IDPs) and refugees. Another organization is Al Fanar, which offers psychosocial assistance to refugees. SIHA, a regional network working on women's rights, has a number of projects focusing on migrant communities, including girls and young women. Again, the girls who participated in the research knew nothing about these initiatives, although our research alerted several of the girls and young women to these organizations, who then approached them for assistance. One of the Eritrean researchers was trained at SEEMA on gender-based violence and subsequently became a point of reference in her community. She was able to identify and refer several adolescent girls and young women who had experienced gender-based violence to SEEMA. In this way, the participation in the research became a learning opportunity for her, which served a wider Eritrean refugee community in Khartoum.

Ethiopian migrant girls working as domestics in the Middle East have very limited sources of support and protection. There is almost no legal protection of their rights and, where there is, girls do not know how to take advantage of them. Domestic work is not covered by the labour laws in the Middle East so migrant girls who run into problems have no recourse to complain about their working conditions. There are very few NGOs that protect the rights of migrant women in the Middle East, in particular on the Arabian Peninsula where CSOs are strictly controlled by the state and migrant organizations even more so (Fernandez and de Regt 2014). In cases where migrant girls are able to leave the employers' house to seek help, they contact the Ethiopian embassy, but assistance is offered only to those with legal status. The fact that adolescent girls often enter the country undocumented or with false documents affects their chance of receiving assistance. Ethiopian Associations, which are linked to embassies, sometimes provide financial and legal assistance and offer temporary accommodation but they lack the capacity to help large numbers of girls and women. This was also the case in Khartoum. The Ethiopian Association offers a more specialized service for young women and girls and runs the only shelter open to migrant women and girls. At the time of the interview in May 2016, there were some seven women staying at the shelter, most of them with small children. The majority had experienced sexual violence, abandonment by their families, or had children outside marriage. The Ethiopian Association also provides financial and legal assistance to those who want to return to Ethiopia but do not have the necessary papers or sufficient funds. In some cases, it offers legal assistance to Ethiopians who have been raped. It was also involved in the highly publicized case in 2014 of an 18-year-old girl who was gang-raped and then imprisoned and prosecuted for 'adultery' and 'indecent behaviour' and breach of the Public Order Law.[2] Although the Ethiopian Association is one of the oldest and most active community organizations operating in Khartoum, none of the Ethiopian girls and women interviewed for the research ever used its services or knew about what type of assistance it offered. Thus, such official assistance is often limited in scope, especially for those who are undocumented or are unaware of its existence.

While official institutions at times offer protection to migrant and refugee girls and women, it is usually within the framework of gendered vulnerabilities and victimization, rather than perceiving migrant women and girls as deserving protection and assistance based on their rights as citizens, migrants or refugees. Rather than being protected, girls and women sometimes suffered abuse and victimization at the hands of government officials, including being raped by police officers, extortion and threats of deportation. Ethiopians and Eritreans in Khartoum often experienced such treatment due to their more precarious position as foreigners in the country (see Chapter 6).

[2] See http://www.bbc.com/news/world-africa-26286264.

Protecting Themselves: Informal Sources of Protection

In research with or about migrants, the concept of social capital is often used, although in different ways (Fig. 7.1). The concept itself has been criticized both for being too loosely defined (Rossem et al. 2015) and for its political agenda (Cheong et al. 2007). Its theoretical dimension does, however, offer interesting insights for the analysis of how those lacking in official support networks develop their own forms of protection. We use the definition of Portes, who was inspired by Bourdieu's work. He defines social capital as "the ability of actors to secure benefits by virtue of membership in social networks or other structures" (Portes 1998, p. 6). Such networks consist of friends, acquaintances, colleagues, neighbours, family members or other contacts, and means that people belonging to them can mobilize these networks for material gain, protection, status or other valued attributes. Social networks have both enabled migration (Dannecker 2005; Hagan 1998; Massey et al. 1987; Portes and Rumbaut 1996) and helped migrants to settle in (Portes 1995; Portes and Rumbaut 1996), as well as sometimes hindering such processes (see Cranford 2005; Padilla 2006; Portes 1998). While the concepts of social capital and social networks have been widely used in migration research, they have rarely been used in research with young

Fig. 7.1 Ethiopian church in Khartoum, Sudan

migrants.[3] Here, we use these terms to refer to the informal social protection that adolescent girls' and women migrants and refugees establish in each location.

In the absence of institutional support networks, adolescent migrant girls turn to informal sources of protection, such as those offered by social and religious networks. In this way, they build on and extend their social capital and ability to address their vulnerabilities. Religious faith often assumes more importance among migrants, as is also discussed in the literature on religion and migration (see Spickard and Adogame 2010; Village et al. 2017). Religious networks can provide psychological, practical and sometimes financial support. Churches in Ethiopia and Sudan in particular were major sources of support. Ethiopia is a highly religious society, the main denominations being the Ethiopian Orthodox Church, Muslim or Protestant (often Pentecostal). Islam is the state religion in Sudan, but other denominations can practise their religion. There are Catholic, Protestant and Ethiopian Orthodox churches, whose main adherents comprise migrants and refugees (also from South Sudan). When asked whether religion had become more important in migration, an Eritrean girl in Khartoum who had joined a Pentecostal congregation said:

> Of course it has. Most of us here in Sudan, in Khartoum, we are alone. We spend our days worrying and struggling. When we come to the church, we are close to Jesus, we are happy. We can share with others, and we hear from the pastor that we are not alone, that Jesus is with us, even if our lives are difficult, we are not alone. This makes me happy. When I leave the church, I feel happy, I feel uplifted.

For adolescent migrant girls in Addis Ababa the church was mainly a source of psychological support. Tigist, a sex worker whose story was presented in Chapter 6, said: "I love going to church when I am depressed. I love praying to God to help me stop doing this job. Although I never wanted this life, I thank God for everything". She also mentioned, however, that people discriminate against her and criticize her for going to church. "People say: 'How can you go to church while you are doing this type of work?'" Churches in Ethiopia do not offer

[3]For an exception see research on education among migrant youth, e.g., Rübner Jørgensen (2017).

practical or financial support to migrant girls; girls go to church only for psychological support. In Bangladesh, the Catholic and Protestant churches and some missionary congregations active in the capital and in the area of origin of the Garo migrants and are an important source of social security for migrant girls, in addition to providing employment opportunities. Churches are not only places where people can gather. As discussed in detail in Chapter 5, they also offer financial support, accommodation, food and, at times, facilitate further migration. While the help is usually extended to members of the congregation, we found several examples of churches helping others, which was sometimes perceived as a way of gaining new church members, and in Sudan particularly dangerous given the political struggles over religious influences.

Socially, adolescent migrant girls in Sudan and Ethiopia who have freedom of movement sometimes frequent places where they can meet others and obtain support and information, such as Internet cafés, shops, restaurants and coffee places, and in doing so increase their public presence. In Khartoum, for example, Internet cafés are major places to advertise offers of marriage to diaspora members. Cafés and restaurants are also places where Eritreans and Ethiopians can socialize, spend time together, share food, exchange the latest news, meet potential smugglers and be less isolated. Most of these places, however, are inaccessible to the girls and young women due to strict gender norms and the gendered division of space. Unless they work in these places, they are mainly frequented by men who, as a result, have a better access to information. The differentiated access to jobs and public spaces for girls and young women influences their access to information and their ability to create social capital. Consequently, those who work in more isolated jobs (such as live-in domestic workers) have fewer possibilities to expand their range of opportunities.

In Bangladesh, migrant adolescent girls are also restricted in their freedom of movement. First, they have very little free time to go out and visit public spaces, and second, their social reputation is endangered if they are seen in (Internet) cafés or restaurants. Shopping is one of the few leisure activities that are acceptable for them. In view of the restrictions on their mobility, mobile phones have become extremely important in the lives of adolescent migrant girls. Once they buy a mobile phone they start widening their social network and overcoming initial fears and shyness. In Khartoum too, mobile phones play a major role. Ethiopian and Eritrean girls stay in touch with their families, as well as with friends and relatives in other parts of the world. They are often active on Facebook and derive great pleasure from posting pictures of themselves (see Grabska 2016; see Chapter 5). For domestic workers in the Middle East mobile phones are also crucial for keeping in touch with their loved-ones. Domestic workers in Addis Ababa often earn too little to be able to purchase a mobile phone.

Family and friends in the diaspora are usually a major source of support especially for Eritreans, but often migrants become rather disillusioned with the lack of assistance. Tsirite, cited at the beginning of this chapter, worked as a tea-maker. When we visited her with Bana, the Eritrean researcher, she asked whether she had relatives abroad and why they were not helping her to get somewhere else. She commented that Ethiopians are not very good at helping each other, but Eritreans usually are. Bana replied that not all Eritreans are the same. Although she has family members abroad, they had not helped her for the six years she had been in Khartoum. "I have to find ways of helping myself", underlined Bana, stressing her own resilience. As in other cases, there is great pressure from those in the countries of origin or in transit on family members in the diaspora to send remittances or to sponsor resettlement (Al Sharmani 2006). A young Eritrean woman, Salha, who was resettled in Canada when she was 22 years old, after spending five years in Khartoum, and came back to Sudan to marry her boyfriend commented:

> The people here [in Sudan] do not understand that it is very difficult to be a migrant or refugee also in Canada. In Canada, nobody helps you. And you die, if you do not help yourself. You have to work a lot. Since I had been there, for one year now, I have been working two jobs. I do not sleep. I had to make enough money to be able to sponsor my boyfriend and marry. But many of my friends did not understand that I did not have money to help them. They are now upset with me. I can tell you this because you know how it is [referring to Katarzyna]. But they think we are just sitting on our beds and the government gives us money. My plan was to study, but instead, I just have to work to be able to help all these people in Eritrea and in Sudan. It is very exhausting.

Most of the Ethiopian respondents in Khartoum did not have family members outside Africa. They came from families where they were usually the first migrants, or with some connections to migrants in Ethiopia. Thus, they did not receive the same type of support and assistance from community members in the diaspora, and nor did girls and young women in Addis Ababa and Dhaka. However, among the girls who had migrated to the Middle East there were more cases of family members, in particular sisters, who had helped them to migrate as they were themselves already working in the region. They had obtained a visa with the help of a relative and sometimes benefited from their presence.

Building Social Capital

One of the main ways in which migrant adolescent girls and young women support each other is by sharing resources, housing, money and food (Fig. 7.2). Connecting with other migrants, those who have been in the city for a long time, relatives or friends, serves as a major support system. Building social capital was, therefore, a key element in most of the girls' narratives. They often talked about the help that they received from strangers, other young migrants, or community groups, or in the case of Eritreans in Khartoum from church groups. They developed new networks of friendships. Friendships develop easily between girls who are working in the same factory in Dhaka, are sex workers in the same area in Addis Ababa, or share a journey to Sudan or a room in Khartoum. Profound affective friendships may develop into important sources of support in times of need. Tigist, whose story we described in Chapter 6, had a long-standing friendship with Worku. They had met when they had both started working as sex workers, were living together and sharing expenses. Tigist helped Worku care for her two children, who were growing up without their father.

The examples of strangers helping each other point to the ability to recast social and family relations in the place of migration. Almas, a 21-year-old Eritrean refugee who came to Khartoum when she was 17, explained:

> We did not know each other before coming here. But these girls saw me suffering in Shegerab camp [Eritrean refugee camp in eastern Sudan where most Eritrean refugees pass through on the way to Khartoum] and then they helped me to come here. Since then we have been staying together and sharing together. We help each other.

At times, girls would by chance meet neighbours or distant relatives from back home. Others would try to create good relations with their

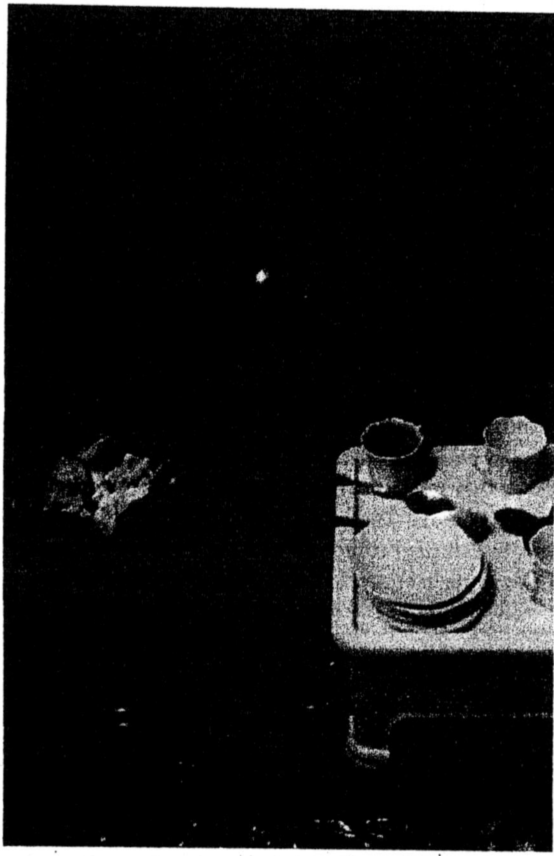

Fig. 7.2 Coffee making and socialising in Addis Ababa and in Khartoum

new neighbours. Mashou, an 18-year-old friend of Tsirite with whom she came to Khartoum from Ethiopia and shared accommodation, explained about the atmosphere at their compound, where she shares a place with her Ethiopian girlfriends:

> All the neighbours who live here love each other. If they make coffee we all drink together. I don't drink coffee normally but if they offer me I drink it out of respect. We build relations with everyone. They [the

> neighbours to the right] are from Eritrea. Two girls work for Sudanese family with me. They are from Ethiopia.

The vulnerability of girls and women is thus minimized due to their capacity to create a safe environment, or the capacity for the environment to be safe.

Domestic workers are more isolated and have fewer possibilities to build social capital. For migrant domestic workers in Addis Ababa attending evening classes can be a strategy to meet other girls and build up friendships, and sometimes they assist and advise them. Their teachers can also be important contacts if they are in need of assistance or advice. Domestic workers who are not allowed to leave the house unaccompanied or who have a very heavy workload have far fewer possibilities to build up social capital. They depend to a large extent on their employers and their willingness to assist them if they are in need (see Chapter 6).

In the interviews with sex workers in Addis Ababa the expansion of their social network was often mentioned as one of the positive sides of their migration (see Chapter 10). It is often argued in the migration literature that social networks among immigrants can be segmented in various ways, such as along gender lines and so have different consequences for men and women (Dannecker 2005; Hagan 1998). In the study among Bangladeshis in Malaysia, Dannecker found hardly any interaction between migrant men and women. Roggeveen and Van Meeteren questioned the existence of a coherent Brazilian community in Amsterdam, emphasizing divisions along the lines of immigration status, nature of work, and often political views (Roggeveen and Van Meeteren 2013). Among migrant and refugee girls and young women in Addis Ababa, Dhaka, and Khartoum, social networks were an important element in building their social capital and also in ensuring their protection. While the networks were segmented across different lines (legal status, nationality or religious denomination), migrants and refugees usually took advantage of the diverse networking possibilities and drew on each network's opportunities to enlarge their access to protection, rights, and security. Girls' ability to draw on various networks increased their social capital and provided an important safety net in their volatile circumstances. Tigist (Chapter 6) was very willing to become a research assistant in our project, and later to participate in the documentary. She had good communication and language skills and used her social network at NIKAT to make use of opportunities that may help improve her life.

Later, when her coffee shop failed, she turned to her old friends, who assisted her finding a place to stay. Clearly, not all migrant and refugee girls and young women are able to take advantage of social networks and boost their social capital. As a result, those who are able to build social capital are better able to protect themselves than those whose social network is very limited.

Locating Social Protection in Translocal Networks

Although there are numerous organizations that support women, young people and children in Bangladesh, Ethiopia and Sudan, few of them focus in particular on adolescent migrant girls. The large number of migrant and refugee girls in these cities makes it also difficult to reach them, if they want to be reached at all. Most of the formal assistance frames adolescent girl migrants and refugees as victims. Thus, in order for them to gain access to it, girls and women have to emphasize their vulnerability, and thus perpetuate the gendered nature of formal protection. In addition, migrant and refugee girls, and domestic workers in particular, are often not aware of the available services and support mechanisms. Sex workers in Addis Ababa are more knowledgeable about the available services and have stronger support networks than domestic workers, but their work makes them very vulnerable to abuse, violence and exploitation.

Despite the rhetoric, there is very little institutional and organizational support for adolescent migrant and refugee girls in all three cases. They therefore depend largely on informal networks. In the next chapter, we discuss the various ways in which migrant girls exert agency and show resilience as a result of their own efforts to protect themselves and their household members, and to cope with situations of vulnerability and risk. Girls' own efforts to stay protected also show that they are not simply victims of risks and circumstances but are able to act upon their own vulnerabilities and minimize them to certain extent.

Another interesting point related to (social) protection, which will be further discussed in Chapter 9, relates to girls' and young women's efforts to ensure the protection of family and household members across locations. By sending (often minimal) financial support to their families back home (within the country or across national frontiers), adolescent girl migrants and refugees are able to enhance the protection of their household members in situations of crisis such as health problems, death, and in investing in their sibling' education, buying land and improving daily access to food for their relatives. In the absence of institutional social protection in many countries of migration or displacement, young people create their own networks and ways of social protection. This discussion adds the perspective from the Global South—and how young people manoeuvre limited or non-existent social protection while increasing protection for themselves and their families and households translocally. They enact a safe and protective environment in the absence of institutional support—and they also contribute to the informal kinds of social protection of their parents and siblings back home. This point of analysis builds on research which takes migrants' simultaneous embeddedness in multiple societies into account and provides us with important foundations upon which to build (Faist 2013, 2014; Glick-Schiller and Faist 2009; Levitt 2012; Levitt et al. 2015; Mazzucato 2011).

This support to families back home often has mixed results on their own social well-being as well as that of their families. The impact on the families left behind is rather minimal, and on the girls often negative, at least in the short term. At the same time, the social protection initiatives developed by the adolescent girls are often beneficial in strengthening their own confidence, agency, autonomy and their own spaces of self-assertion. They are a form of a transition to adulthood—of becoming responsible for themselves (see Chapter 10).

The story of Tsirite and other migrant and refugee girls also provide insights into how social protection is embedded in gendered adolescence: how the migration of young girls is linked to their gendered roles as daughters and young wives or sisters; their obligations and how these change over time, due to the physical move and multilocal lives—and affect their own life trajectories and transitions to adulthood. These themes will be taken up in the concluding chapter.

References

Al Sharmani, M. (2006). Living Transnationally: Somali Diasporic Women in Cairo. *International Migration, 44*(1), 55–77.

Cheong, P., et al. (2007). Immigration, Social Cohesion and Social Capital: A Critical Review. *Critical Social Policy, 27,* 24–49.

Cranford, C. J. (2005). Networks of Exploitation: Immigrant Labor and the Restructuring of the Los Angeles Janitorial Industry. *Social Problems, 52,* 379–397.

Dannecker, P. (2005). Transnational Migration and the Transformation of Gender Relations: The Case of Bangladeshi Labour Migrants. *Current Psychology, 53*(4), 655–674.

Faist, T. (2013). *Transnational Social Protection: An Emerging Field of Study* (Working Papers No. 113). Bielefeld: COMCAD—Center on Migration, Citizenship and Development.

Faist, T. (2014). On the Transnational Social Question: How Social Inequalities Are Reproduced in Europe. *Journal of European Social Policy, 24,* 207–222.

Ferede, A., & Erulkar, A. (2009). *Adolescent Girls in Urban Ethiopia: Vulnerability and Opportunities.* Addis Ababa: Population Council.

Fernandez, B., & de Regt, M. (2014). *Making a Home in the World: Migrant Domestic Workers in the Middle East.* New York: Palgrave Macmillan.

Girma, W., & Erulkar, A. (2009). *Commercial Sex Workers in Five Ethiopian Cities: A Baseline Survey for USAID Targeted HIV Prevention Program for Most-at-Risk Populations.* Addis Ababa: Population Council.

Glick-Schiller, N., & Faist, T. (2009). Migration Development and Social Transformation. *Social Analysis, 53*(3), 1–13.

Grabska, K. (2016). Eritrean Migratory Trajectories of Adolescence in Khartoum: (Im)mobility, Identities, and Social Media. In S. Hale & G. Kadoda (Eds.), *Networks of Knowledge Production in Sudan: Identities, Mobilities, and Technology.* Lexington Books.

Hagan, J. M. (1998). Social Networks, Gender, and Immigrant Incorporation: Resources and Constraints. *American Sociological Review, 63*(1), 55–67.

Levitt, P. (2012). What's Wrong with Migration Scholarship? A Critique and a Way Forward. *Identities, 1,* 1–8.

Levitt, P., Lloyd, C., Mueller, A., & Viterna, J. (2015). *Global Social Protections: Setting the Agenda* (EUI Working Papers RSCAS 78). Firenze.

Levitt, P., Viterna, J., Mueller, A., & Lloyd, C. (2016). Transnational Social Protection: Setting the Agenda. *Oxford Development Studies, 45*(1), 2–19.

Massey, D. S., Alarcón, R., Durand, J., & González, H. (1987). *Return to Aztlán: The Social Process of International Migration from Western Mexico.* Berkeley, CA: University of California Press.

Mazzucato, V. (2011). Reverse Remittances in the Migration–Development Nexus: Two-Way Flows Between Ghana and the Netherlands. *Population, Space, and Place, 17,* 454–468.

Padilla, B. (2006). *Brazilian Migration to Portugal: Social Networks and Ethnic Solidarity* (CIES e-Working Paper No. 12). Lisbon.

Portes, A. (1995). *The Economic Sociology of Immigration: Essays on Networks, Ethnicity, and Entrepreneurship.* New York: Russell Sage Foundation.

Portes, A. (1998). Social Capital: Its Origins and Applications in Modern Sociology. *Annual Review of Sociology, 24,* 1–24.

Portes, A., & Rumbaut, R. G. (1996). *Immigrant America: A Portrait*. Berkeley, CA: University of California Press.

Roggeveen, S., & van Meeteren, M. (2013). Beyond Community: An Analysis of Social Capital and the Social Networks of Brazilian Migrants in Amsterdam. *Current Sociology, 61*(7), 1078–1096.

Rossem, R., Vermande, M., Völke, B., & Baerveldt, C. (2015). Social Capital in the Classroom: A Study of In-class Social Capital and School Adjustment. *British Journal of Sociology of Education, 36*(5), 669–688.

Rübner Jørgensen, C. H. (2017). 'Peer Social Capital' and Networks of Migrants and Minority Ethnic Youth in England and Spain. *British Journal of Sociology of Education, 38*(4), 566–580.

Sood, S., & Shuaib, M. (2011). *Kishori Abhijan Report on Endline Findings*. Dhaka: UNICEF.

Spickard, J. V., & Adogame, A. (2010). *Religion Crossing Boundaries: Transnational Religious and Social Dynamics in Africa and the New African Diaspora*. Leiden: Brill Academic Publishers.

Village, A., Powell, R., & Pepper, M. (2017). Bonding and Bridging Among First Generation Asian Migrants in Australian Protestant Churches. *Journal of Ethnic and Migration Studies, 43*(11), 1943–1963.

CHAPTER 8

Surviving, Resisting and Moving Forward

"*If My Destiny Is to Live I Will Live Abroad, if My Destiny Is to Die, I Will Die Abroad*": Lamia's Story

Lamia was 22 years old when we interviewed her in 2014. We first met her in an FGD with 11 other young migrants in the local office of Aparajeyo Bangladesh. She had been living and working in Dhaka for about seven years and told us openly about her experiences. In the course of 2014, we met her regularly in different places: in the same office, in her room in the Bhola *bustee* where she lived, together with other girls in the botanical garden, and in coffee places in the area near the *bustee*. We also visited her village, where we met her mother and relatives. In 2016, Lamia left for Oman, where she started working in a garment factory.

Together with her father, mother and two sisters, Lamia grew up in a village in Bogra district. Her father was a farmer and her mother worked at home. When she was in class 5, at about 12 years of age, her father died. Her mother could not afford to maintain her and her sister in school, so Lamia decided to become a domestic worker in a nearby household, but their economic situation had still not improved after two years. Lamia overcame her fears of being unable to adjust to city life and decided to move to Dhaka. In the course of the seven years she lived there, her own situation and that of her family changed frequently, as did her aspirations and objectives. When she arrived, she stayed with a family

K. Grabska et al., *Adolescent Girls' Migration in The Global South*, Palgrave Studies on Children and Development,
https://doi.org/10.1007/978-3-030-00093-6_8

in a '*mess*'(hostel). She worked as a domestic in exchange for food and accommodation but was not happy:

> After coming I wasn't happy. Tears were pouring from my eyes all the time, thinking of my mother and sister. I was suffering a lot. After working all day they would give me only *dal* (lentils) and *bhat* (rice) to eat, and some fried vegetables, *dal* was just water, I couldn't eat that, but with a lot of pain, I managed to cope, people in Dhaka are so selfish! They didn't give me fish, they could at least give me the sauce…I couldn't eat, then I would call my mother and ask her how she was. I couldn't tell her how bad I was so I was lying saying that I was all right: I am fine, you don't worry.

Lamia's first attempts to find a job failed because, although she was aged 14, she did not have an identity card and looked much younger. She finally got a job in a garment factory through a friend. She spent some months doing two jobs, in the house and in the factory:

> I was feeling really tired I couldn't rest, I was feeling pain all over my body, when I was getting up in the morning I didn't feel like going to work…but then I was thinking about my sister and then with a big effort, I went.

After some months, Lamia moved to the Bhola *bustee*. During one of our first encounters, she said:

> I am fine now because I earn enough to help my mother and sister. I want my sister to keep studying and I want to buy some land for my mother next to our house. Marriage is not in my plan because if I marry I won't be able to help my mother and to pay for my sister's study [as]I will belong to someone else. I'll be dependent on someone else. I will have to do what my husband says. After marriage, I will work only if my husband allows me. That's why I don't think about marriage; if I got married my mum and sister could be in danger. I came to Dhaka so that my sister can do what I was not able to do. I want to make my sister educated. That's my decision.

Lamia's situation and objectives changed significantly a few months later. In August 2014, her sister became ill with terminal cancer. She borrowed some money from a friend for her sister's operation. Fifteen days after the operation, her sister died. Lamia said:

> Now that my sister is dead I have to think of my mother and myself. In this job, I don't earn enough to secure a future for us; I bore with a lot of hardship (*koshto*) in my life, now I have to think about myself. I want to stop struggling and suffering.

In September 2015, Lamia started the migration procedures through a *dalal* (broker) with a short-term contract to Mauritius, where she hoped to work in a garment factory. When she received her documents, she realized that the visa stamped on her passport was for Oman. When the NGO informed Lamia that the salary in Oman would be lower than in Mauritius and with worse working conditions, she thought of staying in Bangladesh. But since she could not get the money back from the *dalal*, she went to Oman to work in garment factory. At the end of 2015, she told us by phone:

> I decided to come here because in Dhaka I had no future. There is not much that I could do for myself and my mother with 12000 taka (US$145) per month. Here[in Oman], I miss my mum a lot but after two years I will have saved some money and I will be able to go back to Bangladesh, return to my village, buy some land for my mother to cultivate and a little grocery shop for myself. Before leaving I thought: let's go, if my destiny is to live I will live abroad for some time, if my destiny is to die, I will die abroad.

In June 2017, Lamia went back to Bangladesh for a month's holiday, bought some cattle for her mother to rear, repaired their house that had been damaged by the monsoon rains and went back to Oman for two more years. This time, the employer started mistreating her and her friend. Their pay was reduced and when they protested and refused to go to work, they were beaten up and their passports were confiscated. With limited alternative options, they decided to say nothing and continue working until the contract ended.

> It is better to keep quiet. We'll have to bear with this for the next two years. My mum would get mad if something happened to me. There is nothing to do. We just have to work, so that they don't mistreat us, come back, eat, sleep and wait for time to pass. Once I manage to go back to Bangladesh, I will not leave any more. I'll find another job in a garment factory.

Like Lamia, most of the migrants interviewed in Dhaka, Addis Ababa and Khartoum had to deal with and respond to different risks and setbacks throughout their migratory trajectories (see Chapter 6). In Chapter 4, we discussed elements of agency and pressures in the choice to migrate and in how the decision to migrate is taken. Faced with extremely difficult circumstances at home or in their country of origin, they left with the hope of earning a better living, prospects for the future, their own and their families' security, and their own or their siblings' education. In doing so, the girls exercise different degrees and types of agency. As shown in Chapters 6 and 7, they encounter numerous risks and vulnerabilities throughout the migratory trajectories, but are also able to create a limited protective environment for themselves and their families by building their social capital. In this chapter, we look at how they deal with the limited options and constrained choices that their different contexts offer and discuss their resilience and agency in coping with their living conditions and in carving out for themselves new life options and trajectories. We look at their actions and locate them within the "politics of small things" (see Goldfarb 2006), revealing how "small things" matter in their daily survival, resistance, and moving forward.

Resilience: Capacity to Deal with Adverse Circumstances

Resilience as "the process of, capacity for, or outcome or successful adaptation despite challenging or threatening circumstances" (Masten et al., quoted in Rutter 2006, p. 39), and as an increasing capacity to deal with different kinds of difficulties and challenges, characterize the migratory experience of most of the migrants and refugees interviewed in the three countries. To better understand how resilience is constructed, but also how it changes over time, and how it is individual and yet dependent on external factors, we use insights from Ungar (2012) and Theron et al. (2013). We combine Ungar's Social Ecology of Resilience Theory with writings on youth resilience in the context of countries in Africa (see Theron and Theron 2010; Theron et al. 2013). We extend the notion of individuals and their social ecologies co-constructing resilience to include how resilience relates to gender and the life cycle. Several studies have argued that resilience is a complex construct that places responsibility not only on the individual but also on institutions and society (Hart et al. 2016; Masten and Monn 2015). Institutional support, through organizations, religious networks, and government aid, as we have seen in Chapter 7, is important in enhancing the capacity of migrants and refugees to deal with adverse situations. This is also combined with other informal sources of support, often generated by the girls and young women themselves. Thus, the "person–environment interaction" (Ungar 2012, p. 14) reflects the complexity of resilience and also suggests that social-ecological support is essential and outweighs individual contributions to resilience (Bierman et al. 2004). Further, the complexity and diversity of human experiences and human needs reinforce the interaction between individuals and environments as a source of resilience.

Ungar (2012) shows how external factors (protective factors and interventions) have greater value in accounting for the individual capacity to confront challenges, but he also makes clear that the available opportunities are useful only in relation to individual strengths and challenges. It is then that the individual component acts as an intermediary between the available resources and resilience. As Gopal and Nunlall assert, "it is not the mere interactions with the resources but the quality and meaningfulness of the resources and the availability thereof to the individual" (2017, p. 64). Thus, the trajectory of individual responses to adversity not only implies a challenge for existing systems but also calls for a system (individuals, families, communities) to adequately respond to adversities/disturbances (Masten and Monn 2015). Resilience is therefore based on individual strengths coupled with ecological resources that support growth. As we saw in Chapter 7, at the institutional level in the three countries there is a lack of assistance for migrant and refugee girls and young women to ensure more positive experiences of migration and exile. At the same time, girls' positive experiences during childhood, for example, or better social networks in the places of migration enabled them to be more resilient in the face of adversities and challenges.

Lamia's narrative is punctuated by frequent reference to the *koshto* (hardship, suffering difficulties, problems) she had to bear for most of her life. From her words, however, a strong determination emerges to struggle to improve her own and her family's situation. During the seven years she spent working in Dhaka she had been gaining confidence in herself despite the volatility of her situation, which culminated in the death of her sister. She improved her circumstances by changing accommodation, job and eventually even country. Volatility and precariousness as discussed in Chapter 6 have been always present in Lamia's and others' lives. The initial plans needed to be reworked and adjusted significantly throughout their trajectories. To understand Lamia's resilience, we first have to look at her determined approach to life which comes out clearly in her words, for example: "when you are born, you only die once". Second, access to social networks (friends) enabled her to move to Dhaka, find a job, and eventually helped to improve her work and living conditions and played an important part in her resilience to face her sister's death.

The importance of the external environment and better knowledge about the context is also visible in the increasing resilience of migrant and refugee girls over time. For example, Ethiopian girls who migrated to Addis Ababa, Khartoum or the Middle East initially found themselves in the unexpected situation of being abused and exploited as domestic workers by brokers, employers or their relatives who had promised to send them to school. For many of them, running away has been the only way out, often encouraged by others. Meseret (see Chapter 5), who was raped by her uncle and did not dare to tell her aunt, saw a concrete alternative to that situation and was able to take the risk and escape.

> I felt very sad and angry. To lose your virginity this way is the worst feeling for a young girl. The pain of the actual incident and the pain of having my virginity taken by someone I had high regards for were unbearable. I didn't tell my aunt fearing that I would disrupt her marriage but also fearing that she would not believe me. I thought she would think I was making up stories. It's not a story that I could easily tell anyone let alone my aunt. The fact that I kept quiet actually encouraged him to try and rape me again and again until I left. After seven months in that house I told some girls that I met around the school what had happened to me. They told me that it was good for me to leave the house after such a bad experience. They told me that I could stay with them and at that time it seemed a better alternative to me. I left that house without even telling my aunt.

Meseret, like many other girls in Addis Ababa who run away from domestic work, started doing sex work. She consciously chose to do so: "I needed money to survive so I gave in". Her decision to leave an abusive family shows her resilience and ability to make a choice, even if a very limited one, often entailing risks.

In Sudan too, domestic workers run away from exploitative situations. While some manage to open tea-selling services on the streets, others start doing sex work. In Chapter 5, we discussed the difficulties that newcomers to the city with no links to networks face in the first months.

In Khartoum, a large number of Ethiopian girls arrived through middlemen who arranged their journeys (Abbas 2012; see Chapter 4). As they did not know anything about or anyone in the city, they had to rely on the agents for basic survival and had to accept to work as domestics. Some of them, as the story of Tsirite (Chapter 7) shows, worked for no salary to repay their initial debts. All those whom we interviewed, however, eventually fled from the abusive employers and from the agents. Salam, who was aged 17 when she arrived in Khartoum, managed to run away after two years of exploitative employment: "Once we knew the language, and a bit about the city, and met other Ethiopians, we ran away". Employers in these cases not only lose their domestic worker, but also the money they have paid to the employment agency. The sponsorship system, which is used in many Arab countries, including Sudan, is meant to tie migrants to their employers and prevent them from escaping, yet the numerous stories of runaways show that the system is not effective (Jureidini and Moukarbel 2004; Pande 2013). Running away may have different consequences in different contexts. In Saudi Arabia, law enforcement is much stricter than in Sudan, Lebanon or Yemen (de Regt 2010), where migrant workers can also live undocumented for a considerable period of time. In Saudi Arabia, there are regular campaigns in which undocumented migrants are arrested, imprisoned, and deported. We interviewed 15 young women who migrated to Saudi Arabia when they were under 18 years of age, and who were deported to Ethiopia in a large-scale deportation campaign at the end of 2013 (see Chapter 6). They said that their experiences in prison were worse than anything else they had experienced during their stay. The cruelty of the Saudi authorities was beyond imagination, and some were clearly traumatized. Hayat, for example, was living in a house with eight other Ethiopian girls when the Saudi police entered and arrested them. She was imprisoned for three weeks and told us in detail about her experiences. She had hardly any clothes, covered herself with a shawl, and had to sleep outside. The Saudi guards and policemen slept next to them and the risk of being sexually abused was ever present. She was constantly on the alert and scared every night. She considered herself very lucky because she was not sexually abused or physically harmed and returned "with her hands and her legs". She was happy to be back in Ethiopia but disappointed that her stay abroad had not been more lucrative (see Chapter 9).

Salam's (see Chapter 6) narrative also reveals how with time and increased knowledge about the environment the girls have greater capacity to take action in the face of adverse circumstances. Thus, resilience is dependent on time and place. Some girls, including Tsirite, mentioned how they deliberately misbehaved at work in order to 'punish' their employers for abusive treatment or how they negotiated their salaries and treatment with employers who were keen on keeping them. When Tsirite was verbally abused by her employer, she took cooking oil and 'cleaned' the TV in her employer's house with it. Others would add too much salt to their employer's food. Tea-sellers often prepared tea or coffee that was too hot or too sweet for clients who were abusive. In Ethiopia and Sudan, some sex workers spoke about their strategies for dealing with clients, trying to convince and argue with them when the clients wanted to do things that they did not like. As we observed in a tea-house that served as a brothel in Khartoum, some would be overwhelmingly charming with their clients, in order to get better tips and avoid forced sex. Others, like 16-year-old Genet, who worked there, were always badly dressed and mainly prepared the drinks but without serving them. Genet's poor appearance protected her from clients who insisted on engaging in sexual relations with her. As the sex workers explained, however, in the case of drunken and violent clients their agency was very limited (see Klocker 2007; see Chapter 4). They were often beaten up and could not do much against it. Meseret said:

> I don't feel there is protection from the government or the police for people in our line of work. The police either try to use us for sex like any other guy or come to rescue us after we have been badly hurt by someone.

Yet, these "small things" (see Goldfarb 2006) that girls and young women resorted to point to the various ways in which migrant and refugee girls used their marginal positions to negotiate their liminal status and showed resistance through acts of disobedience. Goldfarb, in *The Politics of Small Things*, engages with the significance of politics at the micro level to understand how turning points in the recent history of, for example, dissent in the Soviet bloc was often enacted by people on the streets in Bucharest, Prague and Warsaw in 1989. His attention is to the "small things" that contribute to larger processes of transformation. At a different scale, the "small things" that adolescent girl migrants and refugees did were thus similar to the "weapons of the weak" (Scott 1985).

In all the three cities and in the Middle East, the recently arrived girls and young women had few skills and a limited network of support and contacts. They had little power to negotiate employment, and so had to resort to jobs that their relatives, or acquaintances or agents could offer them. With time and experience girls were able to accumulate human capital, in terms of learning new skills and ways to survive in an unknown environment. Thus, for example, in Khartoum, once they could speak Arabic, and acquired some small financial and social capital, they usually moved to other jobs, including setting up their own tea stalls. In Dhaka, many Bengali girls like Lamia, who had initially been hosted in a sort of hostel where she couldn't cook her own food, or by relatives who were limiting and controlling their movements, moved to a different kind of accommodation.

Some girls are more resilient and stronger in responding to abuse than others. We also found that those who are very submissive usually experience greater exploitation. Girls who had worked since they were very small, came from harmonious and protective households, and were better educated found it easier to deal with adverse circumstances. Their particular experiences during childhood, family relationships and past experiences were thus elements in the degree of girls' and young women's resilience.

Selfhood and Self-Confidence: Understanding and Learning to Take Care of Oneself

In all three contexts young migrants' sense of self before migration was deeply embedded in their social relations within the family, in the reciprocal obligations and expectations towards parents, siblings and close relatives.

With time and experience migrant girls become better able to understand their contexts, the constraints and opportunities they offer, their own position in them and how to improve it. In Khartoum, young migrants and refugees were proud to say that, despite their hardships, they had learned to take care of themselves. Tsirite, whose story was presented in Chapter 7, despite the setbacks and challenges she was facing, said: "If I go home now, even if I have not made a lot of money, I have seen many things in my life, I have faced many hardships. I learned how to take care of myself". Her confidence in her abilities and pride in her achievements pointed to her awareness of herself as an individual. Growing self-confidence was also seen in other girls. As one of our Eritrean researchers, Ruta, who was 25 years of age, came to Khartoum when she was 18, mentioned:

> I did not know anything about life before I left. But then I came here, I went through many things, and faced many challenges. I learned a lot, not only about myself, but also about others. Through this research project, I learned that other girls are suffering more than me. This gives me strength to push forward. I can see that although my situation is difficult, others have to face more hardship.

Gaining confidence and inner strength was mentioned by migrants in all three contexts as a positive outcome of migration. The psychological transition of adolescence, "already charged in terms of gender and sexuality" (Durham Meenakshi 2004, p. 141) affects and is affected by migration. In Bangladesh, for example, according to the survey, for about two-thirds of the migrants, migration and work had a positive impact on their sense of selfhood and self-esteem, on their mobility and on greater decision-making power in their daily life. Some migrants expressed this sense of personal growth in terms of a greater capacity 'to understand' (*bujha*), an important concept that can be understood as the knowledge that derives from experience and the consequent ability to perform one's duties and behave according to social norms, but also as the capacity to assume adult responsibilities. As a village girl who had just arrived in Dhaka Tasmina felt lost: "I am a village girl. I didn't know anything. At that time I didn't know anything. I was afraid, I got lost, I was standing in the street and crying". As a working woman who can support her parents she now 'understands' and she is in the position of deciding that she wants to postpone marriage. Tasmina said:

> Now, you have to consider that I work independently, I stand on my own feet, I earn money, I can help my parents. Now I understand everything. I will not marry now, a bit later, it's not time now. I want to keep working.

On the one hand, when parents say about an obedient and respectful child that she or he 'understands', '*bujha*' seems to imply conformity: the knowledge and respect of social norms and the capacity to adhere to and behave according to social expectations. Our data show that when 'understanding' is related to working, being able to live in Dhaka without one's parents while keeping one's reputation intact, it also means being able to manage one's life and act in one's own interests. It presupposes the individual capacity to assume responsibilities in different domains and activities, not necessarily according to what the hegemonic gender norms prescribe. It is associated, then, not only with the adherence to social obligations, but also to the ability to negotiate them and exercise a degree of agency. Understanding in this context is also linked to transitions in the life course, and the move from the status of a dependent child to a 'person' who works and earns her own living.

The narratives of girls and young women in Sudan also reveal that migration and the geographical shift it entails have been a way to develop a new sense of self in the place of migration, and in the wider world. This is also illustrated by girls' awareness that there is really no option of going back. While for Eritreans, becoming a person is linked to moving ahead in the world (see Treiber 2014), for Ethiopians, it is the sense of change in their own personalities as a result of migration. As Salam said, commenting on her experience of returning home from Khartoum for a year when she was 15, "once you left your home, once you have seen other places, you cannot just go back and sit at home". Almas, a 26-year-old, who first migrated from Addis Ababa to Khartoum when she was 18, and then went back twice (once for 18 months when she got married, and then to see her daughter whom she left in Addis Ababa), said: "When you go back, you just sit. And you have to be able to move in your life to achieve something. There is no chance (*mircha*) in Ethiopia. So, it is better to migrate". The idea of not sitting still, constantly moving, is also linked to the findings of research by Marco Di Nunzio (2014) among young people in Addis Ababa. 'Constantly moving to stay alive' was a notion that permeated the lives of the young men hustlers and street vendors in Addis Ababa. The 'knowing' and the 'self' are thus positioned transnationally and linked to both spatial mobility, but also acquiring selfhood as part of migratory trajectories. Here, physical mobility appears to be an important element in social mobility and transition into adulthood. This also explains the aspirations of some of the girls we interviewed to migrate further, and the frustrations of those who felt "stuck" in the places of migration (see Chapter 10).

Moving Forward or Waiting: Aspirations and Frustrations

For the migrant and refugee girls and young women in the three case studies, migration has intersected with personal growth, with the development of a different sense of selfhood, increased self-esteem and a capacity to deal with everyday challenges and decisions. For some it has also opened the way to more defined and realistic aspirations and new life trajectories. Further migration is one of these. The determination with which Lamia pursued her decision to migrate abroad shows her increased capacity to make a decision and a choice for her life. This is also linked to the enabling environment and access to networks that facilitated her move to Oman to be able to earn more money and save for her imagined future. Salma is another young migrant whom we met in August 2014 when she was about to leave Bangladesh for Mauritius. She had joined her older sister's family in Dhaka five years before, had been working in a garment factory for three years and was determined to improve her situation after hearing about the experiences of some colleagues who had been working in garment factories in Jordan. She felt encouraged by their words and confident enough that nothing unpleasant could happen to her since her intentions were good.

> I used to be afraid in the past. I am a woman, so I feared moving around too much. But after hearing from other girls [about their migration] I am not afraid anymore. I found their choice good. I think that if I am a good person, the people around will be good to me. It all depends on me. I got information about going abroad to work. One of my relative's daughters also went abroad for work. She inspired me to go, so I prepared my documents.

Despite the stigma attached to it, and the actual abuses to which they are subjected, the number of women who migrate from Bangladesh to Middle Eastern countries is increasing (ILO 2014) (see Chapter 3). Women's international migration is subject to strict laws and regulations so that formally only women over the age of 25 can obtain the necessary authorizations from the government for formal migration. This does not mean that younger women do not migrate abroad but adolescents are certainly a minority. From the FGDs conducted with two groups of women who were about to migrate to the Middle East it emerged that most of them were either divorced or abandoned and were seeking a better livelihood abroad, or were young married women whose husbands had agreed to or even encouraged their migration because the associated costs are lower than for men. Only a few of the participants in our research expressed the intention of migrating abroad.

In Ethiopia, most people view women's migration to the Middle East as very negative (Jones et al. 2014; LSHTM 2016). Similar to Bangladesh, almost everyone knows about the large-scale violations of human rights, such as sexual abuse and exploitation, but adolescent girls and young women are attracted by the possibility of earning more money than they do as internal migrants. Selam, a 24-year-old sex worker who left her home town when she was 13 years old said:

> I want to stop this work. I want to borrow money and go to one of the Arab countries. Whatever abuse I have there I want to go and work there in order to change my life. If I stay in Addis I will not change my life. Life is very expensive here. I can't afford to pay 2000 Birr for rent.

Selam was one of the few internal migrants who aspired to migrate abroad. Most of the girls we interviewed in Addis Ababa did not express an interest in further migration. Domestic workers wanted to continue their education and get a better-paid job, and sex workers wanted to stop doing sex work and get a 'normal' job. Yet, during an FGD with adolescent girls in Shashemene, a town 200 kilometres south of Addis Ababa, migration to the Middle East was seen as the best option to improve one's life. They were convinced that migration to Addis Ababa would not help them to improve their lives because the available jobs are domestic work and sex work and the salaries are too low to make structural changes in one's life. According to them, parents are grateful to those who are working in the Middle East because they send remittances. But those who migrate to Addis Ababa are not able to change their own lives and those of their families, and sometimes even disappear. The girl referred to the fact that many people think that those who migrate to Addis Ababa become sex workers. One of the participants said:

> When she comes from an Arab country they respect her and when she passes by greet her, but if she comes from any place in Ethiopia, they don't respect her and they disgrace her because they don't think she worked hard to earn money. They think she was a sex worker.

Migration abroad was seen as the only way to improve one's living conditions (see Mains 2012; Jones et al. 2014; LSHTM 2016; Dom 2017). In some parts of Ethiopia "a culture of migration" is developing, in which international migration turns "into a crucial and necessary social act, that is quasi compulsory for certain social categories. For example, it can become the foremost marker of the process of transition to adulthood, having functions that are similar to a classical rite of of human rights, such as sexual abuse and exploitation, but adolescent girls and young women are attracted by the possibility of earning more money than they do as internal migrants. Selam, a 24-year-old sex worker who left her home town when she was 13 years old said:

> I want to stop this work. I want to borrow money and go to one of the Arab countries. Whatever abuse I have there I want to go and work there in order to change my life. If I stay in Addis I will not change my life. Life is very expensive here. I can't afford to pay 2000 Birr for rent.

Selam was one of the few internal migrants who aspired to migrate abroad. Most of the girls we interviewed in Addis Ababa did not express an interest in further migration. Domestic workers wanted to continue their education and get a better-paid job, and sex workers wanted to stop doing sex work and get a 'normal' job. Yet, during an FGD with adolescent girls in Shashemene, a town 200 kilometres south of Addis Ababa, migration to the Middle East was seen as the best option to improve one's life. They were convinced that migration to Addis Ababa would not help them to improve their lives because the available jobs are domestic work and sex work and the salaries are too low to make structural changes in one's life. According to them, parents are grateful to those who are working in the Middle East because they send remittances. But those who migrate to Addis Ababa are not able to change their own lives and those of their families, and sometimes even disappear. The girl referred to the fact that many people think that those who migrate to Addis Ababa become sex workers. One of the participants said:

> When she comes from an Arab country they respect her and when she passes by greet her, but if she comes from any place in Ethiopia, they don't respect her and they disgrace her because they don't think she worked hard to earn money. They think she was a sex worker.

Migration abroad was seen as the only way to improve one's living conditions (see Mains 2012; Jones et al. 2014; LSHTM 2016; Dom 2017). In some parts of Ethiopia "a culture of migration" is developing, in which international migration turns "into a crucial and necessary social act, that is quasi compulsory for certain social categories. For example, it can become the foremost marker of the process of transition to adulthood, having functions that are similar to a classical rite of to migrate to Europe and North America. There is a clear hierarchy of destination countries, based on wages and legal regulations, which inspire further migration. This also applies to the Eritrean girls who participated in this research, all of whom wanted to pursue further education, to get a good job, and to be able to help their families. Khartoum and Sudan were not the dreamed places of destination, and not even offering more services would change this. Thus, for Eritrean girls wasting time pertains to a specific situation. Their options are visibly constrained: no possibility of returning to Eritrea (and risk potential life imprisonment or even death), lack of opportunities to pursue a (desired) life in Sudan, and the risky and often deadly journey to another place. This exemplifies the enormous absence of choice and sense of accomplishment in the lives of young Eritreans.

For Ethiopian girls in Khartoum, there was a larger range of scenarios for the future. Almost all mentioned the option of eventually going back to Ethiopia, building a house and starting a business. Some wanted to have a trading company, some to sell clothes, others thought about opening hairdressing salons. Although Ethiopians have the possibility of visiting their places of origin, in reality most of the girls and young women could not do so. This was due to very low salaries and the lack of legal documentation, as well as restrictions on migration for young people from Ethiopia to Sudan. The girls also realized that in Ethiopia they had limited work opportunities. Agaresh, a 35-year-old Ethiopian woman first came to Sudan to follow her boyfriend when she was 18 but decided to return for good and open a beauty salon in Addis Ababa. She took her three children and went back. When we visited her in Addis Abba she told us that she had been staying with her parents and was unemployed. The costs of opening up a business in the capital were too high, and she lost some US$1500 just trying to find a place. After seven months, she decided to return to Khartoum. She was planning to join her husband who was going to be resettled in Australia, and was herself later resettled through a humanitarian programme and lives with her family in Adelaide.

The interviews with young women who had migrated to the Middle East and returned to Ethiopia show that even those who had been abroad for only a few years had sometimes moved from one country to another. While the mobility of migrant domestic workers in the Middle East is often severely restricted during their employment, they are very mobile and change employers and countries quickly. Sara, for example, migrated to Saudi Arabia via a legal agent and worked for six months in Mecca. She ran away and went to Riyadh where she worked freelance for six different employers. She was undocumented and lived by herself. In November 2013 she was deported to Ethiopia. While Sara moved inside Saudi Arabia, other girls migrated from one country to the other. Bortukan is 28 years old and migrated when she was 17. She had worked in Abu Dhabi, Bahrain, Dubai and Qatar. She said:

> Dubai was my first destination. I was cleaning 18 separate rooms, 6 bathrooms, I did the laundry and prepared food for the whole family. I was doing all these tasks alone. After finishing my contract they decided to send me back without any reason. When I was in Dubai airport I ran away to Abu Dhabi and I worked there with a runaway status for one year. The police caught and arrested me while I was working and they deported me to Ethiopia. After deportation my plan was to migrate again. I decided to migrate to Qatar. I paid 7000 Birr to a local broker. In Qatar the madam didn't want me to keep my personal hygiene but I always kept myself clean. When I would clean myself the madam would get upset as she considered it the behaviour of a prostitute. But the rest of the family was nice to me. The madam sent me back because she wanted me to be dirty.

Back in Ethiopia Bortukan decided to migrate to Bahrain, but she did not have enough food there and decided to return home again. After a while she migrated to Sharjah, but again got too little to eat and ran away to Abu Dhabi. In Abu Dhabi, she was arrested because she was undocumented and returned home with the help of her brother.

The mobility of Ethiopian girls and young women who migrated to the Middle East stands in stark contrast with the immobility of Eritrean and Ethiopian girls in Khartoum. When asked about their experiences in Khartoum, most of the girls and young women talked about 'no change' (see Chapter 9). They usually referred to the slight impact of migration on their lives. "We came here to change our lives, but look at us, not much has happened. We are still the same", said Salam, aged 23, who has been in Khartoum for nine years. While they did not talk much about wasting time, some of them did refer to the fact that they were 'losing their age and time'. Salam explained it clearly:

> I do not want to lose my age and time too, and as you know the age of a girl short, so I do not want to count age with nothing. If I stay more here, there will be no change. What I mean is I could not change the life of my

> family or I did not get married and have children. So what is the use to stay more than these years in Khartoum? I do not want to lose my time without being successful. I spend my time like this, what is the use? Then it is better to go back to Ethiopia, even if it is not comfortable for me in Ethiopia. Then, I can also go to Saudi Arabia.

Ethiopian girls and young women were very clear about the fact that if all things fall through, they could return to Ethiopia, even if they had to pay fines for leaving their country irregularly. They were in greater of control of their own destinies despite their more precarious economic condition than those from Eritrea. They did not express the same feeling of being stuck in Khartoum, as the Eritreans did, even though they had little potential for social and financial improvement. They saw themselves as living there temporarily, but with the potential of moving somewhere else.

'Small Things' and 'Small Steps'

Migrant and refugee girls, as discussed in previous chapters, face enormous challenges, risks, and setbacks at their places of destination, in their living, working, and social environments. They confront gender-based violence, marginalization and frequent harassment on a daily basis, owing to their gendered and age-specific vulnerabilities. Yet to focus exclusively on the negative experiences would be to deny the capacities and the abilities of the young women to make sense of these tensions.

As we have shown, despite constantly facing adversity and volatility, these young migrants show their resilience and their capacity to navigate uncertainty and unpredictability in their lives. Young migrant girls are vulnerable but at the same time they "may possess—or acquire—protective factors that alleviate the risks to which they may be vulnerable" (Ensor and Gozdziak 2010, p. 15). Their actions in relation to the abuse and risks they face in their everyday life are evidence of agency, albeit "thin" (Klocker 2007; see Chapter 4).

As the narratives and actions of research participants in the three cities show, migration has intersected for them with a process of personal growth and development of an adult identity with an increased capacity to decide about the direction of their life. For some of them, we can say that migration has contributed to broadening the range of options and to opening alternative life trajectories; their actions and choices are evidence of a "thicker" agency (Klocker 2007).

Migrant adolescent girls' and young women's self-assertion and growing capacity to act is also linked to their resilience. In all three countries, the life history and the longitudinal approach to the study of the migrant girls' experiences confirmed the relationship between individuals and their ecological systems (see Ungar 2012).

By doing "small things", migrant adolescent girls and young women also demonstrate small steps towards carving out their own present and future, their own social positions as young women. As our research shows, however, resilience is also fluid and changes over time. The life-course perspective also reveals its gendered dynamics. For example, at the time of leaving, girls' migration objectives, plans and motivations were embedded in their childhood social relations and closely interlinked with their status as girls, with their particular birth and sibling order. Over a period of time, however, the power relations based on gender and age shift, as a result of the physical shift linked to migration and their experiences at their destination. Despite ambiguities and contradictions, girls in Dhaka, Ethiopia and Khartoum challenge and question established ways of becoming and being an adult woman and moving ahead. This is true even for young migrants in Khartoum despite their perceptions of immobility and lack of opportunities. Young Eritrean and Ethiopian girls are in fact actively doing things while waiting. They are acting on their state of perceived immobility. For example, they contribute to changing gender relations and identities by challenging girls' established trajectories into adulthood. For them, as well as for migrants in Dhaka and Addis Ababa, other ways of becoming an adult woman become possible through gaining independence, such as living away from their family, making their own decisions, controlling their own earnings. Thus, the idea of being stuck does not reflect the actual experiences of migrants and refugees in Khartoum. Brun (2015) refers to this as "agency in waiting".

References

Abbas, R. (2012, August 22). Ethiopian Servants in Sudan at the Mercy of Middle Men. *The Niles*.

Bierman, K. L., Coie, J. D., Dodge, K. A., Foster, E. M., Greenberg, M. T., Lochman, J. E., et al. (2004). The Effects of the Fast Track Program on Serious Problem Outcomes at the End of Elementary School. *Journal of Clinical Child and Adolescent Psychology, 33*, 650–661.

Brun, C. (2015). Active Waiting and Changing Hopes: Toward a Time Perspective on Protracted Displacement. *Social Analysis: Journal of Cultural and Social Practice, 59*(1), 19–37.

de Regt, M. (2010). Ways to Come, Ways to Leave: Gender, Mobility, and Il/Legality Among Ethiopian Domestic Workers in Yemen. *Gender & Society, 24*(2), 237–260.

Di Nunzio, M. (2014). Embracing Uncertainty. Young People on the Move in Addis Ababa's Inner City. In L. Cooper & D. Pratten (Eds.), *Ethnographies of Uncertainty in Africa*. Basingstoke: Palgrave Macmillan.

Dom, C. (2017). Migrating for Work from Rural Communities. In A. Pankhurst (Ed.), *Change and Transformation in 20 Rural Communities in Ethiopia: Selected Aspects and Implications for Policy*. Addis Ababa: WIDE.

Durham Meenakshi, G. (2004). Constructing the "New Ethnicities": Media, Sexuality, and Diaspora Identity in the Lives of South Asian Immigrant Girls. *Critical Studies in Media Communication, 21*(2), 140–161.

Ensor, M., & Gozdziak, E. (Eds.). (2010). *Children and Migration: At the Cross-Roads of Resiliency and Vulnerability*. Basingstoke: Palgrave Macmillan.

Goldfarb, J. C. (2006). *The Politics of Small Things: The Power of the Powerless in Dark Times*. Chicago, IL: University of Chicago Press.

Gopal, N., & Nunlall, R. (2017). Interrogating the Resilience of Women Affected by Violence. *Agenda, 31*(2), 63–73.

Hart, A., Gagnon, E., Eryigit-Madzwamuse, S., Cameron, J., Aranda, K., Rathbone, A., et al. (2016). Uniting Resilience Research and Practice with an Inequalities Approach. *Sage Open, 6*(4), 1–13.

Horváth, I. (2008). The Culture of Migration of Rural Romanian Youth. *Journal of Ethnic and Migration Studies, 34*(5), 771–786.

ILO. (2014). *Gender and Migration from Bangladesh. Mainstreaming Migration into the National Development Plans Form a Gender Perspective*. Dhaka: International Labour Organization.

Jones, N., et al. (2014). *Rethinking Girls on the Move: The Intersection of Poverty, Exploitation, and Violence Experienced by Adolescents Involved in the Middle East 'Maid Trade'* (Report). London: Overseas Development Institute.

Jureidini, R., & Moukarbel, N. (2004). Female Sri Lankan Domestic Workers in Lebanon: A Case of 'Contract Slavery'? *Journal of Ethnic and Migration Studies, 30*(4), 581–607.

Klocker, N. (2007). An Example of "Thin" Agency: Child Domestic Workers in Tanzania. In R. Panelli, S. Punch, & E. Robson (Eds.), *Global Perspectives on Rural Childhood and Youth: Young Rural Lives*. New York and Abingdon: Routledge.

Liebelt, C. (2008). On Sentimental Orientalists, Christian Zionists, and Working Class Cosmopolitans: Filipina Domestic Workers' Journeys to Israel and Beyond. *Critical Asian Studies, 40*(4), 567–586.

LSHTM. (2016). *"They Changed Their Lives Because They Went to Arab Countries": Local Perceptions of Women's Overseas Migration for Domestic Labour in Amhara Region*. London: London School of Hygiene & Tropical Medicine.

Mains, D. (2012). *Hope is Cut: Youth, Unemployment and the Future in Urban Ethiopia*. Philadelphia: Temple University Press.

Massey, D. S., Goldring, L., & Durand, J. (1994). Continuities in Transnational Migration: An Analysis of Nineteen Mexican Communities. *American Journal of Sociology, 99*(6), 1492–1533.

Masten, A. S., & Monn, A. R. (2015). Child and Family Resilience: A Call for Integrated Science, Practice, and Professional Training. *Family Relations, 64*(1), 5–21.

Ossman, S. (2013). *Moving Matters: Paths of Serial Migration*. Stanford, CA: Stanford University Press.

Pande, A. (2013). "The Paper That You Have in Your Hand Is My Freedom": Migrant Domestic Work and the Sponsorship (Kafala) System in Lebanon. *International Migration Review, 47*(2), 414–441.

Rutter, M. (2006). Implications of Resilience Concepts for Scientific Understanding. *Annals of the New York Academy of Sciences, 1094*, 1–12.

Scott, J. (1985). *Weapons of the Weak: Everyday Forms of Peasant Resistance*. New Haven: Yale University Press.

Theron, L. C., & Theron, A. M. C. (2010). A Critical Review of Studies of South Africa Youth Resilience, 1990–2008. *South African Journal of Science, 106*(7/8), 1–8.

Theron, L. C., Theron, A. M. C., & Malindi, M. J. (2013). Towards an African Definition of Resilience: A Rural South African Community's View of Resilient Basotho Youth. *Journal of Black Psychology, 39*, 63–87.

Treiber, M. (2014). Becoming by Moving. Khartoum and Addis Ababa as Migratory Stages Between Eritrea and 'Something'. In M. Abdalla, D. Dias Barros, & M. Berthet Ribeiro (Eds.), *Spaces in Movement. New Perspectives on Migration in African Settings* (pp. 189–205). Köln: Rüdiger Köppe Verlag.

Ungar, M. (Ed.). (2012). *The Social Ecology of Resilience: A Handbook of Theory and Practice*. New York, NY: Springer.

CHAPTER 9

Beyond Survival: The Wider Implications of Girls' Migration

"*Nothing Changed*": Arsema's Life in Perspective

Arsema migrated from Gondar in Ethiopia to Sudan when she was 16 years old. By the time we met her in 2015, she was in her forties and had been in Khartoum for 34 years. She came in 1981—during the Mengistu times and the Ethiopian–Eritrean war of liberation—and considered herself a political refugee. Her parents stayed in Ethiopia, and for a while she survived in Khartoum by doing domestic work. Married and with four children, Arsema never returned permanently to Ethiopia. Her Sudanese husband was a truck driver, and she set up a small business selling tea and coffee in front of her house. When we met her, she lived in a small flat on one of the main squares in Deim neighbourhood, in an apartment block in which migrants from Egypt, Eritrea, Ethiopia and Syria resided. The square was filled with piling rubbish and construction of new housing. While she faced various obstacles and setbacks in Sudan, she managed to educate her children and buy a small piece of land in Ethiopia for her extended family. Arsema felt obliged to support her family members in Ethiopia, but given her meagre earnings, as well as her growing family responsibilities in Khartoum, she could seldom send money for her siblings' education, for family emergencies, and finally to purchase land. Despite the fact that she was unable to save enough to move to Ethiopia, the idea of one day returning to her homeland was

K. Grabska et al., *Adolescent Girls' Migration in The Global South*, Palgrave Studies on Children and Development,
https://doi.org/10.1007/978-3-030-00093-6_9

always on her mind. When we asked her whether her life has changed over the years in Khartoum, she looked rather doubtful:

> Look at me, the life here and there is the same. It is tough. It has made no difference for me. I cannot tell you if it would have been different if I stayed in Ethiopia. Because I am here, so I cannot evaluate this. In 2000, I went to the UN [United Nations High Commissioner for Refugees], I had an interview, and I am still waiting for their response. You see. Nothing has changed.

Arsema is one of the few older women we were able to interview who had migrated as an adolescent girl. While initially we had intended to look into the long-term effects of migration on the lives of the girls as well as on the families they left, we were unable to collect enough data to provide in-depth account of such impacts. It was difficult to find respondents who had been in Addis Ababa, Dhaka and Khartoum for a longer period of time. In Dhaka, we interviewed 11 (out of 47) young Bengali women who had been living there for more than ten years, most of whom (34) had migrated up to five years before. This was probably due to the fact that after some years of work and/or after marriage, with a better economic situation, the migrants move to a different area of the city. Second, it seems that most of the young girls who go to Dhaka for garment work tend either to return home after a few years or to migrate further afield. The fact that we found a large number of girls who had migrated very recently (22 of the 47 up to two years before) and that during 2014 eight of the girls interviewed left their jobs and either went back home or migrated abroad, suggests that most do not view garment work as a long-term life choice. Among the Garo migrants, on the other hand, six girls (out of 17) had been in Dhaka for more than ten years, which is in line with the fact that migrants from this ethnic minority are more likely to settle in Dhaka.

In Khartoum, one of the main challenges of the fieldwork was migrants' high mobility (see Chapter 2). Eritrean migrants move both for security reasons and also because they want to migrate beyond Sudan for better life opportunities. It was therefore difficult to find Eritrean and Ethiopian respondents who had migrated as adolescent girls and had spent more than seven or eight years in Sudan. In Addis Ababa, the challenges of finding adolescent migrant girls reduced the time available to find older migrants who had come to the city as adolescents.

The majority of the girls and young women who were interviewed in the three country studies had spent between two and six years in their destination. We interviewed two older[1] Bangladeshi migrant women and one older Garo woman in Dhaka, two older domestic workers in Addis Ababa and five older Ethiopian migrants in Khartoum. This small sample can give only some general trends about the long-term changes in the life course of young migrants. What emerges is that even for those who have spent over ten years in their respective destinations, it is difficult to discern the benefits of migration beyond survival. Most married later, had fewer children, and were also able to have their children educated, just like Arsema.

As we saw in Chapter 4, most girls migrated with the hope of improving their own and their family's lives. In the short term, however, as we discussed in Chapter 5, most were disappointed about their life in the cities and in particular the financial gains of their work. Garment workers earn low salaries, as do domestic workers, tea-sellers, and sex workers. Life is expensive in the three cities and it is hard to save money. When asked about the impact of their migration most migrant girls were rather negative. At the same time, while major positive change might not be visible, small transformations do take place.

In this chapter, we present findings of the survey and the life-story interviews related to sending remittances, supporting family members, investing in the future, the impact on households and on the status of migrants in relation to their families. We use a social transformation perspective (Bakewell 2010; Castles 2010; Grabska 2014) to analyse the changes that have taken place as a result of the girls' migration. We deepen our discussion of the creation of translocal and transnational protection systems (see Chapter 7), paying special attention to gender and generational analysis. We start with financial remittances and investments and then move to a broader discussion of the 'social' impact of girls' migration.

Gradually Supporting Those Left Behind

Many of the debates about migration are located within discussions of the 'impact' of migration processes. In particular, there has been a burgeoning body of literature on the so-called migration–development nexus (Faist 2008; de Haas 2010; Glick et al. 2009; Nyberg-Sørensen

[1] By older women we refer to women in their late twenties or early thirties.

et al. 2002; Taylor 1999). Financial remittances are generally used as the first indicator of the wider impacts of migration. Migrants' ability to remit and financially support those who stayed behind is a dominant paradigm in determining their success. Nina Nyberg-Sørensen (2010) describes in detail their relatives' glorification of Nicaraguan migrants in the US as "migration heroes" while those who failed to send remittances and in addition were deported were referred to as "deportee trash". The discussion about the migration–development nexus is heavily influenced by the increasing number of international migrants, although these are still far outnumbered by internal migrants (King and Skeldon 2010; Castaldo et al. 2012; McKay and Deshingkar 2014). There is, however, hardly any discussion about internal remittances. Internal money transfers are not tracked, or too difficult to track because they go through informal channels, resulting in a lack of statistical data (McKay and Deshingkar 2014, p. 5). As part of the Migration out of Poverty Research Consortium at the University of Sussex in the UK, the relationship between internal remittances and poverty in six countries in Africa and Asia were studied (McKay and Deshingkar 2014). The authors conclude that:

> … international migrants, who have moved further away, are generally more likely to send remittances than domestic migrants, and the average size of the transfer tends to be much larger. But in all cases there are many more domestic migrants than international migrants, which cause the sum total of domestic transfers to exceed that of international transfers, sometimes by a significant margin. (McKay and Deshingkar 2014, p. 20)

Mahler and Pessar (2006) argue that remittances reflect and transmit power, and that there is a need for a detailed analysis to understand the gender dynamics of remittances. The general assumption is that women intend to remit more than men and are seen as more trustworthy in supporting their families (Mahler and Pessar 2006, p. 45; Kunz 2008, p. 1403). The governments of both migrant-sending and receiving countries have also realized the potential financial gains from migration. By comparing the inflows of remittances to foreign investments or development aid, some countries have been actively promoting international migration of their citizens in order to increase the inflow of financial capital (e.g. the Philippines). The migration–development nexus has also been taken up in policy discourses, celebrating migrants' contributions to the development of their communities of origin and, in so doing, to some extent placing the burden for achieving structural changes on the shoulders of migrants.

Increasingly, the study of the economic aspects of the impact of remittances has been integrated with a focus on the social and emotional aspects of the impact on those left behind (Toyota et al. 2007; Mazzucato and Schans 2008; Thieme and Siegmann 2010). These studies also stress that economic choices, such as those concerning the control and use of remittances, are best understood in relation to different socio-cultural contexts and to the social relations that regulate the division of labour and responsibilities, and the reciprocal obligations and claims between household members and wider social networks. Most of these studies, however, look at the social impact of remittances sent by male migrants. Gardner and Zahir (2006) have looked at informal mechanisms of social protection in the context of a village in Sylhet in Bangladesh with a high level of migration to the UK. Rashid (2007, 2008) has dealt with the impact of migration to the Gulf, observing that young wives and older people left behind are particularly vulnerable to abandonment, especially when they belong to small, economically marginal households. Osella and Osella (2006, 2007) also identify changing gender norms and ideas as one of the key changes resulting from migration to the Gulf from the Indian state of Kerala.

In our case studies, the ability to remit and support family members who stayed behind was often part of the girls' migratory project (see Chapter 4). As we have discussed, however, girls also had other reasons to migrate, in addition to the wish to "help the family". We first discuss the answers to the questionnaires, although we are aware that these responses do not always reflect the reality (see Chapter 2). We therefore complement the survey results with data collected in the life-story interviews. In Bangladesh, a little more than half of the survey respondents (33 out of 60) were supporting some family members in their village when we interviewed them. Ten had sent money before and 17 had never done so. Those who were not sending remittances included younger migrants who had arrived in Dhaka only a few months before and who were not yet in a position to send money, older migrants who hardly earned enough to support themselves, girls who had been joined by their families, and girls who had migrated to escape abusive situations and conflict and who therefore did not want to send remittances home. As the remittances are rather small, the impact on the receiving families is usually not very significant. In Bangladesh, two-thirds of the interviewees (31 Bengali and eight Garo) claimed that their family's condition had improved. Thirty-five migrants who mentioned an improvement in the economic situation of their family referred almost exclusively to their being better able to cover basic daily expenses and health emergencies. In spite of the fact that most of the migrants claimed that their objective for the future was to save enough money to invest in assets in their place of origin (e.g. in land) there is not much evidence from older Bengali migrants that they have been able to do this.

Among internal migrant girls in Addis Ababa, a little less than half of the girls said that they send money home (13 out of 30). Those who were remitting money were sending it to their parents, and some to their siblings. Some girls told us that they prefer not to be in touch with their relatives because they are unable to support their parents or siblings. Sex workers also considered the money that they earned "bad money" (or devil's money) because they had earned it by having others "spoiling them" (see Chapter 6). Other girls only occasionally sent money to their parents but they mentioned that the amount was not sufficient to make a substantial change to their lives. They reported that remittances were used for a variety of things, such as daily expenses, health care, education of siblings and the like. Six girls said that they did not know how the money was spent, and seven reported that the condition of their family back home had improved economically. Most argued that there was no real improvement in their family's living condition (20 out of 30).

Among the survey respondents in Khartoum, only 17 out of 48 said they sent remittances to their families back home. Among them, there were four Eritreans and 13 Ethiopians. Ten had sent remittances at least once or in the past, whereas some 21 reported never having sent financial support. Among those, there were 20 Eritreans. These results point to the diverse reasons for girls' migration to Sudan. While for Ethiopians Khartoum is often a destination from where they have to support families, for Eritreans it is a staging post to somewhere else. The amounts sent varied, but were usually very small, about 100–150 SDG (US$8–12) a month. Most of the respondents collected money over a period of a few months and then sent larger amounts using a network of trusted agents, intermediaries, smugglers, and friends. Tea-makers were usually able to send larger amounts than could domestic workers. Usually, women who have been in Khartoum for a longer period have been able to send increasing amounts of money. At the same time, due to the worsening economic situation in Sudan, and the rising cost of living, migrants find it increasingly difficult to support their families in Ethiopia. What they earn is spent on their own survival. Among the older women interviewed for the research (over 30 years old, who had been in Sudan for 20 or more years), two returned to Ethiopia during the course of the fieldwork as they were unable to maintain their families in Khartoum.

The remittances of Ethiopian girls who worked in the Middle East and in Sudan were higher than those of migrant girls in Addis Ababa, which is in line with other studies about internal and international remittances (King and Skeldon 2010). The remittances of girls and young women who had worked in the Middle East were mainly used for daily expenses, education of siblings, improving the house and buying consumer goods such as TV and DVD sets. Even so, the returnees were also often disappointed by the limited structural change in the lives of their family they had been able to achieve. They had migrated abroad hoping to make a significant contribution but their earnings were insufficient to do so. Some said that the time they had spent abroad was too short to be able to save money (see de Regt and Tafesse 2017). Others claimed that only those who enter sex work can really change the lives of their family back home, whereas the salaries of domestic workers are too low to bring about structural changes. These statements must, however, be interpreted in a context in which discourses regarding the success of migration, and in particular the success of women's migration, are related to dominant notions of gender, age and sexuality. Most Eritrean girls in Khartoum did not regularly send remittances to their families. Some sent money occasionally, but others used their meagre earnings to meet their own daily needs. Some also tried to save some money in order to migrate further or supported the migration of their siblings and other family members, as we will discuss below.

In general, in all three country studies, it is evident that the earnings of the adolescent girls and young women are usually small and the costs of living in the city are high. As a result, they are unable to fulfil their dreams of changing the living conditions of their parents in a more structural way, at least in the short and medium term. This finding supports Derks' conclusions about the remittances of migrant girls in urban Cambodia (2008), emphasizing the link between the amount and frequency of remitting and the type of employment, family situation and life phase. In the case of Cambodia, single daughters were more inclined to use money for their own consumption while those whose parents were taking care of their children were remitting more money. In our research this link was also very important. In addition, most of our respondents were young single women without children, thus their obligations to remit were mainly framed within their gendered and generational responsibilities as daughters. Another important finding is that while some were not able to remit money immediately following their migration, they were often able to send money later.

Investing in the Future of Others

While many were disappointed about the structural changes they had managed to bring about for their families, some girls proudly told us about the ways in which they were able to support their siblings' education and make other investments, which illustrate the social transformations that take place as a result of adolescent girls' migration (Fig. 9.1).

The importance of remittances for the education of siblings was particularly evident in Khartoum, where girls and young women told us about their younger or older brothers graduating from college thanks to their support. They usually had pictures of their siblings' graduation displayed in their rooms, a visible manifestation of their contributions. Salam, a 22-year-old woman who had migrated first from Humora in Ethiopia to Khartoum at the age of 13 (see Chapter 7), and had been supporting her family for nine years, said:

> I have six brothers and sisters in Ethiopia. I didn't get a chance to learn [she finished five classes] so I didn't want them to lose that [opportunity] even if our family is poor. I want them in a good class, I want them to be well educated. If they are OK then I will be OK. My parents are proud of me, because I am able to help now. My older brother just graduated from college.

Salam's narrative, which was illustrative of other girls' evaluations of their own choices and decisions, demonstrates how the girls' sense of personal self-accomplishment is intertwined with the well-being of their families. Like other migrant girls, Salam was especially keen that her brothers finish their education. It was also recognized that as educated men they will be able to get well-paid jobs and eventually take on the responsibility for their family. The girls' decisions on how to invest in the

Fig. 9.1 Supporting brothers' education, Khartoum, Sudan

future of their siblings were deeply embedded in the prevailing gender norms. While they supported brothers' education, they invested in their sisters' future by supporting their marriage, which often involved under-age girls marrying men they had not chosen. Tsirite (see Chapter 7), for example, sent money to support the marriage of her 16-year-old sister in Ethiopia. When we asked her why she was not supporting her sister's education, she said: "She is already big, she should be a woman now. And if her husband allows her, she can continue education later. Also, for girls it is difficult to get well-paid jobs, even if they are educated". Thus, the investment in boys' rather than girls' education seemed to be a better move, both reflecting the gendered structures of the labour market, but also permeating gender norms and identities (see Derks 2008).

Supporting their siblings' education was seen as an important investment in the future of the family as well as positive way to improve its social position. This was particularly so for migrant girls in Dhaka and Khartoum, and for Ethiopian girls who migrated to the Middle East. Most of the Ethiopians in Khartoum were supporting their brothers, while in Bangladesh it was a combination of supporting sisters and brothers. Among 39 respondents in Bangladesh who claimed that the situation of their families had improved, 19 said that this improvement concerned the education of siblings or their children left behind. Girls saw investing in others' education as a longer-term strategy to improve the prospects of their families. According to Bengali social norms, a married woman becomes part of her husband's family and is not supposed and usually not allowed by the in-laws to look after her parents. For this reason, some migrants have decided to postpone their own marriage to be able to help their parents and younger siblings in their studies. Many girls and young women said that their parents could not rely at all on their married brothers even though these should be responsible for their elderly parents and younger siblings. Garo social norms about the responsibilities of grown-up children are different. They frequently continue to support their parents even after they have married. The newly wed Garo couple usually settles on its own in town and in-laws usually live in the village. In the case of Garo in Dhaka, long-term migration has visibly changed the villages of origin. In some villages, every household has one or more members who have migrated either to Dhaka or to other towns and the flow of remittances has been substantial. Brick houses have been built in the villages of origin where in some cases only the elderly reside for most of the year.

As in Bangladesh, supporting siblings' education meant that Ethiopian and Eritrean migrant girls decided often to postpone their own marriage in order to provide a better and more stable future for their younger brothers and sisters. At the same time, some Eritrean young refugee women decided to accept the pressure of the family to marry men in the diaspora in order to be able to settle in a European or North American country. This was also a form of investment that the girls were making for their families, as their marriage was a promise of greater ability to support family members financially or with access to legal migration abroad. Providing financial help for their siblings' marriages was another important investment that the girls and young women were making. At a more general level, as migration has become a popular way of improving the household's conditions and reducing its vulnerability in Bangladesh, Eritrea and Ethiopia, having a successful family member in the city or abroad improved the family's social status.

Another major contribution, especially of the Eritrean girls and young women, was a financial and social network provided to their siblings to enable their migration to Khartoum and further on to Europe. This was, however, a huge burden and a responsibility, creating much stress for the young women. Ruta, who was 26 years of age, struggled for five years to survive in Khartoum. First, her brother arrived without informing her beforehand, and she had to provide ransom and pay his trip from Eritrea, which cost her about US$3500. The brother then left through Libya to Italy and on to Germany, finally claiming asylum in the Netherlands. This onward trip cost her again US$4500. She was very stressed, as she had to borrow money and was constantly thinking about how to repay her debts. A few months later, her younger sister showed up from Eritrea and she had to pay for her trip as well. Her mother eventually came in an attempt to join the younger brother, and applied for asylum in the Netherlands. Ruta had to provide for all these family members and was under a lot of pressure. Her cousin, Meriam, a single mother of a two-year-old and who arrived in Khartoum six years earlier explained:

> It is very hard to be here in Khartoum. It is hard for girls here. They have to support their siblings who come and want to go to Libya. Like Ruta, look at her, she supported her brother first, and then her sister. The brother is now fine. I saw his photos on Facebook; he is in good condition. He is in Holland. Have you seen Ruta's sister? She is also strong, not like Ruta. Ruta is suffering because of all of them. The same for me. Look at me, I am a single mum and have to support the whole family who also came [to Khartoum] after me.

These findings tie in well with the discussion about the gender and generational aspects of social support systems. In Chapter 7 we discussed social protection, and the ways in which girls build up social capital to protect themselves in a context where there is limited legal and institutional support. We also mentioned that even though the financial support to their families is relatively small, adolescent girls and young women are able to protect their relatives in times of crisis, such as health issues or death, and are sometimes able to invest in the education of their siblings or in land, and enable the family to buy better quality food. Young people, and in particular girls, play a crucial role in building a safer environment for their relatives at home. While the gendered aspects of the migration–development nexus have been studied quite extensively (Chant and Radcliffe 1992; Bailey 2010; Nyberg-Sørensen 2002; Piper 2009; Thieme and Siegmann 2010), there has been less attention paid to generational aspects. The intersection of gender and age is of particular relevance in the study of migration, with young people, including girls and young women, constituting at least 80% of the total number of migrants (Cortina et al. 2014, p. 2). As we have shown, the increasing number of young and unmarried adolescent girls migrating internally and internationally adds new dimensions to the debate about migration and development. Adolescent migrant girls carry particular responsibilities towards their families back home, since as "dutiful daughters" they are expected to send remittances, however small (Derks 2008; Montgomery et al. 2016). Their migration has mixed consequences for their own self-esteem and social status, however, as we discuss below.

Migrant Girls' Social Status and Self-Esteem

Social status and self-esteem are different but closely connected issues. Social status refers to the social perceptions of migrant girls, while self-esteem refers to girls' own evaluation and perceptions of their lives after migration. Girls' social status affected girls' self-esteem in various ways. Being able to support families back home, through sending remittances, supporting siblings' education or their migration, were in the girls' eyes changing their position in the family and wider community, which in many cases made them feel good. Almas, a 17-year-old who worked as a waitress in a local coffee shop in Khartoum and who had migrated two years earlier from Ethiopia, spoke about the feelings of her family towards her because of the support she has been sending them:

> My family in Ethiopia say that they are proud of me because I am working and sending money to them. I am able to support them. This is what they say. The money that I am sending will not change their lives in big ways. It is only for clothes, food, and the nursery of my daughter. They will have to continue working to survive. If they are sick, I will send all my money to help them.

In Dhaka and Addis Ababa too, many girls and young women believed that the financial support to their families was appreciated and increased their social status. Sangida (see Chapter 8) had been living and working in Dhaka since she was 13, initially as a domestic worker and then as a cleaner for an NGO. She was able to improve her own and her family's economic situation and to significantly help her sisters' education to the point that when we interviewed her at the age of 27, she could proudly say that her parents were now treating her as a 'boy' and that her advice and opinion would be followed by anyone else in the household. This is also an indication of a link between migration, access to jobs and the ability to provide assistance to the household members that reveal alternative ways, beyond marriage and childbearing, of transiting from the status of adolescent daughter within a household to a more respected and autonomous position. We will come back to this discussion in the final chapter.

Young women who returned from the Middle East also often mentioned the importance of their remittances for their families. The ability to remit was strongly linked to the social position of daughters within their households and wider community. Some of them said that their parents respected them because they were sending them money, and that they were very disappointed when they returned home, in particular those who had been deported during the 2013–2014 deportation campaign. Senayt was 23 years old when we interviewed her. She was born in Lalibella, in the north of Ethiopia, and migrated at the age of 14 to Desse, then to Addis Ababa and from there to the Middle East, at the age of 17. She worked in Dubai, Beirut and Qatar, and returned because of problems with her employer. She said:

> The perception of my family was not good when I returned. Their expectations were very high in terms of remittances. They wanted me to invest in building a house for them, like the girls in the neighbourhood did. In our area it is common that migrants do something tangible for their parents but I failed to do that. The perception of the community is also not good, I failed to meet their expectations. They don't know how we get the money, some succeed by doing some other business [sex work]. Migrants like me who don't want to engage in such practices fail to tap into the expectations of the community and the parents.

Internal migrants in Ethiopia also mentioned the importance of remitting for how their relatives perceive them. Tesfanesh, a 23-year-old domestic worker who migrated to Addis Ababa to escape her abusive stepfather, said:

> In the past I used to send money to my mum during the rainy season so that she can buy fertilizer and I did not save at all. But now my employer is encouraging me to save so I have saved up to 2000 Birr. My mum calls me and I help her from time to time. I send her coffee and tea and I also buy clothes for my sisters. The relationship with my stepfather has improved since coming here.

While sending remittances could have a positive effect on their social status, their difficult living conditions and work could also have negative effects. In Bangladesh, the migration of unmarried girls to work in the city is commonly seen with suspicion. Villagers expressed worries about girls' reputation (*man shonman*, honour, prestige) and about the risks of traffickers. The aunt of Sharmeen (Chapter 5) said: "We don't know what kind of people they would meet, they risk marrying with someone and then discover after a while that he doesn't have a position, that he is married with someone else". Dhaka is definitely commonly seen as a dangerous place, unsuitable for young unmarried girls who are supposed to live under the control of their parents and relatives. Their migration is commonly justified only by economic need. Some migrants were very negative about what people think of migrant garment workers. Lamia (see Chapter 8) said:

> If they know that a girl earns 5000 taka per month the people in my village would say: 'she must be a prostitute'. That's what they think, that's why we don't have any more a good reputation in the village. We can't talk to anyone with our head up, we have to talk keeping our head down.

This is in line with the dominant discourses about Ethiopian female migrants, both in Addis Ababa as in the Middle East. Mekdes, a 29-year-old domestic worker in Addis Ababa, thinks that women who have migrated to the Middle East have a special place in the home communities because of the stories about abuse whereas people are not worried about women who work in Addis Ababa because they are not so far away:

> When she comes from an Arab country they respect her and when she passes by they greet her, but if she comes from any place in Ethiopia, they don't respect her and they disgrace her because they don't think she worked hard to earn the money. They think she was a sex worker.

Even so, there is also a clear relationship with remittances from migrants working in the Middle East because they are expected to be higher: "Parents are grateful to those who are living in Arab countries because they send them money. But those who are going to Addis Ababa, they ***may disappear and they may not be able to change themselves and their*** families". Despite the fact that the remittances may be higher, the social status of female migrants in the Middle East is often low. The fact that the girls and young women live without the protection of (male) family members and may experience sexual abuse has a negative effect on their social status. Gender, sexuality and age intersect in the impact of migration on the social status of adolescent girls and young women (see Derks 2008; Hertrich and Lesclingand 2013). The risks and threats of being alone in an unknown and possibly hostile and dangerous environment in which girls' reputation could be harmed affected their social status. This demonstrates even more the importance of their ways of pushing consciously or accidentally for changes in gender order and ideologies by the small things and acts, which stand out even more against the backdrop of the strong gender norms that influence the policing of young women and adolescent girls.

In Khartoum, most girls and young women reported that their social status has improved in the eyes of their families. Some girls have become the main breadwinner and this has significantly improved their position in their family and increased their decision-making power on family matters. Many studies about gender and migration have pointed to the positive effects of women's migration on household decisions, but few have also taken age and life course into account. Only recently have there been some studies showing that migrant girls play an important role in supporting their families (Derks 2008; Hertrich and Lescingand 2013; Montgomery et al. 2016).

Others, like Arsema, who had lived in Sudan for over 34 years, felt unable to respond to the pressures from their families to support them. In several conversations, Arsema mentioned the stress she has been experiencing over the years in Khartoum. She had not been able to educate herself and build a stable future for her family, nor could she send money to relatives in Ethiopia. For this reason, they regarded her as a selfish person who did not want to share.

> In our community, you have a status if you share with others. If you only live for yourself, people do not respect you. But how could I support

> others? I was very young and alone in Khartoum, I married, and God gave me all these children. But I can only do a simple job of selling tea, and my husband also does not earn much. We do not have anyone who helped us, and we barely survive. I often think of suicide, as this pressure of supporting others is too strong.

Migration has thus both opened up possibilities for girls and young women to improve their self-esteem and status in their home communities, but the inability to provide financial support often put them in a disadvantaged position.

In Ethiopia, half of the interviewees considered their life to be better than before migration, while eight said that it was worse. The latter group referred in particular to stress and a lack of self-esteem, and four said that it was economically more difficult. Most, however, said that it had not worsened and had improved in economic terms. Seven women said that they had more self-esteem because of their migration. Those with bad experiences may have had less self-esteem and those with good experiences more, although overcoming bad experiences could also be empowering. Sex workers in particular expressed ambivalent feelings about the impact of their migration. Feven came to Addis Ababa with her aunt two years ago hoping to earn a lot of money as a sex worker, but has not been able to save any money or help her mother. When we asked what has changed in her life she answered: "Nothing changed! I am changed in terms of the clothes that I wear but nothing changed in my life, it is hurting me, burning me. Yet, I have to work in order to survive, I have to eat but I do not have any peace of mind". And Haimanot, a 17-year-old domestic worker in Addis Ababa, said:

> They [people in the village] told me that I would change my life once I get here. But nothing changed except helping my mother with the money that I make. [...] They think that I am lucky because Addis Ababa is a very good place to live. But I keep quiet because I didn't find anything. They think that I have changed and have good things. But as for me, I haven't seen any change yet.

The negative assessment of their migration should be linked to girls' interpretation of "change". They perceived change as something significant and structural, such as buying a piece of land, building a new house or opening a small enterprise with which they or their parents or siblings would be able to earn more and live more comfortable lives.

The analysis of the life stories shows, however, that change comes with "small steps", in line with Goldfarb's "small things" (2006) (see Chapter 8). We therefore argue for the need to pay close attention to how the migrants, refugees and their families conceptualize "change". Change was, for most of the girls, and for their family members and communities, linked to economic rewards. While some girls also valued education highly, they mainly assessed the impact of their migration with reference to what they had earned and the changes that had brought about. Other types of remittances, such as social remittances (Levitt 1998; Levitt and Lamba-Nieves 2011), were rarely taken into account, nor the ways in which their migration had affected their perceptions of themselves and their sense of self. Major changes had taken place in their lives, even though they may not have evaluated them positively. They can be, however, interpreted as "small steps" leading to social transformations.

Small Steps Towards Social Transformation

Gender and age intersect in the motivations for migration, in the experiences of living and working in cities, and in the ways in which migration affects migrants as well as those who stay behind. Adolescent migrant girls are part of translocal and transnational fields (Faist 2008) and play an active role in creating them. They connect people, objects, ideas and knowledge across multiple places by being simultaneously embedded in them. A translocal perspective enables us to study changes at the local level and be sensitive to connections to the national and the global levels (Glick Schiller and Faist 2009; Faist 2009; Levitt 2012; Mazzucato 2011). Faist (2009) calls for a translocal analysis of contemporary relationships of power, moving beyond the discussion on migration and development and focusing on social transformations in the context of changing discourses on the market, state and community. Similarly Castles (2010) and Bakewell (2010 argue that understanding local experiences of migration can be enhanced through an analysis of global social transformations. Castles pleads for the need:

> ... to conceptualise migration not merely as a result of social transformation, nor as one of its causes, but as an integral and essential part of social transformation processes. That means that theories of migration should be embedded in broader social theory. It also means that research on any

> specific migration phenomenon must always include research on the societal context in which it takes place. (Castles 2010, p. 1578)

Such an approach allows us to analyse the interplay between structure and agency in the context of migration, and to move beyond simplistic notions such as "the impact of migration". An intersectional approach of social transformations, in which gender, age and migration are used as analytical lenses, has been remarkably absent. In recent years, a number of studies were published about the impact of migration on families, the formation of transnational families and new phenomena such as "transnational motherhood" (Baldassar 2007; Bryceson and Vuorela 2002; Gamburd 2000; Hondagneu-Sotelo and Avila 1997; Mazzucato and Schans 2008; Parreñas 2005). Children were, however, not visible or recognized as playing important roles in the construction of transnational and translocal families and were therefore absent as agents in migration in research on transnationalism (Huijsmans 2018). Huijsmans (2018) proposes a generational perspective on transnational childhoods, since children participate actively in the formation of transnational (and translocal) social fields.

An example of the ways in which gender, age and migration intersect is the impact of the migration of adolescent girls on the changing composition of households in different locations and the creation of transnational and translocal households and families. This also results in changing positions of women (and men) within the household and power relationships within it. This was particularly striking when an Eritrean mother who came to visit one of her daughters in Khartoum commented on the impact of migration of her children on her life in Eritrea:

> I feel so bad because I am a mother, so a mother wants all her kids to be around her. But in Eritrea the life is too bad. So all my children are leaving. First it was Helen, then her younger brother, now Luam, the younger sister. It is too difficult to be a mother, a parent in one place, and all your children are in another place. For us, it is good to be together in one house. But now we all are in different places. Scattered… Even when I eat food I do not feel it is good for me to eat. I was born and grew up in a big family and now I have a big family [7 children], so I want all my family to be around me. I came here to Khartoum because my children asked me to come. And I want to live with them. But now, I left some children and my husband in Eritrea. This is also not good.

The case of Eritrea is unique because so many young women and men are leaving as a result of the compulsory military service and there are hardly any young people on the streets (see Chapter 4). Several respondents told us that the once bustling streets of Asmara, especially in the evenings, became deserted as young Eritreans left and are now highly visible on the streets of Khartoum, and in many places in Europe. Even in rural Ethiopia, household composition is changing as many young people are migrating, including adolescent girls. In the interviews with parents around Estie, an area in the Amhara region which is known for its high percentage of migration to neighbouring towns, Addis Ababa and the Middle East, we were told that an increasing number of young women want to leave in order to continue their education or find paid work elsewhere. Some of the parents whose daughters had migrated to Bahir Dar or Addis Ababa had lost contact with them and said that they just hoped that they would be happy and able to improve their own lives. They did not expect any remittances. A mother of eight children told us that two of her daughters had migrated. She was against their migration but they insisted and left. The mother expressed her concerns about one of the daughters, in particular: "We worry about her and we are also disappointed that she left because of our incapability to pay for her school. We would have loved it if she was here and continued her education". She is not sending any money to them but the mother considers the fact that she has migrated as help: "We consider helping herself as helping us". The migration of adolescent Ethiopian girls and the loss of contact between parents and children point to an important social transformation for close-knit Ethiopian families. When we compare the findings of the research in Khartoum with those of the internal migration in Ethiopia we can conclude that girls who move internationally play a greater role in the construction of translocal families than girls who migrate internally.

In Bangladesh, there are strong contacts between migrant girls and their families back home, and the fact that many girls aspire to return home in order to get married after having spent several years in Dhaka indicates that family composition is not changing as much as in Ethiopia and Eritrea.

Yet, in all three cases migrant girls have played an active role in shaping social relations as much as they are shaped by them. The backdrop of the everyday struggles of adolescent migrants girls' and young women's is defined by strong gender norms that situate girls' and women's respectability in their reputation as docile, polite, obedient, and virgins. By transgressing these norms through their mobility within or across borders, their access to work and providing for their household members, young women and adolescent girls both gain and lose in their attempt to secure a more autonomous status within the household and the wider community. The underlying justification of policing their respectability is linked to gender, sexuality and age norms that continue to define the respectable potential wives, mothers and daughters in law. How these young women attempt to shape alternative transitions t to adulthood through small steps therefore become more so revealing. We come back to this discussion in the concluding chapter.

References

Bailey, A. J. (2010). Population Geographies, Gender and the Migration-Development Nexus. *Progress in Human Geography, 34*(3), 375–386.

Bakewell, O. (2010). Some Reflections on Structure and Agency in Migration Theory. *Journal of Ethnic and Migration Studies, 36*(10), 1689–1708.

Baldassar, L. (2007). Transnational Families and the Provision of Moral and Emotional Support: The Relationship Between Truth and Distance. *Identities: Global Studies in Culture and Power, 14,* 385–409.

Bryceson, D., & Vuorela, U. (Eds.). (2002). *The Transnational Family: New European Frontiers and Global Networks.* Oxford: Berg.

Castaldo, A., Deshingkar, P., & McKay, A. (2012). *Internal Migration, Remittances and Poverty: Evidence from Ghana and India* (Working Paper No. 7). Brighton: University of Sussex; Migrating Out of Poverty Research Programme Consortium.

Castles, S. (2010). Understanding Global Migration: A Social Transformation Perspective. *Journal of Ethnic and Migration Studies, 36*(10), 1565–1586.

Chant, S., & Radcliffe, S. A. (1992). Migration and Development: The Importance of Gender. In S. Chant (Ed.), *Gender and Migration in Developing Countries* (pp. 1–29). London: Bellhaven Press.

Cortina, J., Taran, P., & Raphael, A. (Eds.). (2014). *Migration and Youth: Challenges and Opportunities.* New York, NY: UNICEF, Global Migration Group.

de Haas, H. (2010). Migration and Development: A Theoretical Perspective. *International Migration Review, 44*(1), 227–264.

de Regt, M., & Tafesse, M. (2017). "Deported Before Experiencing the Good Sides of Migration": Ethiopians Returning from Saudi Arabia. In F. Demissie (Ed.), *Ethiopians in an Age of Migration: Scattered Lives Beyond Borders* (pp. 104–118). Abingdon: Routledge.

Derks, A. (2008). *Khmer Women on the Move: Exploring Work and Life in Urban Cambodia*. Honolulu, HI: University of Hawaii Press.
Faist, T. (2008). Migrants as Transnational Development Agents: An Inquiry into the Newest Round of the Migration-Development Nexus. *Population, Space and Place, 14,* 21–42.
Faist, T. (2009). Transnationalization and Development: Toward an Alternative Agenda. *Social Analysis, 53*(3), 38–59.
Gamburd, M. (2000). *The Kitchen Spoon's Handle: Transnationalism and Sri Lanka's Migrant Housemaids*. Ithaca, NY and London: Cornell University Press.
Gardner, K., & Zahir, A. (2006). *Place, Social Protection and Migration in Bangladesh: A Londoni Village in Biswanath* (Working Paper No. 18). Brighton: University of Sussex; DRC on Migration Globalisation and Poverty.
Glick Schiller, N., & Faist, T. (2009). Introduction: Migration, Development and Social Transformations. *Social Analysis, 53*(3), 1–13.
Goldfarb, J. (2006). *The Politics of Small Things: The Power of the Powerless in Dark Times*. Chicago, IL: University of Chicago Press.
Grabska, K. (2014). *Gender, Identity, and Home: Nuer Repatriation to Southern Sudan*. Oxford: Boydell & Brewer, James Currey edition.
Hertrich, V., & Lescingand, M. (2013). Adolescent Migration in Rural Africa as a Challenge to Gender and Intergenerational Relationships: Evidence from Mali. *The ANNALS of the American Academy of Political and Social Science, 175,* 175–188.
Hondagneu-Sotelo, P., & Avila, E. (1997). I'm Here, But I'm There: The Meanings of Latina Transnational Motherhood. *Gender & Society, 11*(5), 548–571.
Huijsmans, R. (2018). Transnational Childhoods. In H. Montgomery & M. Robb (Eds.), *Children and Young People's Worlds*. Bristol, UK: Policy Press & Open University.
King, R., & Skeldon, R. (2010). "Mind the Gap!": Integrating Approaches to Internal and International Migration. *Journal of Ethnic and Migration Studies, 36*(10), 1619–1646.
Kunz, R. (2008). "Remittances Are Beautiful?" Gender Implications of the New Global Remittances Trend. *Third World Quarterly, 29*(7), 1389–1409.
Levitt, P. (1998). Social Remittances: Migration Driven Local-Level Forms of Cultural Diffusion. *International Migration Review, 32*(4), 926–948.
Levitt, P. (2012). What's Wrong with Migration Scholarship? A Critique and a Way Forward. *Identities, 1,* 1–8.
Levitt, P., & Lamba-Nieves, D. (2011). Social Remittances Revisited. *Journal of Ethnic and Migration Studies, 37*(1), 1–22.
Mahler, S., & Pessar, P. (2006). Gender Matters: Ethnographers Bring Gender from the Periphery Toward the Core of Migration Studies. *International Migration Review, 40*(1), 27–63.

Mazzucato, V. (2011). Reverse Remittances in the Migration–Development Nexus: Two-Way Flows Between Ghana and The Netherlands. *Population, Space, and Place, 17*, 454–468.

Mazzucato, V., & Schans, D. (2008). *Researching Transnational Families, Children and the Migration Development Nexus.* Paper Presented at the Conference on Migration and Development: Future Directions for Research and Policy, Social Sciences Research Council, New York, 28 February–1 March.

McKay, A., & Deshingkar, P. (2014). *Internal Remittances and Poverty: Further Evidence from Africa and Asia* (Migration Out of Poverty Working Paper No. 14). Brighton: University of Sussex.

Montgomery, M. R., Balk, D., Liu, Z., Agarwal, S., Jones, E., & Adamo, S. (2016). Urban Migration of Adolescent Girls: Quantitative Results from Developing Countries. In J. Michael (Ed.), *International Handbook of Migration and Population Distribution* (pp. 573–604). Dordrecht: Springer.

Nyberg-Sørensen, N. (2010). *The Rise and Fall of the "Migrant Superhero" and the New "Deportee Trash": Contemporary Strain on Mobile Livelihoods in the Central American Region* (DIIS Working Paper No. 22). Copenhagen: Danish Institute for International Studies.

Nyberg-Sørensen, N., Van Haer, N., & Engberg-Pedersen, P. (2002). *The Migration-Development Nexus: Evidence and Policy Options.* Geneva: International Organization for Migration.

Osella, F., & Osella, C. (2006). Once Upon a Time in the West: Stories of Migration and Modernity from Kerala, South India. *Journal of the Royal Anthropological Institute, 12*(3), 569–588.

Osella, F., & Osella, C. (2007). Experiences of "Transnationalism" and the Transnational Family: Women and Gulf Migration from Kerala. In S. Koshy & T. Modood (Eds.), *South Asian Diaspora.* Durham, NC: Duke University Press.

Parreñas, R. S. (2005). Long Distance Intimacy: Class, Gender and Intergenerational Relations between Mothers and Children in Filipino Transnational Families. *Global Networks, 5*(4), 317–336.

Piper, N. (2009). *The Gendered Political Economy of Migration* (IMDS Working Paper No. 17). New Delhi: School of Social Sciences, Jahawarlal Nehru University.

Rashid, S. R. (2007). *Lives Without Men, Left Behind Wives of Bangladesh Migrant Workers.* Paper Presented at the Workshop "Gender, Generation and Migration", University of Sussex, Brighton, 20–21, April.

Rashid, S. R. (2008). *Overseas Labour Migration from Rural Bangladesh: Livelihood, Capital and Risk in Two Villages in Comilla.* Ph.D. thesis, University of Sussex.

Sørensen, N. N., & Olwig, K. F. (2002). *Work and Migration: Life and Livelihoods in a Globalizing World.* Abingdon: Routledge.

Taylor, J. (1999). The New Economics of Labour Migration and the Role of Remittances in the Migration Process. *International Migration, 37*(1), 63–86.

Thieme, S., & Siegmann, K. A. (2010). Coping on Women's Backs: Social Capital–Vulnerability Links Through a Gender Lens. *Current Sociology, 58*(5), 715–737.

Toyota, Y., & Nguyen, (2007). Editorial Introduction: Bringing the "Left Behind" Back into View in Asia: A Framework for Understanding the "Migration-Left Behind" Nexus. *Population, Space and Place, 13,* 157–161.

CHAPTER 10

Transitions and Transformations

"I Have a Responsibility Now… I Have Somehow Grown Up": Transitions into Adulthood

The key theme of this book has been the link between migration of adolescent girls and transitions into adulthood. We have examined how migration during the crucial period of adolescence intersects with girls' other important decisions at that time, particularly in relation to education and work. We continue the theme of transitions in this closing chapter, focusing specifically on marriage and on alternative ways of becoming an adult woman that emerge in the context of migration. Ruta, from Eritrea, who has been living in Khartoum for eight years, and whom we met first in Chapter 4, is evocative of such transitions:

> When I left Eritrea, I was still a child, I knew nothing… now, even though my mother wants me to get married because I am 26, I cannot and do not want to do it here[in Khartoum]. I want to study first; I want to get a good job. […] Although I am still single, here I had to grow up very fast. Now, I am responsible for my family in Eritrea. I am the oldest one. I have a responsibility here for them and for myself. I earn money, and I pay for my expenses. I am somehow grown up now. No one else is responsible for me here. I can also decide what I want and how I want to live my life.

K. Grabska et al., *Adolescent Girls' Migration in The Global South*, Palgrave Studies on Children and Development,
https://doi.org/10.1007/978-3-030-00093-6_10

Ruta's narrative shows how some migrant girls and adolescents are slowly carving out alternative ways of becoming adult women, and how their decision to migrate intersects with other decisions at that specific phase in their life. As the three different country studies demonstrate, adolescent girls' migration is not just the result of structural factors but inspired by complex choices and aspirations, both collective and individual. Moreover, migration has positive and negative effects, both for the migrant girls themselves and for their families. In this concluding chapter, we reflect on how the choice to migrate and the experiences of migration have affected the young migrant girls' life trajectories and how they have intersected with their transition to adulthood. Second, we locate our conclusions in the discussion of how the gender order has had profound effects on the decision, experiences and consequences of migration for the girls and their families in the three case studies. We look specifically at social relations and at gender norms using a life-course and generational analysis. Finally, we conclude by reflecting on whether migration is a good option for girls.

Adolescence, Transitions, Life Course and Migration

In Chapter 9 we focused on the links between adolescent girls' migration and wider social transformations. Here, we turn to the particular effects of migration on an individual's life course (Bailey 2009; Brettell 2002), and the links between migration and transition into adulthood. The migration of adolescent girls, whether as part of a household strategy or an individual endeavour, has major implications for their transition into adulthood, because it intersects with other important decisions in their lives. While girls face a number of challenges in their migratory trajectories, migration can also open up new and better opportunities with positive implications for their future. As in the case of the young Bolivians moving to Argentina studied by Samantha Punch (2002, 2015), the transitions for adolescent girls in Bangladesh, Ethiopia and those who migrated to Sudan were not linear. Punch points out that the notion of a linear transition from a dependent child to an independent adult should be problematized in the context of what she calls the "Majority World", where household relationships and between generations tend to be characterized by continuously negotiated interdependencies. For young Bolivians, achieving economic independence goes hand in hand with keeping strong interdependent relationships with their family, thus challenging views that link the transition to adulthood to 'autonomy' and to severing links with parents. Crivello (2009), drawing on longitudinal research among Peruvian girls and boys, argues that migration choices are strongly linked to educational aspirations. Educational achievements are the core of a successful transition to adulthood and migration is a way of "becoming somebody someplace else" (Crivello 2009, p. 23). Guo et al. (2011), discussing the process of reverse and circular migration of young Chinese women to Beijing, argue that the decision to move between rural areas of origin and urban destinations is related to expectations and opportunities for life transitions in different moments in the course of a person's life (Guo et al. 2011, p. 53).

As the narratives of Arsema, Feven, Helen, Lamia, Ruta, Salam, Sharmeen, Tigistand Tsirite—who have been the main protagonists of the book—and those of other girls demonstrate, migration has contributed to challenging established transitions into adulthood for migrating girls and to opening other pathways to become women. This has happened in several ways: through developing a greater sense of selfhood, through obtaining work, through giving up formal education to acquire other forms of knowledge and through postponing marriage or getting married on their own terms. We discuss each of these transitions in this chapter. We show that, as a result of social transformations and transitions in the context of migration, the definitions of gendered adult identities are also being renegotiated. However, the (re)definition of one's adult (gender) identity is fraught with ambiguity and contradiction.

Independent Migration as a Transition into Adulthood

One of the main findings of this research is that the spatial aspect of mobility, linked to the act of migrating, has become part of adolescent girls' transition into adulthood. This observation is not new in research among young male migrants, as several studies have shown how migration becomes a rite of passage and a necessary step in the attainment of the social status of adult men (e.g. Monsutti 2007; Gardner 2009; Osella and Osella 2000). For example, in his research among Hazara Afghan young men in Iran Monsutti demonstrates that:

> ... for many young men, migration offers the opportunity to broaden their social networks beyond narrow kinship and neighborhood ties. It may be conceived as a necessary stage in their existence, a rite of passage to adulthood and a step toward manhood. (Monsutti 2007, p. 169)

Monsutti also argues that the migration of young Hazara men is part of a wider household strategy, as much as an individual endeavour. In a similar way, girls' migration, as we have seen, might sometimes be a way to diversify the household economy and spread risks. While it can be a means to cope, it is also to a certain extent a rite of passage for girls in their transition towards adulthood. As the narratives of migrant adolescent girls and young women and their families presented in earlier chapters show, migration and the related experiences, such as living alone far away from their family, being financially independent and earning money through their own work, as well as at times being able to help family members financially, including helping younger siblings to pursue education and in their internal or international migratory trajectories, were often perceived by girls and their family members as a way to become an adult. For some of the Bangladeshi, Eritrean and Ethiopian migrants, gaining responsibility through the act of independent migration, and thus gaining some level of independence and more opportunities to make their own decisions, gave them a sense of an alternative female adulthood. For these reasons, physical mobility within or across borders has been an important point in the life course of migrant adolescent girls. At the same time, girls' rite of passage is valued differently from boys', as it is subject to stricter gender norms and ideologies that govern the mobility of girls and perceive it as transgressive. In general, however, migration, even in uncertain contexts such as that of Eritrea, is not a rupture but a crucial phase in the life cycle.

This finding builds on the literature on (mainly male) youth migration and points to the importance of to some extent newer phenomenon of girls' and young women's migration. It adds a vital dimension of girls' experiences and grounds the individual and collective experiences of transitions in an intersectional analysis, paying particular attention to the gender and generational dimensions. What emerges is that the act of migrating has to some extent become part of youth transitions and acquiring a new identity. To follow Stuart Hall's seminal statements on "identity" (e.g., Hall 1996), becoming an adult for young migrants is revealed as contextual, situational, relational and processual, or as King and Williams argue, "a process, in other words, of 'becoming'" (2018, p. 4; see also Worth 2009). Migration becomes part of a wider repertoire of transitions to adulthood, and also opens possibilities of becoming and acquiring a different type of gendered adult identity for adolescent girls in Bangladesh, Ethiopia and Eritrea, and elsewhere, as the emerging literature confirms (Agarwal et al. 2016; Crivello 2009; Derks 2008; Hertrich and Lesclingand 2012; Jacquemin 2011). As in the past, and still so to some extent, the process of becoming an adult woman has been predominantly linked to being married and having children. Migration, however, contributes to a more gradual passage towards adulthood, and signifies the element of a journey in "becoming" (Worth 2009).

As King and Williams note in their editorial introduction to the findings from a research project on youth mobility in Europe:

> ... transitions are not only linear or in one, "progressive" direction: there are also "ruptures," "discontinuities," and "yo-yo" transitions (Borlagden 2015; Du Bois-Reymond and López Blasco 2003; Hörschelmann 2011). These alternative transitions arise due to a range of potential drivers varying in time-scale and also social scale, including increasingly flexible labour markets in some countries, the "destandardisation" of both education and career trajectories, the impact of macro-economic shocks such as the 2008+crisis, and personal and family factors. (Walther et al. 2006; King and Williams 2018, p. 4)

Similarly, in our study, migrant adolescent girls did not experience linear and continuous transitions, which were also relational and context-specific. While working girls sometimes perceived themselves as adult women, their neighbours or some family members still saw them as adolescents and categorized them as youngsters. For example, Ruta, whose narrative opened this chapter, was considered fully adult by her mother only once she was married. Ruta's mother told us when she arrived in Khartoum for Ruta's engagement in October 2016:

> I know she has been helping us for a long time, and due to her work in Khartoum the rest of the family could leave Eritrea and reach safer places in Europe. But for me, she has been a child till now. Now, with the marriage, I am happy, she will finally be a grown-up woman, a married woman, a *sabeyti*.

In the same way, for Eritreans who managed to get to Europe by crossing through Libya (including two of our research participants), the fact that they were under 18 years of age put them in the category of "unaccompanied minors" and thus, due to their perceived vulnerability, they were able to claim asylum. This category of minors did not correspond to their experiences and transitions that they had undergone during their migratory trajectories, however. In this way, in their encounters with European asylum procedures, these young women had to adopt an (imposed) identity as children. Hence, the process of transition was often back and forth, highly situational, relational and context-specific.

Capacity to Understand and Take Decisions as a Transition

The narratives of adolescent girls and young women reveal that migration and the resulting geographical shift have been a way to develop a new sense of selfhood as an important transition in their life. Through the new experiences at destination, many girls gained a sense of independence and widened their social world beyond the circle of their own family and childhood relationships. The process of personal growth and development of an adult identity is linked with the capacity to decide about the direction of one's life, even when this does not follow hegemonic social and particularly gender norms. This was expressed, for example, by some Bangladeshi girls in terms of an enhanced capacity "to understand". Sanjida, who was 27 years of age when we interviewed her, migrated as a domestic worker at around the age of 13. She did it unwillingly and under family pressure, because she had already been in Dhaka for a few months when she was only eight years old to do the same job, and she was afraid she might again be abused and mistreated. This second experience, however, turned out to be far more positive than the first one, mainly because of the relationship that Sanjida established with her employer. The 'auntie' (employer) realized how upset Sanjida was about leaving her parents and family behind and tried to console her. This gave her the self-confidence to decide what she wanted when her parents and her 'auntie' insisted that she get married. She was able to explain to them that before getting married she wanted to make a more substantial contribution to improving her family's situation and so needed to work for longer to finance her two little sisters' education as they were still in classes 3 and 4. Finally, Sanjida found a good NGO job and has since been supporting her family and in particular her younger sisters' schooling:

> One of my sisters passed the intermediate exam, found a job and probably she will keep studying. My family is more or less in a good situation. They get more support from me than from my older brother. They respect me

> so much that, as I took responsibility for the whole family, they feel they have to do according to my will. It goes on in this way: they do what I say without complaining and they never asked: you are a woman, why do you talk? My situation now is good, after I found a job there has been a lot of improvement in my family situation, in my personal situation, from all points of view.

On another occasion, she said that she felt that her parents were now treating her as a 'boy', meaning that her status in the family had changed and that she was no longer subordinate to her brother. Even more, her parents were following her suggestions in important household decisions, rather than her brother's. Yet, she was still not referred to as a man or a son, thus showing that her social transition was particularly located within gender norms.

This and other stories of girls and young women in the three cities point to the (re)negotiation of norms regarding gender identities as part of migrant adolescent girls' and young women's capacity to take decisions. Although in their initial responses on the impact of migration on their lives, most girls and young women saw no positive results, when they reflected on small changes, they often referred positively to the fact that, by migrating, they had become responsible for themselves and others and financially independent. The experience of migration had brought changes in their lives and made them redefine their positionalities and priorities, often in contrast with the socially accepted ways of becoming a woman.

Education, Migration and Transitions

Migration is in different ways interconnected with decisions about education. Most Bengali girls in Bangladesh as well as Ethiopians and Eritreans in Sudan had stopped attending school before migrating. Others dropped out because they had decided to migrate. For some girls, however, migration was motivated by the desire to continue studying, for example for Ethiopian girls who migrated to Addis Ababa and for some of the Garo girls who moved to Dhaka. Eritreans' narratives were dominated by the goal to pursue education, if not in Khartoum, then in their intended destination. Overall, our research suggests that in all three case studies, despite the importance that young people and adults attach to education, and despite the migrants' aspirations, migration has mainly coincided with leaving school for good. Only a few migrants have been able to enrol in evening classes (for instance, some domestic workers in Addis Ababa) or specialized courses in their place of destination (a few Eritreans and Ethiopians in Sudan). While formal education remains an aspiration for adolescent girls before and during migration, the realities of their lives in their respective destinations make it unattainable. Thus, girls and young women postpone or abandon their plans for schooling, and instead identify migratory trajectories, as Ruta's narrative at the beginning of the chapter suggests, as a way of acquiring a different type of knowledge.

Migrants in Addis Ababa also pointed out different ways of learning. Elsa was 18 years old at the time of the interview. She came to Addis Ababa to continue her education, as her parents were afraid that she would be abducted in the small town near Debre Birhan. When her aunt and uncle started to abuse her, Elsa ran away and became a sex worker. She is unhappy with her life but has learned to communicate better, thanks to her work:

> Previously I was not good at approaching people. But now the work itself has changed me, it forces me to communicate with people, it makes you meet people and it makes you free. Before I used to get shy talking about sex but now we talk openly about sex, condoms, sexually transmitted diseases. I also teach others about those things.

Fiker is 24 and has been living for a long time in Addis Ababa. She ran away with a friend when she was 13 years old, escaping the restrictive environment of her parents, who were both civil servants. She moved from place to place and finally settled in Addis Ababa, where she started doing sex work. Fiker also thinks that her communication skills have improved: "With regard to my social life, I have learned to communicate with other people and have a good relationship with them. My awareness about many things has increased".

In their study on childhood transitions in Ethiopia, Camfield and Tafere (2011) conclude that there is a large gap between ideals, expectations and experiences of childhood transitions, particularly for girls. They argue that "while girls in Ethiopia are said to be constrained by their lack of opportunities, in fact their likelihood of making successful transitions is reduced by having too many potentially contradictory opportunities too soon" (Camfield and Tafere 2011, p. 259). The expectations to contribute to household chores, the expansion of educational facilities, the rather negative attitude of most parents towards girls' education because of the perceived risk of premarital sex or abduction, and the expectation of getting married and having children are some of these contradictory opportunities affecting girls' transitions to adulthood in rural Ethiopia. As our findings show, migration can be seen as another opportunity in girls' lives, but also a way for girls to deal with these contradictory expectations.

Marriage and Beyond: Alternative Ways of Becoming an Adult

Migration can have a fundamental impact on marriage, particularly in terms of delaying it, as other research has demonstrated (Hertrich and Lesclingand 2012). Marriage is often postponed by Eritrean, Ethiopian and Bangladeshi girls and young women who migrate internally or internationally to escape early arranged marriages and/or to evade constraining gender norms. Marriage is also delayed by most of the young women migrants, both because of financial considerations and because their short- or long-term priority is to earn money and contribute to their families' well-being. In some cases, this sacrifice is made to assist younger siblings to obtain an education (for Ethiopians in Khartoum and Bangladeshis in Dhaka) and to migrate to Khartoum and beyond (for Eritreans). In Bangladesh, Ethiopia and Eritrea marriage remains a cornerstone of womanhood and retains its importance as a social institution and a fundamental step into adulthood. Not only the timing, but also the prospects, decision-making, circumstances and purpose of marriage are now changing, however. For some young women, migration translates into greater capacity to choose a husband and whether or not to marry. Those who had suffered male violence and sexual abuse often did not want to get married.

For some Eritrean girls and young women in Khartoum who felt that their migration meant they could not get married on their own terms and have children, migration resulted in 'getting stuck' in their status as girls as they had to postpone these transitions to a later stage. Eritrean girls who were unmarried and had no children often talked about 'wasting time' (see Chapter 8). Ruta's narrative is evocative of this prolonged and frustrated state of being unable to achieve one's life goals and being stuck:

> Look at us! We are here, we came here to change our lives, and nothing has happened. There is no change here. Me, for example, I am already 26, if I was in Eritrea, I would be married by now, and would have a child. But

> here, how can I get married and have a child here? Even my mother who is in Eritrea, every time when I call she talks to me about marriage, but how can I get married here? I am still a girl (*guol*), people still call me *menesay* (youth). I should be a *sabeyti* (married woman) by now. We are missing our time here.

The issue of time passing was a major problem for some parents as they saw their daughters wasting time and being stuck in adolescence rather than establishing their own families and having children. The idea of time was also related to the social status within the girls' wider community and their transition to adulthood, which could be attained through marriage and having children, as well as their ability to take independent decisions as adult women (within the bounds of household gender and generational hierarchies). Thus, for some, the physical move of migration felt as if it was leading to social immobility. We return to this issue in the next section. On the other hand, while the socially accepted ways of becoming a *sabeyti* might not be easily attainable in Sudan, Eritrean youth are slowly carving out alternative ways. As Ruta's first narrative shows, .escaping from Eritrea offered new changes in the girls' lives. As 16-year-old Luna in Eritrea mentioned, "here I am an adult already. I am here alone, I need to work for myself but also I am responsible for my sick mother back in Eritrea".

Very few of the Bangladeshi migrants perceive the economic independence and the capacity to stand on one's own feet gained by working in a garment factory as leading to life security or, more importantly, to a legitimate adult social identity. Despite saying proudly that her parents were treating her as a boy, and her efforts to save money for her sisters' study, Sanjidahas also been saving to buy gold for her own dowry. She was worried that because of her age, it would be difficult to find a husband. Her independence notwithstanding, like others she is in some ways troubled and not completely at peace with her situation with respect to marriage. Because of her age (27) she would have to pay a larger dowry to the prospective husband's family, which worried her. Sanjida's example shows that becoming 'adult' and independent to the point of being the de facto head of one's family might entail remaining single up to 27 years of age.

Lamia (see Chapter 8) decided to migrate abroad in order to support her mother instead of getting married. She prioritized economic security for her mother and herself, but sometimes she seemed to regret not being able to remarry. On the other hand, having been married before migrating, she had already fulfilled a social and religious obligation, she was already a *mohila* (adult woman) and no longer a *meye* (girl), and this made her feel confident and legitimized her different objectives, such as supporting her sister and her mother. Like Lamia, other Bangladeshi girls were afraid that if they married they would no longer be able to support their families. Some of them were resigned to the fact that their life had already gone "in the wrong direction" and wanted instead to be able to help their younger siblings. Some of the older migrants especially were well aware of the negative experiences of some women who had remarried in Dhaka. They were afraid to be spoiled and cheated by a new husband and for this reason, ruled out the possibility of marrying again. Unlike Sanjida, Lamia and others who had been more successful in terms of work and earning, and those who have been residing in Dhaka for longer, the youngest unmarried Bengali migrants foresee getting married as their main short-term objective, only temporarily secondary to earning an income and contributing to their family's well-being.

In Ethiopia too, marriage is the most important way to make a successful transition to adulthood. Despite the assumption that girls' higher enrolment in secondary school will lead to delayed marriage, young women, especially in rural areas, are often married before they are 18 years of age (Chuta and Morrow 2015, p. 4). Our findings show that migration has indeed led to a postponement of marriage. Both domestic workers and sex workers expressed the need to be economically independent before getting married. One of the main reasons they gave was that economic independence is important in case the marriage does not work out.

Domestic workers were, however, explicit in their wish to marry and have children one day, but they had no idea yet whom they would marry and what their lives would look like as married women. The fact that most of them were still young (around 15 years old) and had migrated recently to Addis Ababa may have affected this. Sex workers doubted that they would be able to marry, at least in the near future. Most of them had lost trust in men because of their experiences in the course of their work, and thought that they would not be able to find a man who would accept them given their history of having been engaged in sex work. Mimi, a 24-year-old sex worker who came to Addis Ababa at the age of 12, said:

> I take marriage as a means to escape this life; I want to get rid of this business through marriage. I believe and want to get married. Marriage is a good thing and I want to get married and if I find a good and considerate man I may even get married now. I guess I haven't been lucky so far because I haven't met the right guy from work or somewhere else for that matter. I don't want to be engaged in a committed relationship while doing this job but I will settle after I begin doing another job like waitressing in cafe etc. If I met a good and caring man, I will marry soon. So far, no one asked me for marriage and neither had I wished a customer for marriage. Being in this life I will not accept any invitation for marriage. It is difficult to get married with a person [once a customer] who knew my life. Anyway I will never try it being a sex worker.

For Eritreans as well, marriage and fertility remain strongholds of womanhood. As a female fighter from independence war in Eritrea explained to Victoria Bernal in her study 'From Warriors to Wives', "Eritrean women are valued according to their degree of fertility" and *tegadelti* (female fighters) could not compete with civilians (Bernal 2001). Many former fighters were infertile because of wounds or the hardships they suffered in the bush; others had sacrificed many of their childbearing years for the struggle. As Dore observes (2002, p. 80) *tegadelti* are easily distinguished from civilian women by their independent spirit, body language, brusque gestures and firm voice. Their behaviour is perceived as being more similar to men's. They can go to bars and drink; and talk back to men. They consider themselves outspoken and with stronger opinions than other women (see Belloni 2015, p. 42).

While some migrants deliberately decide that marriage would not be necessarily their main priority in life, for others this is less of a choice. In Bangladesh, a divorced woman has less chance of finding a second husband unless she abandons her children. The same is true for Eritreans who had been raped or subjected to violence during the migratory journey. For those who become mothers as a result of rape, the situation is even worse. Sex workers in Ethiopia were also aware that their chances of finding a suitable husband were limited because of the stigma attached to their work, while others did not want to get married because of their negative experiences with men. Migration contributes to postponing marriage and it may represent a significant turning point in migrant girls' life trajectories, especially when they are linked to acquiring economic or social autonomy. What also emerges from our data is that the way in which migration intersects with marriage choices and possibilities is *strongly linked to gender orders, both in the places of origin and in the* places of destination.

Migration, Transitions and Being Stuck

Migration does not always lead to a sense of change and transition in the lives of adolescent girls and young women. The sense of being stuck and not being able to attain the desired adult identity was especially strongly felt among Eritrean research participants. "My plan was to come to Sudan, stay a bit, earn some money, and then move somewhere else", explains Elsa, from Asmara, who had spent some six years in Sudan. This plan of "moving somewhere else" is a narrative common to most of the Eritreans and some Ethiopians. They see Sudan and Khartoum as a transit to a better life that can only be attained beyond Africa. This 'serial migration' (see Ossman 2013; Chapter 8) puts the experiences of migrant adolescent girls in Khartoum into perspective, seeing them as part of their migratory trajectories and transitions over multiple international migrations over the course of a person's life. The majority of Eritreans in Khartoum hope for, plan and engage in serial migration. The opportunities to move further are, however, few and far between, so most Eritreans become stranded for years in Sudan. In this transit mode and protracted uncertainty (Horst and Grabska 2015), Eritrean refugee adolescent girls in Khartoum are negotiating time, waiting and forming their identities while hoping to move elsewhere. Ethiopian girls, on the other hand, initially move to Sudan to make money, improve the situation of their family, escape from an oppressive gender order, and eventually hope to return to Ethiopia. However, once in Khartoum, the planned return scenario becomes a more distant option, and girls and women also feel 'stuck', or change their plans to engage in further migration. Eritrean girls who were not married and had no children often talked about 'wasting time'.

The sense of being stuck was less felt by Bangladeshi migrants. Most of the Bengali girls who were working in garment factories did not initially expect the move to Dhaka to be a first step towards further migration. Their aspirations to earn money had been in most cases immediately fulfilled by the availability of jobs in the RMG sector and they foresaw returning home after having earned and saved some money for themselves and their families as the most likely scenario. Only some of the older migrants realized that their income was not enough to secure their future and actively looked for alternative ways to earn before returning home.

Even while waiting for somewhere else, everyday life goes on. Some girls get married, some have new and better work opportunities, some are joined by their sisters or brothers (especially from Eritrea), others get pregnant, some move on, return or migrate further. Frances Pine elegantly describes such moments when she says, quoting Guyer, that the near future "…becomes reinhabited by forms of punctuated time" (Guyer 2007, p. 210), while the more distant future is a place of hope, dreams or intimations of some possible utopia (Pine 2014). To further elaborate on Guyer's nuanced perceptions of past, present and near and far future, the process of migration generates a "time that is punctuated rather than enduring: of fateful moments and turning points, the date as event rather than as a position in a sequence or a cycle, dates as qualitatively different rather than quantitatively cumulative" (Guyer 2007, p. 410).

Being an adolescent girl and young woman in Addis Ababa, Dhaka and Khartoum is punctuated by social restrictions, felt immobility and lack of opportunities, but also with openings and hopes. Migrant adolescent girls and young women are in fact actively 'doing things', small and big, while waiting. They are acting upon their state of perceived immobility, for example, by contributing to changing gender relations and identities, and challenging established trajectories into womanhood. Other ways of becoming an adult woman become possible: through gaining independence such as living away from family, making one's own decisions, and controlling one's own earnings. Thus, the idea of being stuck does not reflect their actual experiences.

Back to Gender Relations and the Life Course: How They Matter in the Context of Migration and Transitions

As this book has shown, a life-course approach to studying migration trajectories and the wider consequences of migration, combined with gender analysis, reveals how migration is experienced in different ways depending on the particular phase in life in which it takes place. The choice to study adolescent girls, their decision-making processes, their migratory trajectories and how they interact with the institutional and structural aspects of migration, illustrate how migration at this specific phase in life intersects with girls' transitions into adulthood as well as affecting their wider communities. In all three case studies, the migratory trajectories and lives of adolescent migrant girls and young women are greatly affected by the gender order and norms, in the place of origin and in the place of migration, and so are their transitions towards adulthood. As we indicated in the introductory chapter, we conceptualized gender as social relations and gender relations as the socially constituted and historically specific form that relations between (and among) women and men take in a given society (see Whitehead 1979). By paying close attention to both the structural aspects of gender relations (gender roles, division of labour in the household and in the labour market) and as well as moral norms and constructions of gender identities and status, our book reveals how migration intersects with social changes in contradictory ways.

Our study has also demonstrated how social identity, including whether being an adolescent girl or a woman, is rather something that "has to be established socially through a set of discourses which are both discursive and practical" (Moore 1994, p. 37). The context of migration for adolescent girls brings to light the importance identity as, what Stuart Hall (1991) argued, building on Foucault, the relationship between subjects and broader discursive practices. In this perspective, as the narratives and experiences of our study's protagonists have shown, adolescence, as much as youth and adulthood are "a socially constructed multiple identity whose relations to other social formations is constantly in flux" (Austin and Willard 1998, p. 3). As we have also demonstrated, "social becoming" in the contexts that we studied is much more a collective endeavour and experience than an individual process. It is a relational process deeply grounded and affected by social relation.

The stories and the narratives of young migrant girls collected in Bangladesh, Ethiopia and Sudan guided us in drawing the contours of their lives on the move, a complex, fluid scenario of choices, constraints, setbacks, risks, aspirations and experiences, in which internal or international migration plays a pivotal role. We emphasized that adolescents and young people are active agents in complex social contexts, engaged in creating their social identities through on-going processes of negotiation within social relations (Bucholtz 2002). Rather than regarding young people either as fully capable of independent agency or in the process of acquiring predetermined adult identities, they emerge as cultural agents in contexts where identities are shaped by elements of local culture as well as by globalization and transnationalism.

As our study emphasizes, gender relations have important implications for how the social phase of adolescence and the process of transition to adulthood are constructed and lived in different socio-cultural contexts. Drawing on Punch's holistic notion of transition as "a time of key changes for many young people" (2015, p. 263) without predetermined content or direction, our findings suggest that gender relations in places of origin as well as destination and/or transit shape these transitions in particular ways. Thus, while perceived as being still adolescent by family back home, the girls might already have acquired the identity of adult women in their places of migration. In this way, our approach to *adolescence transitions* allowed us to explore how concepts of adolescence and adulthood for girls are being transformed in the context of migration, and how contradictory these transformations might be.

Our study reveals a patchwork of relational becoming, meaning that the process of defining one's selfhood is relational and based on "interdependence" rather than on severing links with parents or other family members (see Coleman 2010). As we have seen, while opening up to new social relationships in the place of destination, adolescent girls and young women are still in different ways bound by an "intergenerational contract" (Kabeer 2000) which defines the terms of their relationships with their family members. These relationships are characterized by "negotiated and constrained interdependence" (Punch 2015) and, as our three case studies show, girls' transitions are always embedded in a complex web of social relationships (both in places of origin and destination and/or transit), strongly regulated by gender norms and gender institutions in each geographical location.

A life-course approach allowed us to show how gender matters in specific points in time and place. By showing how adolescent girls are subjected to stricter gender norms in Bangladesh, Ethiopia and Eritrea, and linking this to their experiences that provided the context of their decisions to migrate, we emphasize how gender regulates transitions. A life-course approach also allowed us to elaborate on the importance of the relational approach in understanding girls' agency. The relational nature of the agency (Huijsmans 2016, 2017) of children and young people is important in understanding the interconnectedness of their ability to act. White and Choudhury (2010) and Punch (2015) have shown that, far from being autonomous, children's agency needs to be negotiated, and often supported by adults. In this way, it is more of a collective agency (White and Choudhury 2010) than an individual one. Punch's long-term research among children in Bolivia elucidates the need to understand children's agency in relation to negotiated and constrained interdependencies within (between and among siblings) and across generations (children–parents) (Punch 2016). We argue that in order to understand migrant girls' experiences, the agency they express, the ways in which they tackle the challenges they face, and the kind of social persons they become, we have to take into account how their lives are embedded in multiple relational dimensions. Huijsmans, cited in Chapter 1, highlights age and space as important structuring relations, and that the household is a "key relational space in which migration dynamics unfold and that itself is reworked through migration" (2017, p. 52). As our research shows, gender and the particular phase in a person's life are key structuring relations of these dynamics. In all three contexts, there was an emphasis on commitments to family and complex networks of social relationships that cross-cut class and gender and have profound implications for how young people experience and confront the process of transition to adulthood. Yet, the household is only one space in which transitions take places. Thus a relational approach needs to be qualified to be truly meaningful and embedded in the web of social relations, including those within the household, in the labour market, as well as in the way structural forces that of schooling, policies aïmed at protecting migrants and refugees, and vulnerabilities are structured. Understanding the social embeddedness of agency and the interweaving of gender norms, institutions, identities and gender division of labour allows us to see focus squarely on the agency of adolescent girls. Only by looking holistically are we able to account for social change and continuities as part of migratory processes, for young people, their communities and their host environment.

Is Migration Good for Girls and Is This Really a Good Question?

One of the starting points of the research project on which this book is based was the fact that girls' migration is mainly depicted negatively and girls are presented mainly as victims of trafficking and exploitation. Such depiction is problematic not only because it denies agency to adolescent girls, but more importantly because of what it imposes on them. While portraying girls' mobility as risky, dangerous and seeing moving girls as trafficked and exploited, the prescribed policy response put often girls at risk rather than offering them a way to get out of situations of victimhood. The often cited best solutions for migrating girls advocate reunification with their families and return to places of origin. This is often in denial of the reasons that prompted the girls to leave in the first place. Families are rarely seen as those that pose risks for adolescent girls, as our study has demonstrated. Our findings show a much wider picture of the realities and experiences of migrating girls and that at times migration is the only solution and can make positive changes in girls' lives.

As we have seen, in all three countries each individual situation is complex and depends on the migratory experience, the kind of work in which girls and women engage, and their pre-migration experiences. For all, access to work and a certain degree of economic independence is linked to a wider capacity to take their own decisions and to manage their own life. Migration opens other ways of becoming an adult and most of the migrants, by virtue of earning an income, assumed a different role in the gender division of labour in the household. They often assumed adult responsibilities towards themselves and their family members. As we said above, migrant girls and young women highly value economic independence and the capacity to stand on their own feet. Of course, not all work gives lifelong stability. The Bangladeshi garment workers, for example, do not perceive this occupation as leading to security or a viable means of earning a living in the long term.

By placing the young women at the centre and focusing on their particular phase of adolescence, we have focused on their own perceptions, experiences and aspirations as they had to weave through the complex and multifaceted process of transition, involving physical, psychological and social dimensions. Girls' choices and trajectories, however, can be fully understood only within the complex social networks to which they belong.

There are many economic and political reasons why internal and international migration is increasing and is not going to go away, as now widely recognized. This research has directly addressed the increasing number of adolescent girls on the move within and across borders (Temin et al. 2013; Montgomery et al. 2016). It has also been widely documented that migration can both contribute to and undermine development, depending on the experiences of migration. Yet policies have regularly failed to enable migrants to make the most of these experiences. Changing this would require challenging entrenched power relationships at many levels, including within countries, and internationally.

The importance of looking specifically at adolescent girls has also been recognized by policy-makers and in global development strategies.

For example, the 2030 Agenda for Sustainable Development includes the unique needs and priorities of adolescent girls and examines the critical role that girls play in the development of their communities worldwide. This book shows the importance of listening to adolescent girls' perspectives and their own priorities. As the girls' and young women's narratives suggest, they see migration as an expression of agency and a complex choice, which may be motivated by a desire to improve their own lives or those of their families, or to escape oppressive gender and political regimes.

While girls' mobility might be seen as transgressive according to some gender norms, it has also become a necessity due to changing global labour markets, the growing impoverishment of rural families who need to rely on their daughters' labour, and the increasing lack of local livelihood options. As we have shown, migration generates both opportunities and risks for adolescent girls. In order to assess whether girls' migration is beneficial for them, and for their own communities, we need to have a better understanding of the situation of these girls before they embark on their migratory journey. It is in these circumstances that explanations for adolescent girls' decisions to migrate and their experiences as migrants can be found. Adolescent girls do not see migrating as the first resort to address the difficult circumstances in which they find themselves. As some of the girls' experiences have shown, in some ways, migration is a form of (social) suicide. It is usually the last resort. We argue that it is important it is to understand the particular circumstances of young people living in their own communities, and the type of gender pressures, opportunities and risks to which they are exposed, to understand the imperatives for the migration decisions that girls are making.

Instead of preventing girls' migration the key question is how to ensure a gender-sensitive, safer and more positive migratory experience for adolescents and young women. Much of the current policy discourses and proposals speak of safer migration as gender neutral and thus promote a male privilege without particular attention to gendered dynamics of safety (see Huijsmans 2014). This particular age group is of great importance in terms of when the move takes place. The spatial move is closely intertwined with other life transitions: into work, education, marriage and having children. The existing policy interventions locate adolescent migrant and refugee girls as victims of trafficking, smuggling, abuse and exploitation. There is a need to recognize the complexity of each girl's situation, her age, particular reasons for migrating, her educational level, and the context of her host community. Policy-makers must recognize the diverse potential of migrating girls and young women, and move beyond focusing on their physical vulnerability and the need for reintegration and address directly their individual needs.

For academics, it is critical to show that despite the tremendous suffering and violence often associated with girls' migration, we need to look beyond the immediate effects. While girls' mobility is often framed, and experienced, as being subject to structural gender inequalities and other pressures, their agency, even if fragile, relational and demonstrated as "doing small things" should not be overlooked. The long-term perspective on girls' lives, careful ethnographic and longitudinal research, as this book demonstrates, can and does reveal how migration is linked to transitions and girls' well-being beyond the immediate negative experiences of the journey. Only by understanding the bigger picture of how girls' mobility and immobility are structured by and transformative of wider social processes, can we see the significance of individual experiences of adolescent girls on the move.

References

Agarwal, S., Jones, E., & Verma, S. (2016). Migrant Adolescent Girls in Urban Slums India: Aspirations, Opportunities and Challenges. *Indian Journal Youth Adolescent Health, 3*(4), 8–21.

Austin, J., & Willard, M. N. (1998). Introduction: Angels of History, Demons of Culture. In J. Austin & M. N. Willard (Eds.), *Generations of Youth: Youth Cultures and History in Twentieth-Century America* (pp. 1–20). New York: New York University Press.

Bailey, A. (2009). Population Geography: Life Course Matters. *Progress in Human Geography, 33*(3), 407–418.

Belloni, M. (2015). *Cosmologies of Destinations: Routes and Routes of Eritrean Forced Migration to Europe*. Ph.D. thesis, University of Trento, Trento.

Bernal, V. (2001). From Warriors to Wives: Contradictions of Liberation and Development in Eritrea. *Northeast African Studies, 8*(3), 129–154.

Borlagden, J. (2015). Inequality and 21-Year-Olds' Negotiation of Uncertain Transitions to Employment: A Bourdieusian Approach. *Journal of Youth Studies, 18*(7), 839–854.

Brettell, C. (2002). Gendered Lives: Transitions and Turning Points in Person, Family, and Historical Time. *Current Anthropology, 43*(S4), S45–S61.

Bucholtz, M. (2002). Youth and Cultural Practice. *Annual Review of Anthropology, 3*(1), 525–552.

Camfield, L., & Tafere, Y. (2011). Community Understandings of Childhood Transitions in Ethiopia: Different for Girls? *Children's Geographies, 9*(2), 247–262.

Chuta, N., & Morrow, V. (2015). *Youth Trajectories Through Work and Marriage in Rural Ethiopia* (Young Lives Working Paper No. 135). Oxford: Young Lives, University of Oxford.

Coleman, J. C. (2010). *The Nature of Adolescence*. Abingdon: Routledge.

Crivello, G. (2009). *"Becoming Somebody": Youth Transitions Through Education and Migration in Peru* (Young Lives Working Paper No. 43). Oxford: Young Lives, University of Oxford.

Derks, A. (2008). *Khmer Women on the Move: Exploring Work and Life in Urban Cambodia*. Honolulu, HI: University of Hawaii Press.

Dore, G. (2002). Donne del Fronte eritreo: sessualità e gestione del corpo dalla guerra al rientro nella società civile. "*ERREFFE. La Ricerca Folklorica*", *46*, 73–82.

Du Bois-Reymond, M., & López Blasco, A. (2003). Yo-yo Transitions and Misleading Trajectories: Towards Integrated Transition Policies for Young Adults in Europe. In A. LópezBlasco, W. McNeish, & A. Walther (Eds.), *Young People and Contradictions of Inclusion: Towards Integrated Transition Policies in Europe*. Oxford: Policy Press.

Gardner, K. (2009). Lives in Motion: The Life-Course, Movement and Migration in Bangladesh. *Journal of South Asian Development, 4*(2), 229–251.

Guo, M., Chow, N. W. S., & Palinka, L. A. (2011). Circular Migration and Life Course of Female Domestic Workers in Beijing. *Asian Population Studies, 7*(1), 51–67.

Guyer, J. L. (2007). Prophecy and the Near Future: Thoughts on Macroeconomic, Evangelical, and Punctuated Time. *American Ethnologist, 33*(3), 409–421.

Hall, S. (1991). Old and New Identities, Old and New Ethnicities. In Anthony D. King (Ed.), *Culture, Globalization and the World System*. Macmillan.

Hall, S. (1996). Who Needs Identity? In S. Hall & P. DuGay (Eds.), *Questions of Cultural Identity* (pp. 1–17). London: Sage.

Hertrich, V., & Lesclingand, M. (2012). Adolescent Migration and the 1990s Nuptiality Transition in Mali. *Population Studies, 66*(2), 47–166.

Hörschelmann, K. (2011). Theorising Life Transitions: Geographical Perspectives. *Area, 43*(4), 378–383.

Horst, C., & Grabska, K. (2015). Flight and Exile: Uncertainty in the Context of Conflict-Induced Displacement. *Social Analysis, 59*(1), 1–18.

Huijsmans, R. (2014). Gender, Masculinity, and Safety in the Changing Lao-Thai Migration Landscape. In T.-D. Truong, D. Gasper, J. Handmaker, & S. I. Bergh (Eds.), *Migration, Gender and Social Justice: Perspectives on Human Security* (pp. 333–349). Heidelberg, New York, Dordrecht, and London: Springer.

Huijsmans, R. (Ed.). (2016). *Generationing Development: A relational Approach to Children, Youth and Development*. London: Palgrave Macmillan.

Huijsmans, R. (2017). Children and Young People in Migration: A Relational Approach. In C. Ní Laoire, A. White, & T. Skelton (Eds.), *Movement, Mobilities and Journeys* (Vol. 6, pp. 45–66). Singapore: Springer.

Jacquemin, M. (2011). Migrations juvéniles féminines de travail en Côte d'Ivoire. *Journal des Africanistes, 8*(1), 61–86.

Kabeer, N. (2000). Inter-generational Contracts Demographic Transitions and the Quantity–Quality Tradeoff: Parents, Children and Investing in the Future. *Journal of International Development, 12*(4), 463–482.

King, R., & Williams, A. M. (2018). Editorial Introduction: New European Youth Mobilities. *Population, Space, Place, 24*, 1–9.

Monsutti, A. (2007). Migration as a Rite of Passage: Young Afghans Building Masculinity and Adulthood in Iran. *Iranian Studies, 40*(2), 167–185.

Moore, H. (1994). *A Passion for Difference: Essays in Anthropology and Gender*. Polity Press: London.

Montgomery, M. R., Balk, D., Liu, Z., Agarwal, S., Jones, E., & Adamo, S. (2016). Urban Migration of Adolescent Girls: Quantitative Results from Developing Countries. In J. Michael (Ed.), *International Handbook of Migration and Population Distribution* (pp.573–604). Dordrecht: Springer.

Osella, F., & Osella, C. (2000). Migration, Money and Masculinity in Kerala. *Royal Anthropological Institute, 6*, 117–133.

Ossman, S. (2013). *Moving Matters: Paths of Serial Migration*. Stanford, CA: Stanford University Press.

Pine, F. (2014). Migration as Hope: Space, Time, and Imagining the Future. *Current Anthropology, 55*(S9), 95–104.

Punch, S. (2002). Youth Transitions and Interdependent Adult–Child Relations in Rural Bolivia. *Journal of Rural Studies, 18*(2), 123–133.

Punch, S. (2015). Possibilities for Learning Between Childhoods and Youth in the Minority and Majority Worlds: Youth Transitions as an Example of Cross-World Dialogue. In J. Wynand & H. Cahill (Eds.), *Handbook of Children and Youth Studies* (pp. 689–701). Singapore: Springer.

Punch, S. (2016). Exploring Children's Agency Across Majority and Minority World Contexts. In F. Esser, M. S. Baader, T. Betz, & B. Hunderland (Eds.), *Reconceptualising Agency and Childhood: New Perspectives in Childhood Studies* (pp. 183–196). Abingdon: Routledge.

Temin, M., Montgomery, M. R., Engebretsen, S., & Barker, K. M. (2013). *Girls on the Move: Adolescent Girls and Migration in the Developing World. A Girls Count Report on Adolescent Girls*. New York, NY: Population Council.

Walther, A., Plug, W., Du Bois-Reymond, M., & Chisolm, L. (2006). Transitions from School to Work in Europe: Destandardization and Policy Trends. *New Directions in Child and Adolescent Development, X*(113), 77–90.

White, S., & Choudhury, S. (2010). Children's Participation in Bangladesh: Issues of Agency and Structures of Violence. In B. Percy-Smith & N. Thomas (Eds.), *A Handbook of Children and Young People's Participation* (pp. 39–50). London: Routledge.

Whitehead, A. (1979). Some Preliminary Notes on the Subordination of Women. *IDS Bulletin, 10*(3), 10–13.

Worth, N. (2009). Understanding Youth Transitions as a 'Becoming': Identity, Time and Futurity. *Geoforum, 40*(6), 1050–1060.

INDEX

K. Grabska et al., *Adolescent Girls' Migration in The Global South*, Palgrave Studies on Children and Development,
https://doi.org/10.1007/978-3-030-00093-6

T